Every year, thousands of talented young people aspire to careers in the arts. Vincent Dubois's brilliant sociological analysis of French careers in cultural management reveals the challenges – and often disappointments – which lie in their way. This book will be essential reading across the globe for those interested in how career patterns in the cultural sector are changing.

**Professor Mike Savage,**
*Head of Sociology Department and Chair,*
*London School of Economics, UK*

Many have wondered: what is arts management? Few answers truly satisfy. Vincent Dubois poses a set of fresh questions and manages to answer this and far more in his well-researched, highly readable volume. It should be required reading in our field.

**Professor Constance DeVereaux,**
*Director, LEAP Institute for the Arts,*
*Colorado State University, USA*

*Culture as a Vocation* focuses on the social space of cultural managers, who play a crucial role in the contemporary cultural world. Superbly researched in a Bourdieusian framework, this book provides an insightful view on this occupational universe. Thanks to the nuanced analysis of this strategic case, he sheds light on the changing social settings of culture in contemporary societies.

**Professor Arturo Rodríguez Morató,**
*University of Barcelona, Spain*

This persuasive and challenging analysis of the changing realities in cultural professions offers insightful understanding of the aspirations and motivations of professionals engaged in arts and culture. Dubois' book is a must read for all those involved in education and training of cultural professionals, whether in academia or in centres for lifelong learning.

**Professor Milena Dragicevic Sesic,**
*UNESCO Chair in Cultural Policy and Management,*
*University of Arts, Belgrade, Serbia*

Serious researches on management in the cultural field are rare and still rarer are conceptually sophisticated ones. With his usual mastery Vincent Dubois manages to match in this unique book the seriousness of a solid empirical study on would-be cultural managers with the imaginative insightfulness of the best social theory to provide a must reference for future research and a valuable reading for aspiring as well as practicing professionals in the culture sector.

**Professor Marco Santoro,**
*Head of Sociology,*
*University of Bologna, Italy*

T0300089

## Culture, Economy and the Social
### A new series from CRESC – the ESRC Centre for Research on Socio-cultural Change
### Editors

The *Culture, Economy and the Social* series is committed to innovative contemporary, comparative and historical work on the relations between social, cultural and economic change. It publishes empirically-based research that is theoretically informed, that critically examines the ways in which social, cultural and economic change is framed and made visible, and that is attentive to perspectives that tend to be ignored or side-lined by grand theorizing or epochal accounts of social change. The series addresses the diverse manifestations of contemporary capitalism, and considers the various ways in which the 'social', 'the cultural' and 'the economic' are apprehended as tangible sites of value and practice. It is explicitly comparative, publishing books that work across disciplinary perspectives, cross-culturally, or across different historical periods.

The series is actively engaged in the analysis of the different theoretical traditions that have contributed to the development of the 'cultural turn' with a view to clarifying where these approaches converge and where they diverge on a particular issue. It is equally concerned to explore the new critical agendas emerging from current critiques of the cultural turn: those associated with the descriptive turn for example. Our commitment to interdisciplinarity thus aims at enriching theoretical and methodological discussion, building awareness of the common ground that has emerged in the past decade, and thinking through what is at stake in those approaches that resist integration to a common analytical model.

Series titles include:

**The Media and Social Theory (2008)**
*Edited by David Hesmondhalgh and Jason Toynbee*

**Culture, Class, Distinction (2009)**
*Tony Bennett, Mike Savage, Elizabeth Bortolaia Silva, Alan Warde, Modesto Gayo-Cal and David Wright*

**Material Powers (2010)**
*Edited by Tony Bennett and Patrick Joyce*

**The Social after Gabriel Tarde: Debates and Assessments (2010)**
*Edited by Matei Candea*

**Cultural Analysis and Bourdieu's Legacy (2010)**
*Edited by Elizabeth Silva and Alan Ward*

**Milk, Modernity and the Making of the Human (2010)**
*Richie Nimmo*

**Creative Labour: Media Work in Three Cultural Industries (2010)**
*Edited by David Hesmondhalgh and Sarah Baker*

**Migrating Music (2011)**
*Edited by Jason Toynbee and Byron Dueck*

**Sport and the Transformation of Modern Europe: States, Media and Markets 1950–2010 (2011)**
*Edited by Alan Tomlinson, Christopher Young and Richard Holt*

**Inventive Methods: The Happening of the Social (2012)**
*Edited by Celia Lury and Nina Wakeford*

**Understanding Sport: A Socio-Cultural Analysis (2012)**
*By John Horne, Alan Tomlinson, Garry Whannel and Kath Woodward*

**Shanghai Expo: An International Forum on the Future of Cities (2012)**
*Edited by Tim Winter*

**Diasporas and Diplomacy: Cosmopolitan Contact Zones at the BBC World Service (1932–2012)**
*Edited by Marie Gillespie and Alban Webb (2012)*

**Making Culture, Changing Society (2013)**
*Tony Bennett*

**Interdisciplinarity: Reconfigurations of the Social and Natural Sciences (2013)**
*Edited by Andrew Barry and Georgina Born*

**Objects and Materials: A Routledge Companion (2013)**
*Edited by Penny Harvey, Eleanor Conlin Casella, Gillian Evans, Hannah Knox, Christine McLean, Elizabeth B. Silva, Nicholas Thoburn and Kath Woodward*

**Accumulation: The Material Politics of Plastic (2013)**
*Edited by Gay Hawkins, Jennifer Gabrys and Mike Michael*

Theorizing Cultural Work: Labour, Continuity and Change in the Cultural and Creative Industries (2013)
*Edited by Mark Banks, Rosalind Gill and Stephanie Taylor*

Comedy and Distinction: The Cultural Currency of a 'Good' Sense of Humour (2014)
*Sam Friedman*

The Provoked Economy: Economic Reality and the Performative Turn (2014)
*Fabian Muniesa*

Rio de Janeiro: Urban Life through the Eyes of the City
*Beatriz Jaguaribe*

The Routledge Companion to Bourdieu's 'Distinction'
*Edited by Philippe Coulangeon and Julien Duval*

Devising Consumption: Cultural Economies of Insurance, Credit and Spending
*By Liz Mcfall*

Industry and Work in Contemporary Capitalism: Global Models, Local Lives?
*Edited by Victoria Goddard and Susana Narotzky*

Lived Economies of Consumer Credit: Consumer Credit, Debt Collection and the Capture of Affect
*By Joe Deville*

Cultural Pedagogies and Human Conduct
*Edited by Megan Watkins, Greg Noble and Catherine Driscoll*

Culture as a Vocation: Sociology of Career Choices in Cultural Management
*By Vincent Dubois*

Topologies of Power (forthcoming)
*By John Allen*

Unbecoming Things: Mutable Objects and the Politics of Waste (forthcoming)
*By Nicky Gregson and Mike Crang*

E·S·R·C
ECONOMIC
& SOCIAL
RESEARCH
COUNCIL

Centre for Research on
Socio-Cultural Change

# Culture as a Vocation

Vocational occupations are attractive not so much for their material rewards as for the prestige and self-fulfillment they confer. They require a strong personal commitment, which can be subjectively experienced in terms of passion and selflessness. The choice of a career in the cultural sector provides a good example of this. What are the terms of this calling? What predisposes individuals to answer it? What are the meanings of such a choice? To answer these questions, this book focuses on would-be cultural managers. By identifying their social patterns, by revealing the resources, expectations and visions of the world they invest in their choice, it sheds new light on these occupations. In these intermediary and indeterminate social positions, family heritages intersect with educational strategies, aspirations of upward mobility with tactics against downward mobility, and social critique with adjustment strategies. Ultimately the study of career choices in cultural management suggests a new take on the analysis of social reproduction and on the embodiment of the new spirit of capitalism. The empirical findings of this research conducted in France are set in a broader comparative perspective, at the European level and with the USA.

**Vincent Dubois,** sociologist and political scientist, is currently Professor at the Institute for Political Studies in Strasbourg (France). His research fields include cultural sociology and policy, language policy, poverty and welfare. He belongs to the SAGE research unit and to the University of Strasbourg Institute for Advanced Study, and is associate member of the Centre for European Sociology founded by Pierre Bourdieu in Paris. He is a former member of the Institute for Advanced Study in Princeton, NJ, USA, school of social science (2012–3) and of the Institut Universitaire de France (2007–12). He has published 8 books, 2 of which have been published in English translation (*The Bureaucrat and the Poor*, Ashgate, 2010; *The Sociology of Wind Bands*, Ashgate, 2013). He has published around 80 scientific contributions in edited volumes and journals including *International Journal of Cultural Policy, Cultural Sociology, Poetics, Social Analysis, Current Anthropology, Critical Policy Studies, Actes de la recherche en sciences sociales*.

# Culture as a Vocation

Sociology of career choices in
cultural management

**Vincent Dubois**

**with the collaboration of Victor Lepaux**
**Translated from the French by Jean-Yves Bart**

Routledge
Taylor & Francis Group

LONDON AND NEW YORK

First published 2013 by Liber/Raisons d'agir, Paris

2 Park Square, Milton Park, Abingdon, Oxfordshire OX14 4RN
52 Vanderbilt Avenue, New York, NY 10017

*Routledge is an imprint of the Taylor & Francis Group, an informa business*

First issued in paperback 2019

*British Library Cataloguing in Publication Data*
A catalogue record for this book is available from the British Library

*Library of Congress Cataloging in Publication Data*
Dubois, Vincent, 1966–
[Culture comme vocation. English]
Culture as a vocation / by Vincent Dubois.
  pages cm
  1. Arts administrators–France. 2. Arts–Management–Study and teaching–
France. 3. Occupations–France. 4. Arts and society–France. I. Title.
NX770.F7.D8313 2015
706–dc23
2015019910

ISBN: 978-1-138-81998-6 (hbk)
ISBN: 978-0-367-87058-4 (pbk)

Typeset in Times New Roman
by Sunrise Setting Ltd, Paignton, UK

# Contents

*List of illustrations*                                                     *x*
*Foreword*                                                                  *xi*
*Preface*                                                                   *xiv*
*Acknowledgements*                                                          *xx*

Introduction                                                                1

1   Culture in the space of career choices                                  12
    *How cultural occupations became attractive  12*
    *Training and the genesis of vocations  25*

2   Who wants to be a cultural manager?                                     38
    *A largely feminine vocation  38*
    *Higher social backgrounds  42*
    *Educated applicants  45*
    *Well-rounded applicants  48*
    *The space of applicants  50*

3   The meanings of a career choice                                        56
    *Leaving doors open  56*
    *A third way between art and teaching  73*
    *The social rationales of a career choice  81*

4   Intermediate dispositions and adjustment strategies                    97
    *Between cultural legitimism and eclecticism  97*
    *Reinventing the artist's life  106*

    Conclusion                                                              119

*Appendix*                                                                  *123*
*Bibliography*                                                              *131*
*Index*                                                                     *142*

# Illustrations

**Figures**

2.1   The space of applicants                                      51
3.1   The space of prospects                                       60
4.1   Cultural tastes and practices                                99

**Tables**

2.1   Social backgrounds                                           43
2.2   Main sectors of activity of the parents                      44
2.3   Cultural outings over the previous thirty days               49

# Foreword

The British sociology of class and stratification is now massively resurgent. Over the past ten years, British sociologists such as Harriet Bradley, Fiona Devine, Diane Reay, Beverley Skeggs, Alan Warde and numerous others have once more put the study of class at the heart of the discipline. Compared to the 1990s, when it was widely argued by luminaries such as Ulrich Beck and Anthony Giddens that class had lost its analytical purchase, this body of work has emphasized the entrenched power of class divisions, and the way that they mark numerous dimensions of cultural and social life.

Yet, in reinstating the power of class, this was a very different vision of class analysis from that which commanded international attention during the middle decades of the twentieth century, as enshrined in the pivotal contributions of T.H. Marshall, John Goldthorpe, David Lockwood, Stuart Hall, Paul Willis and others. This earlier generation of class analysis was rooted in its direct heritage in twentieth-century industrial capitalism. Classes were rooted in a relatively fixed division of labour characterized by the dominance of agriculture, manufacturing and extractive industries. Professional and white-collar employment took on a middle-class identity in striking contrast to these blue-collar occupations. Studies of work and employment therefore lay at the bedrock of class analysis.

It was precisely changes to the nature of work – de-industrialization, the rise of service employment, the development of more flexible forms of labour – which seemed to mark the end of the class order. Those commentators who proclaimed 'the end of class' did so on the basis that class divisions could no longer be etched so directly in the experience of the employment relationship. Instead, the new generation of proponents of 'cultural class analysis', inspired by Pierre Bourdieu, focused on the role of cultural capital and educational processes in the generation of advantage and disadvantage. It is thus the analysis of culture, lifestyle, consumption and identity that has been the central feature of more recent work on class – notably in works such as *Culture, Class, Distinction* (Routledge 2009), of which I was co-author along with Tony Bennett, Elizabeth Silva, Alan Warde, Modesto Gayo Cal and David Wright.

This new generation of class analysis has had only limited engagement therefore with the study of work, employment and industry – a very different situation from that which was found in the classic sociology from the 1950s to the 1980s, when it would have been unimaginable to have held these apart. Some exceptions to this generalization, such as Valerie Walkerdine, might be explained by their focus on the world of declining manual employment, such as in the Welsh industrial districts.

Further, the new generation of cultural class analysis, with its emphasis on how people disidentify with class, and perform class obliquely, through practices of consumption, is also very different from the previous focus on how positive forms of consciousness can be read as defined by active class identities, rooted in occupational experiences.

We should note that the experience of French sociology is very different. Here, Pierre Bourdieu was not used as part of a dominant trend towards emphasizing the significance of consumption and lifestyle, and it is possible to identify a much closer association with research on work and employment. It is precisely this approach which Vincent Dubois exemplifies so well in this important book.

British research on the sociology of work and employment is now reviving, as in the important contributions such as those by Miriam Glucksmannm, Susan Halford, Lynn Pettinger, and Tim Strangleman. Vincent Dubois's study is an exemplary example of how it is possible to link elements of Bourdieusian theory to a sophisticated sociological study of employment to ensure that we understand not only the spheres of consumption, but also those of production as fundamentally organized around social class.

Dubois shows how it is possible to use a Bourdieusian frame to recognize how the division of labour is itself the product of powerful symbolic and cultural forces. Dubois's key platform is a version of social constructionism. Rather than treat the division of labour as a fixed structure from which classes can be derived, Dubois takes the constructionist move of seeing how passions, desires and aspirations are themselves implicated in the making of occupations. Using a specific focus on the rise of the cultural management profession, Dubois argues that this occupation is popular as a means for the upwardly mobile to define an arena in which they 'express themselves'. They are thus attracted to gaining cultural qualifications which lock them into a growing cultural sector which turns out to be a niche.

In many respects, Dubois's study reminds me of the pivotal contributions of Paul Willis and Beverley Skeggs. Like them, he is interested in how young people seek to be 'free', how they desire to take on positions of their own to rid them of what they see as dull constraints around them. Again like Willis and Skeggs, Dubois shows how in fact these freedoms come to inscribe social inequalities, though in ways which can be oblique to those engaged in such battles. Cultural management is an arena which appears to offer possibilities and the chance of upward mobility, but in fact such aspirations are implicated in the new 'spirit of capitalism', which has the unintended consequence of extending the managerial writ more widely. What emerges from this account therefore is the need to see culture as not simply linked to issues of lifestyle and consumption, but also to the world of work, career, and employment.

In an era when it is increasingly clear that young people are facing severe labour-market difficulties, and where career pathways into professions and management are more turbulent and less predictable, Dubois's study shows clearly the value of a Bourdieusian perspective. He emphasizes how young people cannot simply be seen to be following a pre-defined path, and can exercise creative energy; yet at the same time he demonstrates how their plans are marked by their history and social conditions.

Finally, I want to draw attention to Dubois's preoccupation with time. The sociology of class, as sociology more generally, struggles with endemic cross-sectionalism. Thus class is defined as one's present occupation. More broadly, we confront epochalist accounts of social change which present contemporary conditions as fundamentally different from those which preceded them. Dubois insists on placing trajectory, forward thinking, and aspiration at the heart of his account, and thereby we can see structure and agency as interrelated. Through this deft move, we are able to see in turn how emerging forms of work and employment can only be understood with respect to their longer-term historical forbears.

Mike Savage
*London School of Economics, May 2015*

# Preface to the English Edition

Which social factors are involved in making educational and occupational choices? How do these individual choices reveal the adjustment of social reproduction strategies to the new realities of higher education and the employment markets in the neoliberal era? This book addresses these questions by exploring vocational attitudes towards occupations in the cultural field. As culture serves as a vehicle for the expression of 'principles of vision and division' of social space – albeit sometimes sublimated or negated – and of the ways in which to define one's role in that space (Bourdieu 1984), the choice of pursuing a cultural occupation is a particularly telling reflection of the aesthetic, ethical and political preferences that define relationships to the social world. In this book I consider cultural vocations, both as a topic in its own right and as a starting point to address broader sociological issues.

While workers in the cultural sector hold a wide range of positions and social statuses, from unskilled employees to craftspeople, professionals and managers (Hesmondhalgh and Baker 2010: 67), cultural occupations strictly speaking are typically held by members of educated fractions of the middle and upper-middle classes, which have been a major locus of social change over the last decades (on the UK see Savage *et al.* 1992; Bennett *et al.* 2009: 177ff.) They epitomize the changing role of cultural intermediaries, which has recently been revisited in studies on specific sectors and national contexts (Smith Maguire and Matthews 2012; Solaroli 2014; Jeanpierre and Roueff 2014; Lizé *et al.* 2014). Here, I focus on the cultural intermediaries who have been labelled 'cultural managers' or 'arts managers' since the mid-1960s. Cultural managers are 'intermediaries' in three senses: in terms of their position in social space, as they are located between the middle and upper classes; in terms of their activity, which operates across the relations between various social fields (in particular art and culture, the political field, non-profit and for-profit economic fields, bureaucracy, the media); and in terms of the intermediation function they fulfil, by connecting cultural projects and their funders, events to their public and artworks to their prospective buyers. These three levels of intermediateness intersect and interact one with another. Cultural managers must grapple with certain contradictions and make compromises, most notably when it comes to the traditional opposition between art and money. This essential feature of their work relates to structuring factors, which define their positions in social space: the relations between economic and cultural capital. In other words, their social status reflects the dilemmas they face, the interactions between the social universes they cross and the mediation work they accomplish.

Starting with the questions of educational and occupational choices and of reproduction strategies, the analysis presented in *Culture as a Vocation* mostly draws on empirical research focused on the cultural sector, and more precisely on cultural managers, in France. A few salient features of the French case therefore need to be recalled to assess the possible generalization of my findings and to compare them with other cases (the latter approach being the one I prefer). At this stage I will not get into the questions of cultural employment, which are addressed in the beginning of the first chapter, nor will I examine the impact of the long-term deterioration of socio-economic conditions, which I elaborate upon in several chapters, in particular by revisiting the question of 'downclassing' (the term used by Bourdieu to refer to the inability of individuals to reach social positions equivalent to their parents – social downclassing – and/or matching their academic achievements – educational downclassing). This preface will merely outline aspects of the educational system and of the social organization of the cultural field that may not necessarily be entirely specific to the French case, but regardless combine in ways that influence the choice of pursuing cultural occupations.

In France, the vast majority of children are educated in free state-funded primary schools and high schools (87 per cent). Students can pick a vocational stream at high school level, but most of them go into one of the three national streams of general education: literature and languages; economic and social sciences; mathematics and natural sciences. Since the mid-1990s the proportion of an age cohort obtaining the national high school degree (*baccalauréat*) has stabilized at around 65 per cent. Eighty per cent of *baccalauréat* holders go on to pursue higher education, for the majority in universities, with around 40 per cent of an age cohort obtain a higher education degree. French universities are state-funded, do not select students on entrance (except for a minority of programmes), and charge low tuition fees. This distinguishes the French educational system from those that sort and select students more systematically at an early stage (junior high school) and/or at entrance to universities. In practice, massive access to higher education does not necessarily translate into democratization. Despite considerable transformations in the system, the social reproduction processes unveiled by Bourdieu and Passeron in the 1960s still operate: social class inequalities of access remain decisive, and the hierarchies of courses and diplomas still reinforce these inequalities much in the way that they did at the time of *The Inheritors* (Bourdieu and Passeron 1979). If massification does not equal democratization, it does result in the production of more numerous graduates in search of a career choice, which is one of the factors steering vocational choices towards cultural occupations, especially in the case of humanities students.

The most prominent and stable features of the French cultural field and the attitudes towards culture associated with it are well known by international social scientists, thanks to the worldwide dissemination of Bourdieu's *Distinction*. The cultural system is highly centralized: the main institutions and instances of consecration are found in Paris. This is connected with the domination of the model of the cultured fractions of the higher (Parisian) bourgeoisie – highbrow culture plays a very important role in marking social and symbolic boundaries – and an inclination towards the sacralization of culture. While over the decades countless studies in cultural sociology have nuanced and refined these observations, they remain relevant in accounting for the social distribution of tastes and cultural practices in France (Coulangeon 2013) in ways that differ from other national traditions, such as the 'loosely bounded culture' of the USA (Lamont 1992). In addition to these aspects, it is worth noting a complementary French specificity pertaining to the role of state cultural policy. As we will see, cultural policy has played a key role in the professionalization of cultural managers, and in the rise of specialized training programmes in cultural management across a variety of national and institutional settings, from organizations at the European level to federal support for the arts in the USA. This has also been the case in France, where cultural policy has had other and more specific impacts on the choice of pursuing occupations in the cultural sector. French national and local cultural policies have created a cultural economy that is largely dependent on public budgets. This takes the form of a direct dependence on numerous public cultural institutions (libraries, theatres, museums and others), and an indirect dependence on subsidies for artists or cultural projects, or loans for film production (*avance sur recettes*). This particular economy has had a direct impact on cultural employment, whose rise from the 1960s onwards is in large part due to public subsidies. The increase in the public cultural budget, especially during the 1980s, has resulted in the recruitment of civil servants in cultural institutions and services, in new paid positions opening up in the non-profit sector, and in more opportunities for employment in the for-profit private cultural sector. In addition to cultural policy, strictly speaking, the unemployment benefits system for workers in the performing arts and the film industry (*intermittents du spectacle*) has been an important factor in the growth of the cultural labour market (Menger 2005a). Cultural policy has not only boosted cultural employment and brought about a new division of cultural labour leading to the professionalization of cultural managers; it has also promoted cultural occupations in the preferences and anticipations of newcomers on the labour market. It has mapped out the boundaries of cultural management as a professional sector, which in France is more closely linked to the public and state-subsidized sectors, and less to the arts market or the 'creative industries', than it is for instance in the USA or in the UK. Although these trends have been weakened by the stagnation or decline of cultural public budgets in recent years, as well as by the internationalization of curricula and careers and by the dissemination of a more 'entrepreneurial' model of cultural worker, they remain notable.

While this emphasis on social reproduction strategies and the structure of cultural management as a career choice that are specific to the French case may reduce the empirical generalizability of this study, it does not lessen its broader sociological relevance. My analytical proposals are formulated in such a manner that they can both accurately reflect the empirical case under scrutiny and yield insights that can be applied to other cases and broader issues. In order to move fluidly from empirical discussion to generalization and back, I have included as many points of comparison as possible, following Passeron's thesis that socio-logical reasoning is based on assertions that are specific to a certain time and space, and disputable in a comparative perspective (Passeron 2013). Several of the trends and questions I discuss are relevant to other professional worlds beyond cultural management; this book addresses them as such whenever possible, espe-cially when it comes to occupations and employment sectors where the question of 'vocation' arises in similar ways – namely cases that combine an expectation of non-monetary rewards and the pursuit of moral values or common goods with high levels of cultural capital.

My intention, then, is to present my findings on the French case in ways that they can be useful beyond it, drawing comparisons with other national contexts, even if the lack of similar research often limits them to sketches of what a proper comparison should be. The generalizability of my empirical findings (by defini-tion limited in space and time) should not be confused with that of my socio-logical results (which must be assessed on the basis of the research questions they help to formulate): the processes I observe may display forms specific to my fieldwork, but these processes and the way I analyze them reflect general issues. It is my hope that readers will follow me in this approach by complementing this comparative sociological reasoning with their own knowledge and reflections, and by looking at this book not only as a study of the French case (which it is), but also as a set of proposals to be tested in other contexts (which it aims to be).

Smith Maguire and Matthews argue that 'research on cultural intermediaries has followed two different (although not incompatible) directions: cultural intermedi-aries as exemplars of the new middle class, involved in the mediation of produc-tion and consumption [...]; and cultural intermediaries as market actors involved in the qualification of goods, mediating between economy and culture' (Smith Maguire and Matthews 2012: 551). Nixon and du Gay referred to two roughly similar directions ten years earlier: 'there is a serious need for more substantive work on cultural intermediary occupations in order to empirically ground claims about both their place in the occupational structure and the role they play in eco-nomic and cultural life' (Nixon and du Gay 2002: 498). Most recent Anglophone research on cultural intermediaries focuses, however, on the functions they fulfil in various markets for symbolic goods. This is what Smith Maguire and Matthews do when they conflate the defining features of cultural intermediaries and the roles they play: framing the qualification of goods; exerting expertise; contrib-uting to the construction of the legitimacy and the value of these goods (Smith Maguire and Matthews 2012). Even though they mention social dispositions and habitus, they neither address the mechanisms of their formation and actualization nor consider the backgrounds and trajectories of cultural intermediaries associ-ated with their dispositions and habitus. In other words, as with most Anglophone scholars (this is different in French sociology), they envision cultural intermediar-ies from the point of view of what they do, rather than from the point of view of what they are (sociologically speaking). As a result, despite frequent references to Bourdieu's *Distinction* from which the very notion of cultural intermediaries is borrowed, most Anglophone sociological research on cultural intermediaries contributes to the sociology of the markets of symbolic goods more than to the sociology of stratification and class (Conlin 2014: 2).

At odds with the bulk of existing research, then, the research presented in this book essentially pertains to the sociology and stratification and class. My contribution draws on Bourdieu's framework, but this does not mean I aim to simply reiterate his analyses. While I revisit his notion of the 'new petite bourgeoisie', for instance, I reach significantly different conclusions, showing that access to the loosely defined occupations of cultural intermediaries now requires a high level of educational capital, even for children of the high bourgeoisie, and is increasingly difficult for lower-class children – even achieving ones (Dubois 2014, and Higher social backgrounds (p. 42) and Dreams of social mobility (p. 81) in this volume). While Bourdieu remained fairly general in his sociology of cultural intermediary occupations (Smith Maguire 2014), I examine a specific subset of holders of such occupations. The empirical case of cultural managers offers the theoretical advantage of avoiding the use of the category of cultural intermediaries in a watered-down form – as a 'descriptive catch-all for seemingly any creative or cultural occupation or institution' (Smith Maguire and Matthews 2012: 552). Indeed, in addition to dealing with 'culture' in the strict sense of the term, cultural managers are cultural intermediaries in three respects (as previously mentioned: their position between social classes and class fractions, their activity at the crossroads of various social fields and their intermediation function between culture, its publics and supporters). Another criticism of the category of 'cultural intermediaries' consists of questioning the 'newness' it supposedly accounts for: 'new' middle-classes holding 'new' positions in expanding occupational sectors (Nixon and du Gay 2002). There would be no point in simply stating that arts and cultural managers are entirely 'new' positions. Nonetheless, I do sketch out the historical process of their invention, show their quite recent rise as compared to well-established professions and account for their expansion in the last decades. But in my view, the question is less about newness in itself than about the features of the positions observed. While they have experienced some of the trends characterizing the establishment of classic professions (the increasing role of specialized training, the formation of professional organizations, the use of a specific jargon, common references shared via specialized press, books and conferences), positions in cultural management still share many characteristics of other 'new' occupations. This professional galaxy remains quite heterogeneous. There has been little standardization of jobs and paths of access and, as is the case with new positions, the individuals who hold them still have leeway in their definition. The book will show that this is a significant part of what makes these occupations attractive.

As Smith Maguire and Matthews note, the social stratification approach to cultural intermediaries is not incompatible with analyzing them as market actors involved in mediation activities. While I do not directly discuss these activities, I conceived this research as a first stage of a research programme ultimately designed to include the practices and functions of cultural managers. For instance, the sociology of cultural tastes I propose in chapter four primarily envisions taste as an indicator of position in the social space and of attitudes towards social space. In addition to that, and because individual preferences do matter in the work of cultural managers, my aim is also to ground the analysis of these taste-makers' professional activities in a sociology of their social dispositions.

In my view, in order to fully understand the role cultural managers play in the social organization of culture, as taste-makers, experts, gatekeepers and organizers, we need to look at them as a professional group and in terms of their position in social space. This book is intended as a step towards this research agenda, which will include two comparative facets. The various forms of organization and definition of cultural managers as a professional group shape the structures of national cultural sectors, from the French state-funded arts to the British celebration of 'creative industries', and shed light on these structures in their turn. As a complement, the sociology of cultural managers could be approached as a cross-national comparison of class structures. The challenge of these occupations for a social stratification analysis lies in the fact that they can both be viewed as a galaxy spanning across several classes, and as a distinct fraction of the upper-middle class. As we will see, the relative indetermination of these positions, the often relatively low level of economic capital associated with them and the complex socio-professional trajectories frequently including precarious work likens them to the 'emergent service workers' of the new UK social class model, but with a higher level of legitimate cultural capital; they also share features of the 'established middle-class', but with a lower level of economic capital (Savage *et al.* 2013, 240–2, 234–6). As for their position in the internal structure of the middle classes, cultural managers could be considered from the point of view of the variations in the balance between the 'cultured' and the 'moneyed' fractions of these classes, which take place between one national society and another (Bennett *et al.* 2009; Lamont 1992).

This book contributes to this research programme by offering a sociology of career choices in cultural management as a first stage towards a yet-to-be-written sociology of positions in this field. To do this, I use a sociological reformulation of the common-sense notion of 'vocation', which I use as an ideal-type to account for the specificity of these career choices. My analysis of the social structures grounding cultural vocations is also conducive to comparative analysis of national cases, touching on labour markets, higher education systems, class structures and the economies of cultural fields. I focus on the internalization of these structural patterns and on their translation into attitudes and choices, that, especially in the case at hand, individuals come to consider as the expression of their personality. As future cultural managers look for self-fulfillment through work, grapple with the contradictory urges of working on individual 'projects' and expanding 'networks', combine references to good management with critical attitudes towards finance and capitalism, I was led to consider them as embodiments of 'the new spirit of capitalism' (Boltanski and Chiapello 2005). In that sense, this sociological portrait of would-be cultural managers is also a reflection on this new spirit at work.

Vincent Dubois, Luvigny, 24 April, 2015

# Acknowledgements

*Culture as a Vocation* was greatly facilitated by the *Institut universitaire de France*, of which I was a member when I conducted this research, and by the Institute for Advanced Study in Princeton, where I finished writing this book. Both institutions offered exceptional working conditions. Many people helped, in some cases decisively, at various stages in the process; my warmest thanks go out to them. By agreeing to submit the questionnaire to applicants, the directors of master's programmes in cultural management allowed us to obtain a sample upon which much of this research is based. Jeremy Ahearne, Anne-Marie Autissier, Marc Lecoutre, Ugo Lozach, Sébastien Michon and students in the *sciences sociales du politique* master's programme of Strasbourg's Institute of Political Studies (class of 2010–11) contributed at various stages in this study by providing additional material or documentation. Antonin Dubois helped in recoding questionnaire responses. Camille Marthon conducted most of the interviews, and processed the applications with me. I had the opportunity to present this research in several workshops and conferences, upon invitations by Celia Bense Ferreira Alves, Annie Collovald, Philippe Coulangeon, Julien Duval, Christophe Gaubert, Joël Mariojouls, Gérard Mauger, José Luis Moreno Pestaña, Frédéric Poulard and the International Conference on Cultural Policy Research. A number of colleagues commented on earlier drafts of the book, including Jérôme Bourdieu, Stéphane Dorin, Franck Poupeau, Olivier Roueff and Jérémy Sinigaglia. Morgane Paris has completed the index. Last but not least, I am immensely indebted to Victor Lepaux, research engineer at the laboratory SAGE (UMR 7363), who participated in this research from the earliest stages. He collected data that was often hard to locate, performed the statistical processing whose results are presented in the book and discussed my interpretations. This book would not have been possible without his availability and rigour. This English-language edition was improved by remarks and suggestions made by Constance DeVereaux, Anita Kangas, Per Mangset, Eleonora Redaelli and Anna Uboldi, and by the support of Tony Bennett and Mike Savage. It is once again the outcome of a collaboration with the translator Jean-Yves Bart, with whom I still greatly enjoy working.

# Introduction

Some occupations are attractive not because they ensure material comfort in terms of job stability and income, but rather because they bring recognition and self-worth to the people who hold them and offer the promise of self-fulfillment. They are *vocations*, based on a strong personal commitment that can be subjectively experienced as a form of selflessness, insofar as material wealth is not top of the list of priorities and rewards expected from such occupations. They should not, however, be defined solely in the negative by laying emphasis on the lower value that those who pursue them attribute to material rewards. Likewise, we should not take for granted the enchanted life histories that retrospectively depict professional trajectories as responses to some internal call or need – such narratives are magnified forms of 'biographical illusion' (Bourdieu 1987a).

Under this definition, vocations consist of a combination of three features.[1] The first pertains to individuals' relationships to their own social determinations. This relationship cannot be reduced either to the calculating individualism of rational choice, or to subjectivist approaches in terms of 'project' or 'motivations'. It is characterized by a relation between specific social conditions in which 'objective chances' are 'situated between absolute necessity and absolute impossibility' and subjective expectations that favour investment, interest and *illusio* (Bourdieu 2000). One of the objectives of this book will be to identify the conditions that allow for a reflexive relationship to one's own determinations, which lead individuals to seek to distance themselves from their most likely future by using the capitals at their disposal or seeking to acquire those they lack (Bourdieu 2014) In this sense, the vocational process is not a matter of denying one's fate, but of making investments (relational, educational, cultural, etc.), which although they relate to objective factors (social background, gender, educational performance) allow the individuals who make them to see their career as the result of deliberate choices – even if that may be an illusion.

Second, such a manner of 'following one's inclination, provided it leads up hill', in the words of André Gide in his 1925 novel, *The Counterfeiters*, also comes with a distinctive relationship to work. A vocation requires specific dispositions that lead individuals to envision their professional activity as a means, or at least an opportunity, to achieve self-fulfillment. This conception comes hand in hand with the lower value attributed to material wealth and is crucially opposed to the 'alienated labour' theorized by Marx. Work is seen as a source of multiple rewards: being substantial and interesting, offering opportunities for social relationships, a lifestyle, a status and prestige. The conditions that make such a conception of work possible and those ensuring that work can actually be experienced in this way are not distributed randomly across society (Baudelot and Gollac 2003); clearly vocations do not develop within a social vacuum.

Third, the relationship to work ties in with a broader set of beliefs. Beyond the work itself and the personal rewards it may bring, vocation involves a reference to a political, aesthetic or moral horizon; such occupations are defined in reference to universal social values and functions. Vocation may thus be doubly defined as a strong *illusio*, i.e. a belief in the games specific to a given social microcosm which grounds the investment in these games (Bourdieu 2000) and as the translation of this *illusio* into a discursive register of the common good or a mission – helping those who suffer, working for justice, serving the cause of science or art.

Redefining the concept of vocation on the basis of these three features requires going beyond the observation of individuals' discourses of self-justification and striving to identify the objective conditions making their trajectories and aspirations possible, as well as analyzing 'vocation work', i.e., the transformation of these conditions into motivations (Suaud 1978: 9). By adopting this approach, I do not mean to lump the occupations discussed in this book under the same label. I do not contend that all the trajectories under study fit the vocation model, but I interpret them in the light of this ideal type (Weber 1992: 183). What leads individuals to pursue such occupations? How is vocational work performed? Which social, collective and individual conditions facilitate it? These questions will constitute the core concerns of this book.

Here, they are applied to a specific category of professional activities – cultural sector occupations, whose objective and subjective logics of access currently display some of the features characterizing vocation under the aforementioned definition. The focus is placed more precisely on cultural managers, more often called arts managers in the American context. These occupations are primarily defined in the negative: they are neither about artistic creation (actor or writer), nor about technical work (lighting designer or proofreader), commentary or analysis (critic, historian of literature) or teaching (music or arts teacher). Even if they bear some similarities to them, cultural managers differ from the better established cultural intermediaries, such as librarians and museum curators in that their positions emerged much more recently and that for these occupations there is no unified course of study to attain a specific status and become part of a professional corps endowed with its own collective representation.

Within the labour force, cultural managers constitute the organizational component of the 'support personnel' who, according to Howard Becker, make artistic creation and its presentation to the public possible but do not have a creative activity (Becker 1982). Their tasks range from fulfilling strictly administrative and organizational duties of diffusion, communication and outreach ('cultural mediation') to managing cultural facilities and curating programmes. Here, they will be examined primarily in terms of their position within social space. At first glance, cultural managers appear to belong to the cultured fractions of the upper social classes, or at least to the upper middle class, if only with respect to their high levels of educational attainment. In the nomenclature of the National Institute for Statistics and Economic Studies (INSEE) in France, which. as I will later show is very imperfect, they are categorized within these groups. Their social statuses and salaries however vary widely both within their organizations and according to their organizational size and resources: although they may have the same job title and perform similar tasks, there is a huge gap between the manager of a major national theatre and one leading a small company. In France, cultural manager positions are more frequently found within the subsidized public sector than in the private sector, even though the 'cultural industries' of publishing, film and the art trade are part of their professional worlds.

Cultural manager is not a profession in the strict sense; rather, cultural managers form a professional group (Demazière and Gadéa 2009). Considering the extent to which members of the group are scattered, it may be considered as a 'professional galaxy', i.e. a weakly objectivized set of interdependent positions and activities. The cohesion of this 'fluid group' (Boltanski 1987) is ensured by the shared belonging of its members in the field of culture, whose unity is in itself very relative. The cultural field is indeed institutionally and professionally structured by sector; each sector has its specificity, from the various sub-sectors of the performing arts to heritage, publishing and the broadcasting sector. Its boundaries are porous and sometimes change, for instance with the 'creative industries' trend leading to a rapprochement between arts, fashion, advertising and the media as economic activities based on knowledge and information, or with the rearrangements induced by the rise of new information technologies. Some cultural managers hold positions situated at the crossroads of culture and other fields, such as tourism, international co-operation or local development; these multiple group memberships suggest the unity of the group is relative.

These features probably account for the scarcity of sociological research on cultural/arts managers. Most sociological studies focus on occupations or professional groups with more clearly established boundaries (Peyrin 2010), or on cultural intermediaries. In the latter case, they conduct a cross-sector investigation of the activities involved in the socio-economic organization of cultural worlds (Jeanpierre and Roueff 2014; Lizé, Naudier and Roueff 2011; Lizé, Naudier and Sofio 2014), or explore cultural intermediaries in a broader sense, including a various range of occupations, from book retailers to public relations practitioners (Smith Maguire and Matthews 2014; Solaroli 2014), but do not focus on cultural managers. One of the main references on the sociology of these occupations remains Paul DiMaggio's study on US arts managers, defined restrictively as the managers of cultural institutions (theatres, symphonic orchestras, cultural centres) (DiMaggio 1987). The few other sociological studies on cultural managers only rarely and cursorily analyze their social trajectories and characteristics (Herron 1998; Tchouikina 2010), generally focusing on their function, often considered under the angle of the tensions between art and management (Chiapello 1998; Kuesters 2010). Most of the scholarship in the field of arts and cultural management does not follow a sociological orientation. It is mainly practice-oriented, either for the purposes of training (Jeffri 1983; Hutchens and Zoe 1985) or to enact the norms of cultural management and turn it into a genuine discipline in addition to a professional activity (Evrard and Colbert 2000; DeVereaux 2009; DeVereaux and Vartiainen 2009; Kirchberg and Zembylas 2010). The International Association of Arts and Cultural Management (AIMAC) organizes conferences and supports the *International Journal of Arts Management* following a comparable orientation. The critical reflections sometimes found in this literature (see for instance DeVereaux 2011) are generally inspired by personal experiences and thoughts rather than on empirical sociological research.

The research presented in this book was not meant to fill this gap, as it focuses on applicants to cultural management positions and is not strictly speaking concerned with the sociology of cultural managers as a professional group and of cultural management as an activity. Yet, it indirectly contributes to this under-investigated sociology, insofar as aspirants to careers in the cultural management sector give us an anticipated reflection of what these careers are, or at least of what they represent socially. In this perspective, retracing the genesis of these career choices allows us to identify who invests in them and what is involved in them, and in the process to establish the role played by these occupations in strategies of social reproduction or upward mobility and to explain what working in the cultural field means to those who want to do so.

Occupations in the cultural sector attract many candidates. They are routinely featured among young people's lists of 'favourite jobs' published in magazines. In local government organizations, 'cultural' positions are generally the most prized. Courses preparing students for these jobs attract applicants in particularly high numbers, sometimes several hundred for 20 or 30 master's students accepted. The reason for this seems self-evident: cultural sector jobs are attractive because culture is a socially valued and rewarding world. Yet, merely stating this is tantamount to raising the question in different terms: why, for whom and to what extent does the social worth ascribed to the cultural sector inspire professional aspirations?

To answer these questions, I chose to focus on the applicants to cultural management training programmes – specifically master's degrees specialized in that field.[2] There were several reasons for this choice. It was first made to reflect the predominant role played by specialized training programmes in determining educational trajectories and access to employment. This empirical approach also allowed us to build a substantial and homogeneous sample in terms of status and age (students in initial training beginning their fifth year of academic education, aged 22 to 25), liable to provide a clear picture of the variables that account for choosing the cultural sector in this age and status group. Having a homogeneous population in terms of age, sharing certain conditions of socialization (particularly in the light of the state of the education system and of the job market) allowed for a generational analysis conducive to the historicization of the variables mobilized and of the resulting interpretations. For the purposes of maintaining this homogeneity, I decided to disregard private training programmes and only consider those offered by universities, which are currently largely in the majority in France anyway (Martin 2008). Studying job applications would have allowed us to account for career changes and professional promotion trajectories that lead individuals to apply for cultural management positions without necessarily pursuing specialized training first. This option would, however, have involved considerable methodological hurdles – specifically it would, for instance, have been difficult to have access to the applicants and the sample would probably have been very heterogeneous; additionally the design of our research required us to focus on new entrants. Not only did the analysis of students' applications to training programmes specifically preparing them for these jobs meet that requirement, it also enabled us to take into account the generalization of the demand for academic degrees in the field and to consider aspects pertaining to the education system and its transformations (choice of studies, effects of branches of education on professional career choices, adjustment to 'inflation' and 'devaluation' of degrees, etc.).

The reader will find a methodological appendix at the end of this book, providing a detailed description of the data and methods I used, which I will only briefly present here. I also include some methodological explanations in the main text where directly necessary. A questionnaire intended for applicants to cultural management master's programmes provided the bulk of the material for this research. We retained the responses of 654 individuals, which, because of multiple applications, amount to a total of 1,470 applications and to a response rate of c. 65 per cent. We processed these responses using cross-tabulations, multinomial logistic regressions and, most importantly, multiple correspondence analyses (MCA).

MCA is a form of geometric data analysis (Le Roux and Rouanet 2004). The technique involves reducing a large dimensionality space and projecting it onto a two dimensional plane in order to capture the main principles that structure the dataset. Overall, it is meant to represent proximities and distances (between individuals, between variables) within the dataset. The axes on the graph are the vectors (a linear combination of the existing variables) that preserve most of the variance of the initial space. They need interpretation. To do so, one has to look at the variables that contribute most to the creation of any given axis. Data is categorical: each column contains a certain number of 'modalities' (the levels of the qualitative variable). There are two types of variables. Active variables are used in the calculation of the MCA, they contribute to establishing the structure of the 2D plane. Supplementary variables are plotted into this 2D plane. Although they do not contribute to its structure (they are not taken into account at the moment of calculation), they add useful information for interpretation. This inductive method shows how multiple variables (e.g. gender, educational background, artistic practices and expectations about work) combine in the distribution of positions, practices and attitudes into the geometric space of the graph, in order to shed light on their actual distribution in social space. The first MCA establishes the structure of the social space of would-be cultural managers on the basis of the applicants' main features (social and educational backgrounds, gender, cultural socialization, professional experiences). The second identifies the structure of their prospects regarding training and employment, while the third accounts for their cultural tastes and practices.

In addition to the questionnaire, this research relies on secondary analysis of data on cultural employment from the Ministry of Culture, the Ministry of Labour and from the National Institute of Statistics and Economic Studies (INSEE), mainly used in the first chapter, to specify the profiles of cultural workers and the main characteristics of their employment conditions. The database of the French Ministry of Education was occasionally useful to compare the characteristics of the applicants to those of students registered in cultural management master's programmes. Three types of qualitative material complemented these statistics: a corpus of 45 application files for one of the programmes in our sample, especially useful to analyze the applicants' modes of self-presentation and their narratives of vocation; direct observations of 50 selection interviews for the same master's programme, and 20 interviews with successful or unsuccessful applicants.

The analysis presented in this book takes into consideration the major factors involved in the social genesis of vocations. The first factor is the characteristics of the professional world under study. The choice of pursuing activities that confer recognition but at the same time offer uncertain prospects in terms of career and salary is classically explained by the importance of the non-financial rewards they may afford.[3] This is undoubtedly an important factor, as in the artistic vocation model that some agents pursuing careers in cultural management have renounced, and that they regularly encounter in everyday work relationships (Freidson 1986; Abbing 2002; Sapiro 2007b: 5; Menger 2014). Yet cultural management affords lower material uncertainty but also lower hopes of self-fulfillment compared to 'creative work' (this is one of the key differences between this study and Menger's analysis). At any rate, the importance of this factor can only be assessed by relating these symbolic rewards to the objective conditions that permit a reasonable chance of securing them. In this case, the number of positions in the French cultural sector has sharply increased over the past few decades. New professional positions have appeared (mediator, sponsorship consultant…). As the result of a combination of demographic growth and of the creation of new occupations, working in the cultural field and in cultural management in particular is now a more achievable professional goal than it was 30 years ago. Although generally such professionalization processes reduce access to the field and lead to more rigid positions, for the most part the definition of cultural occupations has remained open and free from exclusive specialization. Instead, these occupations encompass a wide array of activities and skills; accordingly individuals with varied backgrounds may pursue them. Likewise, the 'costs of entry' to the field remain low, as for most artistic occupations (Mauger 2006a, 2006b). Since the early 1990s, the levels of educational achievement of aspirants have risen, as have requirements for specialized training. Yet, there are still multiple paths of access to these jobs; applicants are therefore more likely to believe they will find a path than for instance those pursuing scientific occupations (Convert 2006). Barriers to entry remain difficult to identify (unlike for the positions that require passing an entrance examination). Cultural occupations are therefore attractive not only because they offer hopes for symbolic rewards, but also because their development conditions and some of their characteristics make them, if not 'realistic aspirations' (Bourdieu 1984), at least conducive to fostering that 'natural confidence which every man has, more or less, not only in his own abilities, but in his own good fortune' as Adam Smith put it in explaining the choice of careers where success is uncertain.

For occupations to be 'attractive' there needs to be a significant number of agents displaying characteristics that predispose them to be attracted. Here, individual ('passion') or psychological ('desire') explanations are often favoured, especially as applicants often themselves express their 'motivations' in such terms: in many cases they are encouraged to do so given that formulating a 'plan' is now expected in educational and professional settings. My approach consists instead in resituating personal social histories within their social and historical contexts. The global characterization of the population of applicants will be a first step in that direction. Cultural administration shares with other vocations like journalism (Lafarge and Marchetti 2011) or humanitarian work (Dauvin and Siméant 2012) the specificity of attracting applicants with high levels of educational capital. This raises the question of relationships – which are anything but linear – between investment in studies and professional career choices. Additionally, the fact that women constitute the vast majority of aspirants to these jobs suggests that the role of gender in making professional 'choices' deserves investigation.

Things would be much too simple if the aspirants formed a perfectly homogeneous group and had a single reason for opting for a career in cultural management. While some frequently recurring features are identifiable (including the importance of current or past artistic practice), they have diverse backgrounds that map out the social space of applicants and attest to the variety of rationales behind their applications. This variety also reflects the diversity of positions pursued, from public relations positions, which require a background in communications, to managing theatre companies, which requires legal skills, or curating festivals, which requires artistic knowledge. The similarities between the social space of aspirants and the space of the positions to which they aspire is thus characterized by fragmentation: the diversity of trajectories and dispositions converging in cultural management is both the cause and the consequence of the diversity of aspirations brought about by cultural management, which might arguably account for the extent of this fragmentation.

No single hypothesis, then, accounts for the variety of rationales behind the choice of pursuing cultural occupations. In order to understand how the vocation to work in cultural management works, we need to map out the space of thinkable and possible career choices and to achieve a sense of the desirability of a given option in relation to other possible options. Cultural employment can, in particular, constitute a desirable prospect – one that is not necessarily less realistic than others for the many higher education graduates with degrees in literature, languages and the humanities. Their educational capital leads them to raise their professional aspirations; teaching at primary and secondary schools is not only an unattractive prospect (due to the degradation of working conditions and social status) but also one that is often somewhat uncertain (due to decreases in the number of positions offered). Cultural occupations also attract applicants because they may be perceived as a path to salvation within a context of massification of higher education and high youth unemployment.

The transformation of potentially favourable dispositions into aspirations conceived as such is not an automatic process. It hinges on a complex alchemy of experiences and spaces of socialization which, in more or less coherent and fortunate combinations, produces a wide array of 'vocations' taking different forms: from cultural inheritors purposefully building on family legacies (by taking over the family's art gallery), to scholarship holders with aspirations of upward mobility (who become involved in cultural mediation to enable others to have the same access to culture that they received) or the emancipated children from wealthy families who convert the social and cultural capital they have accumulated within their peer groups into a professional future by organizing rock concerts rather than continuing the family tradition. Education – specifically the higher education system – plays a prominent role here. My hypothesis is that it does not operate through direct prescriptions leading to specific career choices, but rather through more diffuse but nevertheless insistent incentives. Students in literary and artistic courses are for instance subjected to the incentives to become 'professionalized' that characterize higher education today. For them especially, 'cultural mediation' and 'communication' may serve as responses to requirements to present a career plan, in a context where the choice of doing research or pursuing literary studies tends to be discouraged – especially as specialized training programmes leading to cultural jobs have flourished in the past few years, particularly in departments of arts and humanities. Insofar as academic supply contributes to creating demand and shaping professional prospects, the proliferation of programmes has been a factor in making these occupations a conceivable professional option. The academic system itself contributes to a view that sees the choice of cultural occupations as a means to maximize the professional return of a devaluated educational capital (especially literary and artistic capital). The fact that those who possess such forms of educational capital are for the most part women further explains why more women pursue careers in cultural administration than men.

Although there are factors specific to the sector, the vocational aspiration in cultural management gives us a window into the relationships between gender, social origin, educational capital and career choices – in other words they give us insights into the analysis of contemporary forms of reproduction. Considering the developmental chronology of these jobs – which began in the mid-1960s and has intensified since the early 1980s – aspirants of the 2000–10s are the children of those who occupy many of these positions, or in some cases the grandchildren of cultural management 'pioneers'. 'Passion' for cultural occupations can indeed be inherited and derives from a traditional mechanism of professional reproduction: this is at least partly the case here. Although it is unoriginal, this mechanism deserves examination. First, it is unparalleled in scope considering that these positions are relatively recent. Second, it has limited the proportion of first-generation cultural workers, particularly those with working-class roots, when precisely these jobs served as paths towards upward social mobility for working-class or lower middle-class graduates of previous generations. In practice, applicants to cultural management positions not only possess high amounts of educational capital, but they are also, for the most part, from the upper and upper-middle classes. The defining elements of social downgrading converge: inability to ensure maximal return on educational investments and uncertainty regarding the chances of occupying a social position (at least) equivalent to that held by the parents even despite higher levels of educational capital.

In *Distinction*[4], Pierre Bourdieu showed that in the 1960s and 1970s, the fuzzy and emerging positions of cultural intermediaries were occupied by graduates with working-class roots who were unable to make the most of their educational capital as they had not inherited the necessary social capital, and symmetrically by children of the bourgeoisie who were deprived of social capital required to reproduce the social position of their parents (Bourdieu 1984: 119ff.). Both groups could count on attractive, yet loosely defined, occupations in the fields of psychology, advertising or culture to achieve 'personal fulfillment' and 'freedom' (in contrast to better established positions in banks or administrations, perceived to be rigid and stifling) in order to reach a state of 'social infinitude' liable to offset the effects of the social or educational downgrading that comes with occupying a lower position than they could otherwise expect, considering, respectively, their level of qualification and their parents' occupations. The analytical scheme that supports this interpretation remains very useful to understand the trajectories of later generations, but its application yields slightly different observations. The effects of the second educational 'boom' have now combined with those of long-term mass unemployment and led to significantly lower prospects for upward social mobility and increasing difficulties for newcomers on the job market to match the social positions of their elders (Chauvel 1998; Peugny 2009). In this context, cultural intermediary positions can still offer a refuge to those threatened with downgrading, but as both graduates with working-class roots and inheritors excluded from the education system have fewer chances to access them, they are now in the sights of those who are facing downgrading even though they have both high educational capital and high social backgrounds. Precisely because women are more often in such situations than men, there are more women who apply for such positions (Nauze-Fichet and Tomasini 2005).

We might say, then, that we are not witnessing a 'crisis of vocation' but rather, at least in part, crisis-induced vocations. Aspiring cultural managers in specialized training programmes graduate in large numbers – around 5,000 each year, which is slightly above the number of available positions. This number has greatly increased since the early 1990s and continues to grow (Martin 2008). This is not specific to France, and can be observed in other contexts although there is no uniform pattern of evolution.[5] Beyond individual 'choices', one possible reason for the popularity of these career paths lies in a combination of several lingering crises. The first one (a crisis of social reproduction) consists in the growing difficulty for middle and upper class children to maintain their parents' positions even though they have more education. Depending on the type of curriculum pursued, this uncertainty may lead students to target professional sectors which, like cultural management, are open enough for them to consider carving a space in and over-coming possible failure, but also sufficiently rewarding to allow for forms of symbolic reassurance (cultural managers may for instance 'live out their passion' by organizing contemporary art exhibits) powerful enough to offset a possible sense of decline (which, say, a doctor's daughter might experience when going back and forth between unemployment stints and short-term contracts). More generally, the newer generation is subjected to the combined effects of two other crises: the crisis of the educational system and the crisis of employment. With higher education come higher expectations in terms of both employment (avoiding downgrading) and satisfaction at work (self-fulfillment). The fear of unemployment induces utilitarianism in the choice of educational studies and the pursuit of job security; yet it can, paradoxically, under certain conditions also lead some to go for 'risky' options: at times of crisis, the pleasure principle may seem like a desirable alternative to the utility principle whose implementation yields very uncertain results anyway, especially considering that other options like research and teaching have themselves become uncertain and often less desirable.

The social genesis of these crisis-induced vocations affects the meaning agents give to holding these jobs and the way they perceive them. Depending on the characteristics of those who pursue such occupations, it allows us to establish the importance and the form assumed by these risky career choices, in the sense that there are many applicants for few jobs. In relation to other possible options, such a career choice may in fact appear reasonable and constitute an honorable outcome for literary students with high levels of educational and social capital, or offer hopes of social mobility to average students from low-income families who have small chances of making it, but have nothing to lose if they try. Likewise, the sense of selflessness reported by some aspiring cultural managers is arguably more of a belief than the ideological mask of an advantageous position. Regardless, it does not have the same extent or meaning when success in terms of social status and pay is both strongly expected and statistically probable (for instance for upper-class graduates from business schools or highly selective programmes) and when expectations and objective chances of social success are lowered as the result of the combination of characteristics pertaining to education, gender, rank among siblings and social background (i.e. middle-class girls with lower educational capital whose older brothers and sisters have fulfilled parental hopes). Lastly, regarding different visions of culture, and beyond, of the social world at play according to the trajectories leading to these career choices: some have primarily technical or practical outlooks derived from initial experiences of cultural management; others have the missionary zeal of the newly converted; and yet others see culture as a social alternative – a means to find some relief from the harshness of the capitalist system or even, in some cases, a venue to criticize it.

This book is divided into four chapters. In the first one, I identify the main structural factors for career choices in the cultural sector, and, more precisely, in cultural management. I retrace the development of cultural employment over the last decades, and the invention of new positions in this domain. I also show how transformations in the higher education system and the rise of specialized training programmes in cultural management favour such a choice. In chapter two, I show how these objective and collective conditions fit with social dispositions of specific agents in order to explain the transformation of structural factors into subjective and individual aspirations. To do so, I examine the social features of the applicants to cultural management master's programmes and account for their diverse characteristics and backgrounds. In chapter three, I turn to a qualitative interpretation of the forms and the meanings of vocation resulting from the combination of objective conditions and subjective perceptions. The fourth and final chapter explores, in a broader perspective, social reproduction and how the young would-be cultural managers combine anti-conformism and individual strategies of adjustment to the social order.

Please note that all illustrative examples (case studies and interviews) without a source are from my own research.

## Notes

1 I use the words vocation and vocational in the sense of 'calling', apart from a few occurrences where I explicitly refer to 'vocational training' as the learning of specific professional skills.
2 I use the first-person singular to describe my personal choices and contributions, and the first-person plural when it comes to the collective aspects of this research, especially in collaboration with Victor Lepaux.
3 The fact that professionals in the information, arts and performing arts sectors are the most likely to report being satisfied by their work (over 75 per cent) even though they get paid less than others with an equivalent social status gives an indication of these non-material rewards (Baudelot and Gollac 2003: 74).
4 *Distinction: A Social Critique Of the Judgment of Taste,* by Bourdieu, P. (1984).
5 In Norway, for instance, these programmes were very popular among students until the early 2000s, but most of them nowadays face a crisis of recruitment (personal communication by Per Mangset).

# 1 Culture in the space of professional career choices

Making a career out of culture is now a conceivable option within the space of professional career choices, particularly for higher education graduates. First, the development of numerous new positions in cultural employment has inspired realistic hopes of possible careers in the field. Second, the higher education system has produced students with needs for professional guidance and offered specialized training programmes leading them to perceive cultural employment as a possible project or encouraging them to pursue this path further.

## How cultural occupations became attractive

### The rise of cultural employment

Career 'choices' cannot only be explained on grounds of individual 'motivation' – interpretations in such terms tend to merely reflect the words used by individuals to justify themselves, as in 'motivation letters', or to content themselves with putting a psychological label on processes that require explaining, which is hardly better. What is usually called a career choice hinges on social conditions, and it is subjectively translated into an expression of individual will. The first of these conditions relates to the number and accessibility of positions within reach – in other words to the situation of the job market in the sector under consideration, which, albeit in roundabout ways, encourages or discourages the inclusion of these positions in the space of potential choices. This does not mean that individuals systematically make informed adjustments on the basis of sector-by-sector job market realities. It is highly doubtful that information regarding the quantity and quality of cultural employment shapes short-term individual strategies, let alone accounts for lasting collective choices to pursue occupations in the cultural sector.

I propose a completely different hypothesis. Western European countries have witnessed a massive and continued long-term increase of cultural employment since the 1980s.[1] From 1995–9, the cultural sector in the EU experienced an average annual rate of employment growth of 2.1 per cent, and during the same period employment figures for cultural occupations within the cultural sector grew at an annual rate of 4.8 per cent (MKW *et al.* 2001: 9–10). I argue that this increase, even if not linear, has progressively contributed to making these occupations conceivable career choices for a growing proportion of new entrants to the labour market despite often unattractive employment conditions. This increase, stimulated by cultural policy, was also encouraged by an official discourse on culture as a job-creating sector that was largely echoed in the media, from the early 1980s and Jack Lang's Ministry of Culture, in France, to the promotion of 'creative industries' in the 2000s, particularly in the UK (Ashton and Noonan 2013: 1–8) and at the European level. Rather than the reasoned analysis of reliable information on the state of the job market, I argue that the promotion of cultural occupations as 'regular' jobs, in the sense that they are no longer statistically exceptional and are officially described as employment opportunities, might go some way towards explaining why agents with favourable dispositions effectively pursue them.

I will begin by going into some detail about the extent of the increase of cultural employment in France, before I elaborate on those who see it as a calling and the conditions under which they respond to that calling. I use the concept of 'cultural employment' for lack of a better term: it is not a sociological concept, but rather a category constructed by and for government cultural policy makers. It is used, for example, by France's Department for Studies, Strategic Forecasting and Statistics (DEPS), which is also the main source of information on the subject. These statistics are based on two debatable categorization rationales; they encompass both employment in 'cultural professions' defined as such, and all employment in the 'cultural sector' including jobs with no specifically cultural content (such as accountants) as long as they are performed within an organization that belongs to the cultural sector. The concept is used in particular to measure the evolution of cultural employment; as with any statistical dataset this is based on 'conventions of equivalence' that become increasingly problematic the longer the period covered by the dataset. The objective positions considered as equivalent may change over time as well as their classifications (Desrosières 1992). Beyond the case of 'cultural employment', the same applies to all the statistical categorizations based on occupations and social categories used by the French National Institute of Statistics & Economic Studies (INSEE) in the field. There are more specific issues in addition to this general problem. It is well documented (Moulin and Passeron 1985) that identifying artists, as such, poses difficulties because they tend to self-identify even in the absence of a formal status. Similar issues are encountered with other cultural occupations, particularly outside of technicians (managers, mediators, etc.). There is no specific categorization for these jobs; some of them are considered information professionals while others may be included in various other categories that may vary with time. While there is arguably no sector with clearly defined and unchanging boundaries, those of the cultural sector are more subject to change as their definitions are contested (Dubois 2012a). It is necessary to keep these limitations in mind when discussing cultural employment statistics and their evolution over several decades. Here, I do this essentially on the basis of secondary analysis of INSEE census data from 1962 to 2008,[2] and of available syntheses complementing this approach based on information about professional groups with statistical portraits by sector of activity.[3]

Regardless of the statistical sources considered and definitions used, and despite the aforementioned limitations of available data, it is quite clear that there has been a significant rise in cultural employment. The number of professionals employed in information, arts and performing arts sectors multiplied by 1.7 between 1962–82 and again by 2.5 between 1982–2008; as of 2008 there were 4.2 times as many of them as there were in 1962 – twice that number if the unemployed are also considered. This increase is far greater than that of the labour force in general; over the entire period these occupations accounted for between 0.35–1.08 per cent of the working population.

Depending on the definition under consideration, the cultural sector reportedly accounts for 1.7–2 per cent of all employment in France, which is equivalent to the 2009 European Union average.[4] In this country, the increase in cultural employment was encouraged by a significant rise in public cultural expenditure beginning in the early 1980s; yet it cannot only be attributed to that as previous figures suggest that more money had already been spent in the previous two decades after a sharp decline – although this data is subject to caution due to changes in INSEE's classification of occupations.[5]

This trend cannot be attributed to journalists or more generally to information and communication professionals, who are in the same category as holders of occupations in the arts and performing arts sectors in French national classifications. To take a somewhat rough indicator, if we relate the number of registered, professional journalists to the overall number of professionals in information, arts and performing arts sectors listed in the INSEE census, we observe that their proportion within this category has been steadily decreasing since the early 1980s (c. 16.5 per cent in 1982; 11.5 per cent in 2008). In fact, while the number of journalists rose sharply for a long time,[6] it did to a lesser extent than that of the holders of cultural occupations; after 2003 the increase was slower and ultimately the number of journalists began levelling out and then decreasing in the late 2000s. The sector-by-sector figures on salaried employees in the 1990s and 2000s confirm that the cultural sector strictly speaking grew from around 300,000 in 1992 to over 360,000 in 2007; over the same period, employment in the media decreased slightly, from around 68,000 to 67,000 salaried individuals.[7] This is also indicated by data on professional groups, which confirms the independent rise of arts and performing arts professionals over the 1982–2009 period.[8]

If we consider the 1982–2008 period, the rise of cultural occupations also cannot be explained by the development of the most established positions. The number of state-employed librarians, archivists and curators increased only slightly (by 1.23 over the entire period), and even decreased after 1990. The number of arts teachers, however, increased in similar proportions, if slightly less than those included in the category as a whole (by 2.65). Regarding artistic occupations, the contrast is noteworthy. The numbers of authors, musicians and visual artists increased sharply, yet at a slower rate than the overall number of individual holding cultural and information occupations.[9] It has, however, been well documented (Menger 1998, 2005a) that the number of actors increased at a much faster rate (by 4.12); likewise their proportion within the group of cultural occupations increased substantially, from 8.6–14.4 per cent, which indicates that they made a significant contribution to the overall increase.

As the combined number of those employed in the cultural sector grew, cultural management occupations developed and new related positions emerged, making possible aspirations that were initially inspired by novelty appeal, i.e. the introduction of new professional opportunities, and then gradually came to reflect new divisions of labour established in the cultural field.

### Cultural managers: professional labels and vocations

Cultural management positions essentially expanded in France from the early 1980s onwards as employment in the cultural sector as a whole increased. This does not mean, however, that they emerged as a result of a progress in the division of labour that can be directly traced back to the morphological growth of the sector. Their rise more generally relates to transformations in social space which, starting in the 1960s, led to the development of cultural intermediary positions in the broader sense of the term, as educational capital became increasingly important in reproduction processes (Bourdieu 1984). It also reflects transformations in the functioning of the cultural field, which I will now elaborate upon – specifically the growing importance of managerial activities that have been partly promoted by public cultural policies and, more broadly speaking, induced by more numerous and complex financing schemes.[10]

While organizational activities enabling the production of artworks and their presentation to the public have existed for a long time, it is worth investigating how these activities, which were previously undertaken by artists themselves or by volunteers, became progressively specialized and elicited the development of a professional milieu – in other words the way in which they went from being tasks to complete to fully-fledged occupations that became conceivable career paths. The case of the US, where these jobs appeared earlier, allows us to put the French case into perspective and gain a better understanding of the development of these professional labels and occupations. Richard Peterson showed how arts management experienced a shift, from the early 1960s on, from the highly personalized model of the impresario to the 'administrative' model, relying on professional skills that cannot be reduced to personal qualities (Peterson 1986, 1987). Until the mid twentieth century, theatres, museums and orchestras were led by upper-class impresarios who claimed to have an artistic sensibility but had received no training in the field. They combined charisma and entrepreneurship and maintained ties with donors; one of their key skills was to 'talk to wealthy prospective patrons' (Peterson 1987: 164). There was no distinction between the function and the person who fulfilled it or between the institution and the person who led it. The transformation that began in the 1960s first came with the emergence of specialized training programmes. The first appeared in 1966 at Yale and Florida State University; they were followed by programmes that initially focused on theatre management but were then progressively extended to all the arts, in arts colleges and business schools alike. Like their functions, the backgrounds of arts administrators became increasingly standardized: they progressively shifted from using social skills and connections to maintain rapport with patrons to occupying a more organizational and audience-oriented role, less charismatic and more technical.

These changes were not brought about by organizational factors relating to the size of the arts institutions or the history of their development. Rather, the rise of arts administrators mostly resulted from external factors. The emergence of new sources of funding was the primary cause of the shift, as the expansion of public funding in the mid-1960s and the rationalization of private sponsorship procedures led to an increased demand for accountability, requirements for financial statements and activity reports and, ultimately, transformed the way arts institutions functioned. Paul DiMaggio also emphasized the impact of these new funding methods by pointing to what he calls an 'institutional isomorphism' effect: interacting organizations tend to adopt compatible structures. Orchestras, museums and theatres began operating more like the public administrations or businesses that provided them with funding (DiMaggio 1987). This convergence was directly encouraged by the funders. Business sponsors offered the services of their managers to arts institutions to 'rationalize' their management, and the government supported the development of professional training programmes preparing for the implementation of the new administrative model. Eleonora Redaelli similarly underlines the connection between American cultural policy and 'the rise of a new idea: the professionalization of arts management, envisioning arts management as a distinctive function in arts organizations' (Redaelli 2012: 146). This idea was also promoted by professional organizations such as the American Symphony Orchestra League and later the North American Performing Arts Managers and Agents (established in 1979); the Association of Arts Administration Educators was founded in 1975. The same period also witnessed the creation of specialized journals including *Art and the Law* (1975) and *The Performing Arts Review* (1969).[11] These developments had a mutually reinforcing effect leading to the emergence and unification of a professional world. To some extent this contributed to standardizing cultural management occupations, which in turn facilitated the training of a group of specialists who then taught these professional standards to others. In contrast to the very strong ties between an individual and an institution that prevailed at the time when the impresario model dominated, standardization facilitated the careers of individuals who moved from one institution to another; this mobility contributed to reinforcing the distinction of the function and of its occupant, who had made it possible.

Where France is concerned, a similar long-term historical account remains partly to be written.[12] Yet, from the 1980s on, it is possible to retrace a shift that is to some extent comparable to what happened in the US some 20 years earlier (Dubois 2012a: 337 ff.). While cultural activities experienced a professionalization process that began in the 1960s, it was essentially after the mid-1980s that professional labels pertaining to cultural management occupations were defined and popularized. This was when the terms of cultural *gestionnaire* (manager), *manager*, *ingénieur* and *médiateur* emerged. In part, new positions were created, like those of the directors of cultural affairs in local authorities. Specialized training programmes and publications appeared.[13]

'Status-creating individuals' (Heinich and Pollak 1989), often senior civil servants in the field of culture, provided a model for the reference of those who aspired to occupying positions in cultural management. A case in point is Bernard Faivre d'Arcier, who studied in the prestigious schools HEC, Sciences Po Paris and the National School of Administration (ENA), which trains civil administrators (class of 1972). He became a civil administrator at the Ministry of Culture where he served as director for theatre and the performing arts (1989–92), and also directed the famous theatre festival of Avignon (from 1980–4 and 1993–2003). Some of these prominent figures also actively promoted cultural management occupations, like Claude Mollard. A senior public auditor at the French court of auditors, Mollard was among other things secretary-general of the Centre Georges-Pompidou (1971–8) and then director of the *Musée des arts décoratifs* (1978–80). In 1981, he was appointed as adviser to Minister of Culture, Jack Lang, and then led the newly established delegation for visual arts. After the 1986 change of Cabinet, he founded ABCD (Arts, Budget, Conseil, Développement), the first cultural engineering agency', in which he implemented principles he had introduced in his book (Mollard 1987). In the following year, he created the *Institut supérieur de management culturel* to train future 'cultural engineers'.

The crucial contribution of senior civil servants in shaping and diffusing the cultural management model goes some way towards indicating the role of public authorities in their promotion – a role which in fact extends far beyond that. As in the US, the development of new sources of funding for culture provided conditions conducive to the rise of cultural management. Unlike in the US, however, this funding was mostly public. The recruitment of staff in charge of administrative and management duties was enabled by the significant growth of cultural budgets that began in the late 1970s at the local level, and went on to intensify in the early 1980s under the combined effects of an unprecedented increase in resources for the Ministry of Culture and of decentralization. This was also made necessary, partly in functional terms, due to the increase of administrative workload, but also in more political terms. In practice, increased public spending on culture came with an effort to demonstrate the strict control of expenditure, eliciting the rise of a managerial rhetoric that previously had little currency in the cultural field (there were now incentives to 'manage culture') and the promotion of individuals with 'managerial' backgrounds in what came to be termed 'cultural enterprises'. The establishment of a national network of assistance for the management of cultural enterprises (AGEC) in 1983 reflected this orientation, aimed, in particular, at advising and training staff in subsidized cultural structures. The opening address at one of the conferences organized for the launch of AGEC, held in December 1983, summarized the coming revolution in thinking: 'Economy and culture: these two terms, these two worlds, these two rationales have in the past, all too often, appeared to contradict each other. Yet today it is no longer time to debate on whether or not it makes sense to bring them together; we must now discuss under what forms this will happen'.

As we have seen in the US case, a direct link can be drawn between changes in cultural policy and the invention of new professional positions. The emergence of municipal cultural managers in Norway during the 1970s and 1980s, for instance, resulted from the 'new cultural policy' of Norwegian local authorities at the time (Mangset 1995). Cultural policy discourse and ideas also shape individual choices and the definition of positions. Jennifer Hinves illustrates this influence in a case study showing how the creative turn in British cultural policy from the end of the 1990s onwards could have impacted career orientations and the redefinition of professional identities (Hinves 2012). These effects are clearly visible in the French case. The promotion of cultural management jobs in the 1980s was part of a wider shift in cultural policy orientations at national and local levels. The reference to community-based cultural activities (*animation socioculturelle*) that prevailed on the left, attracting individuals with backgrounds in activism, was abandoned to the benefit of the promotion of artistic creation and professionalism, encouraging the rise of cultural specialists (*techniciens de la culture*, Dubois 2006). The Ministry of Culture's rhetoric extolling the 'reconciliation' of economy and culture gave symbolic validation to this managerial shift. Starting in June 1981 this came with a cultural employment policy aimed at boosting cultural management, presenting public investment in culture as profitable in terms of job numbers. While this policy targeted the cultural sector as a whole, it was a contributing factor in the promotion of the 'new' jobs of cultural administration, management and mediation.

These occupations, which received symbolic and financial support from the cultural policies implemented from the early 1980s onwards, gained considerable exposure at the time. From positions that needed inventing, whose definition and designation played on the novelty (if not the provocative) aspects of importing references to management in the cultural field, they became established components of organization charts of cultural and artistic structures. Where they were once tasks carried out on the side by directors or musicians, these activities were now seen as necessary and to require distinct skills liable to provide their main source of employment to individuals who did not have an artistic activity.

While it is undeniable that cultural management occupations experienced a boost, it remains difficult to establish an accurate numerical estimate of the increase in jobs. As I have noted, these jobs are not featured as such in the classification of occupations. However, the evolution of managers in the press, publishing, audiovisual and performing arts sectors over the period when the classifications remained unchanged provides us with a useful approximation of the increase – which was almost fourfold between 1982 and 1999 (from 3,200–12,363). Over the same period, the number of individuals in cultural occupations that did not involve administrative duties increased significantly less. It is the same case, as we have seen, for journalists, but also for executives in the performing arts sector (whose numbers were multiplied by 1.8, reaching almost 8,000); only technical executives in the performing arts and broadcasting sectors (who also include administrators) are comparable in terms of numbers and increase (from 4,240–14,818). The high number of members of the newly established category (as of 2003) of directors, programmers and producers in the broadcasting and performing arts sectors confirms the significant progression of these jobs in those sectors, and the increasing number of those working in the performing arts and broadcasting sectors in general, numbering 22,350 employed individuals in 2008, including artistic executives (with no further distinction in terms of sector) but not press and publishing executives.

### An attractive sector despite poor employment conditions

Working in the cultural sector in general and specifically making a career out of cultural management may have become a realistic pursuit in view of the increase in the number of available positions, but employment conditions in the sector nevertheless often remained poor, and in some cases worsened (Neilson and Coté 2014). This contradicts the utilitarian view purporting that workers make professional choices on the basis of a rational calculation aimed at maximizing their interests; it is actually *despite* poor conditions that the sector became attractive.

The increase in the number of jobs did not come with a stabilization of employment. Arguably the opposite happened: as in the case of the performing arts, which accounts for a significant share of the sector,[14] the labour supply increased at a faster rate than the volume of activity, leading more and more people to alternate between periods of increasingly short-term employment and unemployment, to the detriment of the number of hours worked and, accordingly, to their level of remuneration (Menger 2003, 2005a). Although it is important to be mindful of the very sharp disparities within the performing arts sector and between the different cultural sectors, the general picture of employment conditions in the sector as a whole is mostly unflattering (Gouyon 2010; Gouyon and Patureau 2012). Those who pursue these occupations can hardly be said to be lured by the promise of a stable and well-paid job. A 2001 official report mentions increases in atypical, precarious employment in the cultural sector at the European level, a trend which certainly worsened during the following period (MKW *et al.* 2001: 12).

First, cultural occupations face high levels of under-employment and unemployment. In the late 2000s in France, under-employment reached 12 per cent in the arts and performing arts sector, i.e. over twice as much as in the labour force at large (5 per cent).[15] In the second half of the 1990s, these occupations were found twice as much in the population of job seekers (4 per cent) as in the labour force at large (2 per cent).[16] The situation has worsened since: the number of job seekers in the arts and performing arts sectors increased by nearly 50,000 between 1997 and 2009.[17] In practice, this results in a particularly high job application rate (18 per cent, against 10 per cent for the overall population), especially for skilled occupations, and in a higher proportion of long-term unemployed (registered for at least a year) among the overall population of job seekers (44 per cent against 27 per cent), even though these unemployed individuals are often more skilled (42 per cent of job seekers in the sector have two years of higher education or more, compared to 17 per cent for the overall population).[18] An exceptionally high turnover rate has also been observed (273 per cent in 2007–9).[19] This rate can be explained by the specificity of the unemployment insurance system in the French arts sector (*intermittents du spectacle*), and more broadly by the massive recourse to fixed-term contracts (contract terminations account for 95 per cent of exits from employment). The proportion of these contracts, which is high in the performing arts and in broadcasting as well as in heritage conservation occupation, indeed strongly increased, particularly in the 1990s, [20] reaching 31 per cent in cultural occupations and 25 per cent in the cultural sector regardless of occupation in 2007.[21] The share of non-salaried workers, which has traditionally been high in the sector, is around 30 per cent; they form a vast majority of those employed in literary and visual arts.

These employment conditions do not systematically result in precarity: at least for a minority of individuals, intermittent employment translates into a succession of regular contracts intercut with short periods of compensated unemployment, ultimately ensuring a stable and occasionally high income level (Menger 2005a). Yet overall, remuneration levels in the cultural sector remain fairly modest for work under often difficult conditions. As a recent research has shown in the case of 'creative labour' in the UK, 'the large reservoir of labour from which the cultural industries can select its employees [...] enables a form of exploitation of junior workers in the form of low pay, especially when we take into consideration the number of junior workers who are willing to gift their labour to companies in order to accrue the experience needed to eventually attain (better) paid positions', (Hesmondhalgh and Baker 2010: 114–6). This also applies to the French case. In 2007–9, over half (58 per cent) of the full-time salaried professionals in the arts and performing arts were paid under 2,000 € a month; the median salary was 1,800 €, which is higher than the labour force as a whole (1,600 €), but lower than that of teachers (2,000 €) and information and communication professionals (2,300 €).[22] Individuals employed in the field must also be highly flexible. In addition to the recourse to fixed-term contracts, there are high levels of part-time employment (27 per cent, compared to 17 per cent for the entire labour force; 45 per cent in the performing arts in 2006–8), which have become increasingly high over the past two decades.[23] At the same time, professionals in the arts and performing arts more often work on Saturdays (69 per cent and 53 per cent respectively) and Sundays (59 per cent and 30 per cent); additionally, more of them work over 40 hours a week when they are employed full-time (51 per cent and 40 per cent).

Lastly, professionals in the cultural sector are characterized by their 'multi-activity' – over half fall into this category, which is ten times more than in the labour force as a whole.[24] It consists not so much of the diversification of activities within the same work group (polyvalence) or within the cultural field (pluri-activity), but rather in 'poly-activity', in the sense that 90 per cent of the employees in this category also work outside of the field (Rannou and Roharik 2006; Bureau, Perrenoud and Shapiro 2009). In addition, the majority of them are in different occupations (Gouyon 2010). In other words, even if working in the cultural field or pursuing a cultural occupation results from a deliberate choice, this choice is far from exclusive and entails diversification, which is generally forced upon these individuals rather than actively chosen by them.

Cultural management occupations share some characteristics of the employment conditions in cultural occupations and in the cultural sector as a whole, but in several respects they offer more stability. This is suggested by trends observed in the 1990s for executives and technicians in the performing arts, which include administrators.[25] Over that period, the share of non-salaried employees decreased significantly (from 34–26 per cent), even as it increased among artists. The increase of part-time work was lower than in the labour force at large and in cultural employment in general (from 26–8 per cent compared with, respectively, from 12–18 per cent and from 21–4 per cent). Lastly, while the share of fixed-term contracts sharply increased over the decade and was significantly higher than in the labour force at large, it remained smaller than among artists (48 per cent in 1999 compared with 68 per cent for artists in the performing arts and 15 per cent of all those employed). Employment conditions appear comparatively better for directors, programmers and producers in the broadcasting and performing arts sectors: as of 2008, 77 per cent were salaried full-time (67.8 per cent under open-ended contracts or as civil servants), compared with 10 per cent of non-salaried and 14.4 per cent of part-time workers.

Unattractive overall but comparatively better for management positions, employment conditions in the cultural sector are characterized by their heterogeneity, reflected for instance by the very sharp disparities among performing artists. In such cases, Pierre-Michel Menger showed how uncertainty could be a driving force in the pursuit of creative activity, in part because it offers an antidote to routine and increases satisfaction in cases of success, but also because it allows these individuals to hope for success – in this sense uncertainty should not only be seen in terms of low probability; it keeps the door open (Menger 2014). While this does not entirely work in the same way for activities that are not creative in the strictest sense, some in neighbouring fields, such as cultural management, may exhibit common traits. There the uncertainty of careers, the inequality of positions and the heterogeneity of employment conditions may in a sense allow individuals to maintain their confidence in their 'good fortune', as Adam Smith put it, and ultimately, as we will see, serve as seemingly paradoxical factors in the attractiveness of these jobs.

*The attraction of uncertainty*

In 1987, Paul DiMaggio wrote that the new arts managers trained and recruited in the US from the mid-1960s onwards had not become professionals in the strictest sense of the term, requiring the certification of skills by a degree and a peer accreditation scheme – he called their professionalization process 'unfinished' (DiMaggio 1987: 7). In France, some ten years after the launch of the ministerial cultural employment policy promoting the professionalization of organizational and management activities, specialists and actors in the field also observed that tasks remained weakly specialized and that their professional world still had little unity and structure (Dubois 2012a: 376). Twenty years later, this observation still largely holds, which might mean that we are not witnessing an unfinished professionalization process, but rather that the relative indetermination of these occupations is one of their lasting features.

The development of cultural management positions has, in effect, resulted in little standardization of jobs and paths of access to positions.[26] Unlike professional bodies previously formed by librarians and museum creators, these occupations remain somewhat ill-defined. The diversity or vagueness of job titles (cultural manager, administrator, mediator, development officer, project designer, etc.), the absence of statistical classification and their presentation in directories of occupations give some indications of this.[27] Due to the heterogeneity of contractual arrangements (civil servants, contract workers, employees of associations, employees under standard contracts), the strong internal divides within the cultural field between artistic disciplines and sectors (theatre, visual arts, conservation, etc.) and the vast number of employers with differing status,[28] there are now unified recruitment channels. The definition of functions remains largely open and a great diversity of skills comes into play. This indetermination can only be considered a flaw if one takes the most formalized professional sectors as a yardstick by which to assess all professional groups (Abbott 1988; Demazière and Gadéa 2009). Instead of a passing imperfection that requires fixing, it might very well be one of the factors explaining why individuals pursue these jobs: the diversity of paths of access makes cultural management look like a fairly open sector, and the flexible definition of these occupations allows for the commitment of agents with varied dispositions, offers them a degree of freedom in their jobs and makes the possibility of failure appear more distant.

Like artistic occupations, cultural management jobs may require a high cost of entry, but as they vary widely and are only vaguely defined, they do not discourage the strategies of those looking to try their luck (Mauger 2006a, 2006b). In this field as in others (Millet and Moreau 2011), the possession of a specialized degree plays an increasingly important role, if only because of the increase in the number of degree holders among applicants due to the rise of training programmes since the mid-1980s, which has contributed to heightening competition for access to jobs and to transforming the field by introducing specific educational capital that did not exist previously. Like holders of cultural occupations in general, cultural managers have high levels of education; they tend to be even higher for the youngest generations.[29] Despite the increasing weight of education and the higher levels of attainment, having a degree is far from systematically expected. Access to these positions requires the combination of various forms of capital, which varies according to generations and positions. Educational capital, characterized by the possession of a specialized degree, is only one of them; its importance may be growing but it varies. Other important forms of capital include social capital (having relations in the field), incorporated cultural capital (dispositions acquired though familiarization with artworks and personal practice i.e. mainly outside of school, Bourdieu 1979; Serre 2012), and a specific capital consisting of past experience in associations, doing internships or working other jobs, etc.

As there are virtually endless combinations of these forms of capital, very few of those who have accumulated a certain amount of cultural capital, regardless of their past training or trajectory, will feel as though they do not have what it takes to access these positions. Indeed, a very wide variety of backgrounds can be found in cultural management, including artists reinventing themselves as managers by cashing in on their cultural dispositions in theatres or museums, students with literary majors who pursue cultural jobs as a logical extension of their school-ing or others with a more general training that seek to put their polyvalence to use, science graduates who shift from research to scientific and technical cultural mediation, etc. Additionally, until recently, a cultural management position was rarely someone's first job; rather, these occupations were held by agents who had previously exercised related jobs (artists, teachers, social workers, journalists) and more broadly by those with affinities with the cultural world through personal dispositions and practices rather than because of their professional activity, liable to see cultural management as a desirable path for their 'second career'. These career shifts deserve further analysis, in particular to assess the evolution of their relative weight among cultural managers, which is likely significant and contrib-utes to the diversity of the paths of access to these functions.

This diversity of backgrounds and paths of access is sustained by the low level of formalization of recruitment and positions, even in the public sector. The cultural branch of the French local civil service created in 1991 gives an indication of this. It codified the recruitment and career paths of staff in the fields of heritage conservation, libraries and art teaching, i.e. around two thirds of cultural occupations in local government, but not those of numerous functions in the sector, such as those of the cultural departments of local administrations, in which some managers are recruited on a contractual basis and others are local civil servants with no cultural degree.[30] The absence of systematic requirements in terms of status (such as a *concours* [competitive exam] serving as a barrier to entry) and the maintenance of varied paths of access, combined with the extensive development of local cultural policies over the last decades, have con-tributed to encouraging career choices of agents with varied backgrounds who pursue somewhat undefined jobs in 'local cultural development' and 'cultural action'. Similar processes are at work outside of local government in all cultural management occupations.

These occupations accordingly benefit from the particular form of attraction at work in all cultural fields, these 'uncertain places in the social space (...) whose most significant properties include the extreme permeability of their boundaries and the extreme diversity in the definition of the positions they offer' (Bourdieu 1991: 15). It is 'because they offer ill-defined positions (...) [that they] attract and welcome agents who differ widely in properties and in dispositions and therefore in ambitions' (Bourdieu 1991: 15). I elaborate on this in the following chapter: cultural management occupations are liable to attract agents with very varied characteristics. We have just seen that this is the case regarding their conditions of entry and their educational and professional trajectories. This also applies to social origins: these jobs may be held by possessors of a small amount of cultural capital accumulated during their education or within their peer group or by inheri-tors of high levels of cultural and sometimes material capital alike. These different backgrounds are matched by potentially opposed dispositions – hybridization and purism, creation and conservation, cultural democratization and elitism, social and political emancipation and managerial rigor. It is therefore hardly surprising that those aspiring to work in the cultural sector have very variable sets of skills; arguably this is merely the translation of social gaps in 'professional' language (Mathieu 2011: 217).

While a trend towards the standardization of profiles has been denounced, the dialectical adjustment between the characteristics of a function or a job and the dispositions of those pursuing that function tends to compound the relative fluidity of cultural management as a well-defined occupation. This fluidity, or indetermination, attracts applicants with varied backgrounds, and in turn they contribute to sustaining this indetermination by bringing their heterogeneous dispositions into play. Indeed, another reason for the attractiveness of these fuzzy positions is that they leave those who pursue them the possibility of defining their outlines by expressing their own socially constructed 'personality'. The *attractive* uncertainty of a weakly codified world that allows very diverse agents to envision success is complemented by what we might call *projective* uncertainty, in the sense that individuals project their own properties onto the positions they seek. Like social work in the late 1960s, these cultural management jobs contrast with 'occupations that hold no surprises, in which the future is played out in advance' by offering, instead, 'positions with fuzzy outlines, institutions conducive to innovation, and careers where you can always feel like you are inventing your life' (Muel-Dreyfus 1983: 202). There are multiple examples of indeterminate professional statuses and/or practices, from 'mediators' who organize 'encounters between the public and artworks' (Montoya 2008; Peyrin 2010), art agents and the other intermediaries of the art worlds, whose work is characterized by the 'vagueness of their roles, the heterogeneity of the rationales of action to co-ordinate and the relational complexity of the activities' (Lizé, Naudier and Roueff 2011). This indetermination can become problematic, particularly when it affects employment conditions. Yet it also contributes to making these jobs attractive: polyvalence and pluri-activity are antidotes to routine; individuals are often, to some extent, able to define their activity on the basis of orientations that are personal or experienced, as such, instead of merely fulfilling pre-established functions. In short, their work gives them the opportunity to achieve self-fulfillment.

Lastly, indetermination can also be attractive in that it offers protection against possible subjective feelings of failure; instability may be perceived as desirable mobility in a world where discovery and change are valued. It reduces the cost of transitioning from one activity to another, which is always lower in cases of smoother transitions between positions that are partially undefined. The ambiguity of the positions spares their holders the disinvestment and reinvestment entailed by the 'shift from a vocation of philosopher to a vocation of philosophy teacher' (Bourdieu 1984: 175); instead of brutal changes, their career, which they experience as a 'personal project', moves in imperceptible combinations and shifts.

## Training and the genesis of vocations

Together with the development of cultural employment and the characteristics of these occupations, the transformations of higher education and specifically the development of training programmes specialized in cultural management have contributed to making these jobs a conceivable professional prospect.[31] The provision of training has contributed to shaping choices of education and professional projections.

In France, universities are state-funded, and, except for specific programmes and at the master's level, there is no selection at entrance. Tuition fees are low (approximately from 200–400€ per year depending on the degree), and around 40 per cent of an age cohort obtain a higher education degree. Over the past three decades trends in higher education have contributed to producing students whose resources and dispositions make them possible aspirants to cultural sector occupations. I will begin by briefly outlining the main features of these general trends (Convert 2010). First, the increase in student populations and longer periods of schooling have produced cohorts of graduates looking for professional guidance.[32] This is especially the case in the general degree courses, including in the humanities and literary subjects, which despite fluctuations in enrolment still make up a very high proportion of the student population.[33] Due in part to the decoupling between these degree courses and the recruitment competitions for teaching positions in secondary education that were their 'natural' extension, bachelor-level graduates have had to seek out alternatives that fit their training and give them the opportunity to access positions that limit the risk of educational downgrading. The choice of culture is a possible response to this twofold quest; most of the applicants to cultural master's courses have this background.

From the perspective of the provisions of training, incentives to 'professionalize' universities have become increasingly widespread. This process, which began many decades ago,[34] intensified considerably in the 2000s with the implementation of reforms induced by the Bologna process. In the humanities and social sciences especially, this has increased the disaffection of students with non-vocational courses steered towards research and teaching (in secondary and higher education) to the benefit of the so-called 'professional' training courses, preparing for work outside academia. Students have been increasingly asked to devise a 'career plan' beginning in the early years of their studies; some of them endowed with literary or artistic educational capital that is more difficult to convert into professional resources in other worlds might find pursuing a career in culture a suitable response to this requirement. The same mechanism is at work for teachers of literature and the humanities. Under the combined effects of strategies to retain undergraduate students, preserve courses and research-oriented programmes, teachers in these disciplines, reputed to be underperforming in terms of employment rates place more value on the so-called 'professional' programmes (Soulié 2008). Therein lies one of the explanations for the rise of training programmes steered towards cultural occupations, which are primarily the product of incentives to professionalization for teachers in the humanities.

These programmes have been successful in terms of recruitment and the creation of new degrees in part because they provide a way out for students seeking professional salvation and a solution for the sustenance of university positions threatened by academic policies that promote 'useful skills' and place emphasis on finding a job. These are mutually reinforcing phenomena: while high student enrollment numbers ensure the creation and maintenance of courses, the opposite is also true. While it may be an oversimplification to put this in terms of 'supply creates demand', it can be argued that the existence of specialized training programmes contributes to informing and steering the educational and professional choices of students disposed to pursuing this path. Unlike established occupations, for which training is a restrictive form of regulation (see the *numerus clausus* in medical studies), the availability of training might contribute, in these cases, to an uncontrolled increase in the number of aspirants. I will explore this hypothesis further by retracing the genesis of culture-oriented training programmes, establishing the structure of this supply and considering its possible effects on career choices.

### The development of specialized training in cultural management

Training programmes specialized in the management and administration of culture began appearing in the early 1960s in American universities. In keeping with Paul DiMaggio's analysis of the professionalization of arts managers, Eleonora Redaelli shows that 'the distinctive cultural policy in the United States is in large part responsible for the rise of arts management programmes' (Redaelli 2012: 155). Most of these programmes are brought together in the Association of Arts Administration Educators,[35] whose activities include the unification of training programmes and the maintenance of relationships with the relevant professional sector, and which also acts as a venue for the discussion of teaching practices and programmes. Despite this structure acquired at an early stage, long-term stability was not ensured; the programmes were in particular weakened by the drop in public cultural funding in the 1980s (Dorn 1992; Sikes 2000). There is 'considerable curricular convergence' among these programmes, although they are proposed in various educational settings (Varela 2013: 74). In Europe, similar programmes appeared in the 1970s and developed mostly after the 1980s, with support from international organizations like UNESCO and the Council of Europe and then the European Union (Moulinier 1983) at the European level (Sternal 2007: 72–7). In the early 1990s, the Council of Ministers of Culture adopted a resolution on the training of arts administrators,[36] and the European Network of Cultural Administration Training Centres (ENCATC) was established.[37]

France followed a roughly similar chronology. Projects aimed at rationalizing the training of *cadres culturels* (cultural managers), who were then called *animateurs*, were formed in the immediate post-World War II period and revived in the early 1960s with the development of policies at the Ministry of Cultural Affairs. Still, most did not amount to much. The creation of training programmes specialized in cultural management came later, beginning in the early 1980s, as part of the broader professionalization of the cultural sector promoted, at the time, by government policies (Dubois 2012a: 353–66; Girard 2012).

Ministerial policies in support of cultural employment included promoting new programmes, particularly in the area of management, offered mostly by the *Association nationale pour la gestion des entreprises culturelles* and its regional branches, which provided training sessions for staff already in place. Cultural management training programmes were also offered by a variety of structures such as the *Association technique pour l'action culturelle* (ATAC), created in 1966, which became the *Centre national pour l'action artistique et culturelle* (CENAC) in 1986, the *Centre de formation nationale d'Avignon* (CFNA) created in 1983 to train 'cultural project management executives'; the *Association nationale pour la formation et l'information artistique et culturelle* (ANFIAC) merged the two organizations in 1987. Other types of programmes progressively emerged.[38] General curricula within and outside of universities included optional courses in cultural management, for instance in business schools such as the top ranking *Ecole des hautes études commerciales* (HEC). As had been the case shortly before in the field of communication (Georgakakis 1995, Neveu 1994), from the mid-1980s when numerous private schools offering preparation for executive positions in cultural management and administration were created: the *Groupe des écoles d'art et de culture*, the *École supérieure des métiers de la culture*, the *Institut d'études supérieures des arts*, the *Institut supérieur du management culturel*, the *École supérieure internationale d'art et de gestion*, the *École d'art et de communication*, the *Institut de la culture de la communication et du management*, the *Institut supérieur de communication et de développement culturel* and yet others, including some that disappeared or were merged, and some created more recently such as the *Agence européenne du management culturel*.[39] Lastly, specialized training programmes also began appearing in the mid-1980s; there were about 20 specifically focused on cultural management as of the early 1990s. Most awarded a professional post-graduate degree (DESS). While some were geared towards the cultural industries (*DESS de Gestion des institutions culturelles* at the University of Paris-Dauphine) or local civil service (*DESS d'Administration locale* in Reims), these programmes prepared trainees for work both in the private and public sectors across the entire cultural field, for example the *DESS de Direction de projet culturel* in Lyon and Grenoble.

From the early 1990s onwards, the development of these programmes elicited three main criticisms from those invested in them and in the cultural world at large: the lack of co-ordination by the Ministry of Culture, which does not have any authority regarding the creation of academic curricula; the lack of consultation with professionals in the sector, who admittedly had little collective structure, in their training and workforce needs; and the disproportion between the number of graduates and the number of jobs available.[40] Still the number of training programmes increased at an even quicker rate over the following years in France and in Europe in general (ENCATC 2003: 15), so that similar criticisms were formulated some twenty years later (Girard, Moutarde and Pébrier 2006: 29; Chaumier 2006; Martin 2008; Mathieu and Patriat 2012). While the provision of cultural employment did increase, the provision of specialized training increased in far greater proportions. According to various estimates, there were ten times as many in the late 2000s as there were in the mid-1980s. There were 282 training programmes on cultural administration by 2006, including 168 at the master's level, most of which were offered by universities (Martin 2008). These figures include programmes preparing for cultural mediation and communication occupations (24 per cent) and cross-disciplinary programmes like 'cultural project management' (40 per cent) and others concerning specific sectors such as heritage conservation (22 per cent) and the cultural industries (19 per cent); yet, they give us a telling indication of the scope of this increase.

Three quarters of these programmes were created after 1990, including 32 per cent after 2004; this development continued after 2010 (Mathieu 2012). Half of the master's level programmes were created between 1991 and 2003 and over a third after 2004 (Martin 2008). This chronology confirms that this development in no way reflects the fulfillment of a need for previously identified jobs; it has much more to do with the changes in the higher education system. The Bologna Process has played a decisive role in the rise of cultural management training programmes in Europe (SECEB 2006). The intensification of competition within the higher education field, particularly when the European standardization of degrees was implemented, was, at least in France, a decisive factor in creating these programmes. Even though in each case specific or partly contingent factors may have had an impact (such as the involvement of a lecturer with relations in cultural circles), the reform clearly heightened competition both within the universities (between teaching staff, disciplines, departments and faculties) and among them, as they fought to attract students, especially at the master's level. This competition was also played out during the Ministry of Higher Education's authorization process – each of these campaigns elicited the creation of new master's programmes in preparation for cultural work. For the reasons stated earlier, these effects are particularly visible in fields reputedly lagging behind in terms of employment rates (literature, humanities and social sciences). The creation of training programmes preparing for cultural occupations, enabled by the negotiation of contracts between the universities and the Ministry, is a response to incentives to develop more 'professional' curricula. In practice, it is in those fields where the vast majority of cultural management programmes are found, while they are most often offered by arts departments more generally in Europe (SECEB 2006), and in the US (Varela 2013). University departments and schools of economics and management, which were not faced with comparable incentives, are much less involved even though the cultural management model directly draws upon these disciplines. Yet, like law faculties, to a much lesser extent, they have by now carved their place in the field after being previously absent – with the notable exception of the University of Paris-Dauphine. While they did so for very different reasons (not to offer tokens of professionalization, but rather to diversify the career prospects of their students), they also contributed to the proliferation of training programmes.

*The structure of the specialized training supply*

Corina Suteu describes three national models that have been adopted by European countries (Suteu 2006: 77, summarized in Sternal 2007: 67–70). The British model, characterized by 'predominant market values' and 'intensive professional training, labour market oriented' is typical of the Netherlands, Scandinavian countries and Baltic countries. By contrast, the French model is defined by 'predominant humanistic values, academic training [and] weak relation between the labour market and training offered', and has been followed in Spain, Italy, Greece, Poland, Romania and Bulgaria. The German model presents a 'balanced mix between humanistic, academic and administrative value oriented education' and is followed in Austria, Switzerland and Croatia. While this typology provides a general picture of training programmes in Europe, which helps contrasting national tendencies, a closer examination of the French case reveals a more complex and nuanced situation.

Having begun in the mid-1980s, intensified during the following decade and continued afterwards, this largely unchecked development resulted in a very large number of training programmes becoming available almost across the entire country, even though there are still significant disparities between regions.[41] There is hardly a university town without its cultural administration or mediation programme; some have several, whose scopes may partially overlap, even sometimes within the same institution.[42] Most of them (60 per cent) are master's level and the vast majority offer initial training (95 per cent), even if some of them include a few professionals already in place pursuing lifelong training.[43] Due to this unchecked growth the supply of training is highly varied, in terms of the types of institutions offering the programmes (universities, business schools, etc.), of content (management, social science, law, art, business and various combinations thereof), of sectors targeted (the cultural field in general, combined or not with tourism, luxury, local development, international trade etc., or a specific sector like music, or two sectors combined like heritage conservation and publishing), and accordingly in terms of employment prospects. Students might work in the private sector or in the public and subsidized sectors, although generally the latter two are particularly targeted (only 13 per cent of programmes are specifically oriented towards the private sector). While there are specific reasons for them, the diversity of programmes and their relative indetermination also reflect those of cultural management occupations. In other areas, the development of specialized training often has the effect of restricting access to the field (Abbott 1988), but this has not been the case for cultural management. In a sense the effect has almost been the opposite, with the multiplication of the possible paths of access (and therefore of entrants' backgrounds) and the diversification of the curricula (and accordingly of their range of professional skills).

There may be multiple ways to enter, but cultural management also has its *grandes portes* and *petites portes*, to borrow Bourdieu's phrase about the *grandes écoles* (Bourdieu 1998). Considering the diversity of these programmes, it is difficult to present a synthetic overview – we may nevertheless make an attempt at a simplified mapping on the basis of a range of distinctive factors: the status and prestige enjoyed by the institution; the disciplinary orientations and place in the hierarchy of disciplines; the extent and form of specialization; the type of jobs targeted. If we put aside the few for-profit private schools, some of which we have mentioned, and some cultural management training programmes offered optionally by public teaching institutions under the helm of the Ministry of Culture in cinema (the film school *La Fémis*) museums (the *École du Louvre*) or theatre (*École nationale supérieure des arts et techniques du théâtre*, ÉNSATT), which are in the minority, a distinction between two main sets of programmes can be observed.

The first, which accounts for the largest number of them, includes university programmes[44] in the fields of literature, the arts, the humanities and social science.[45] Many of them are the professional extension of a given curriculum organized in the corresponding department. This is the case in the artistic disciplines, where graduates of a bachelor's in the performing arts or in musicology may enrol in a master's in 'cultural project management' or 'music management'. This also applies to other disciplines: literature graduates go on to study publishing, history graduates do conservation or archives, ethnology graduates may go for the assembly of exhibitions. In addition to these there are also cross-disciplinary programmes, which have less artistic and discipline-specific content; their audiences and forms are more variable. The majority of them are steered towards cultural communication and mediation; more rarely they connect culture with related areas, such as international trade and tourism. This group has a hierarchy of its own, which depends on the exposure of the university, the age of the programme and its ties with cultural institutions.[46] The hierarchy also hinges on the (not always clearly established) opposition between those preparing for operational, audience-oriented occupations and more curatorial occupations.[47]

The second set of programmes prepares quite clearly for the latter type of jobs. These programmes are offered by prestigious institutions, nearer to the fields of economic and political power, and where specialization in culture comes as the extension of a generalist training. They include the country's leading business schools[48], the Institutes of Political Studies (IEPs or 'Sciences Po')[49] and management-oriented academic curricula, as at the University of Paris-Dauphine. Their students are selected among social and educational elites; aside from the odd exception, they do not have an academic background in literature or the arts. The contents of these programmes are not cultural in the primary sense; rather, they consist in the application to the cultural field of economic, managerial, legal, political, communicational and sociological approaches, presented and combined in various manners. They prepare students for executive positions of cultural management, such as director, secretary-general or administrator of a company, an institution or a cultural enterprise. Programmes offered by the Institutes of Political Studies tend to lead to jobs in the public sector (particularly local government) or at least in the subsidized sector, though some of their alumni do end up in the private sector. The more specifically management-oriented programmes essentially prepare students for jobs in the 'cultural industries' (film, publishing, new technologies) or the art market.

*The effects of the specialization of training*

Since the spectacular increase in the number of training programmes did not happen to fulfil a pre-existing need for skilled workers, one might be tempted to see it as a response to students' 'demand'. In effect, in France and abroad (Rolfe 1995: 32), the success of these programmes among students ensured sufficient enrollment numbers that in turn made possible the creation of new programmes that would be sure to attract enough applicants. However, this 'demand' does not exist independently from the corresponding 'supply'. We must refrain from adopting a unilateral view of things and looking at the 'choice' of training as the consequence of a deliberate career plan to pursue occupations to which these programmes prepare students. Indeed it might be conversely argued that students turn to culture as a career choice *because* of the existence of training programmes in that field. As Marx wrote about commodities, production 'not only creates an object for the subject, but also a subject for the object' (Marx 1993) – in the case at hand, these programmes do not only offer training to candidates who think they need it, but also suggest a possible future career and so contribute to creating applicants among those who have the required dispositions.

The wide diffusion of the idea that one can make a career out of culture through these training programmes, without necessarily being an artist, probably goes some way towards explaining why so many pursue them, especially those who are most uncertain about their career. Whereas marketing strategies in higher education are far less developed in France as they are in other countries, such as the US or the UK (Reay, David, and Ball 2005: 139 ff.), these programmes receive significant exposure in the press – especially in the mainstream cultural press (like the magazine *Télérama*[50]) and in career information magazines and handbooks like those of the National Office for Education and Career Information (ONISEP).

The ONISEP's *Parcours* series regularly publishes a special issue on *Culture et patrimoine* (Culture and Heritage). In the 2008 edition, several pages were devoted to cultural management, complete with portraits and a few warnings on the difficulty of finding work in that field (which requires a network and a high level of educational achievement). The text extols the virtues of jobs that attract passionate, driven individuals: 'Supporting and funding an artist's project, curating and organizing a festival or a concert... these are the everyday tasks of cultural management professionals. They spare no effort to further the cause of art' (p. 28).

Even though the candidates seldom mention it during the interviews, the influence of peer groups comes into play – including, in particular, those who have completed these programmes and inform prospective students about them, giving them an illustration of a possible career path. This was the case for Muriel, a musicology student with no clear professional prospects, whose flatmate was studying for a master's in publishing in a business school, and informed her about the existing programmes and their hierarchies. Likewise, Charlotte, who did not have a well-defined career plan, heard about a cultural master's programme from a friend: 'he told me about that master's and I thought, oh, that's really interesting, well I'd like to do that myself!' (woman born in 1987, mother commercial employee, father technician, international *baccalauréat*, bachelor's in Italian and master's in culture).

We may also present a hypothesis on the effect of the local supply of training on the likelihood of applying. While the questionnaire results do not allow us to establish a direct correlation, they reveal a high proportion of local applications. Obviously there are other factors involved (especially financial ones), but they may be informed by a prescriptive effect resulting from the availability of a training programme, and therefore of teachers of students who embody cultural management as a possible career path: nearly half of the candidates apply only in the area where they live, 20 per cent in their area and elsewhere, and less than a quarter outside of their area when there is a programme available in their area; only 7 per cent apply outside of their area because there is none where they live.

The diversity of the available training programmes leads, in turn, to the diversification of the prospective students who see cultural management as a possible career path. Few other academic curricula are indeed likely to attract the interest of students in history, business and theatre alike. It is not only because the professional world of culture welcomes all of these backgrounds, but also because there are programmes available in each of these disciplines that culture became a conceivable and legitimate career choice for all these students.

While I started with the reverse hypothesis that training programmes play a role in the awakening of vocations, this does not mean that the usual order in the relation between educational choice and professional choice fails to apply – training as a way to access the initial goal of a desired professional position. One of the effects of the development of specialized training is that a degree is increasingly required to access cultural management occupations. While candidates possessing social and cultural resources, but no degree, could, and can still succeed, the rise of these training programmes now places them in competition with those who do have a degree and who may have the equivalent social and cultural resources. This trend fits within the broader process of the increase of the weight of educational capital in access to social positions. It took on a meaning and scope of its own for relatively new professional positions, including those of cultural management. These jobs were for the most part created from the early 1980s onwards; 30 years later, many of them are still occupied by first-generation cultural managers.[51] The fight between generations for jobs is especially bitter, which further reinforces the importance of specialized degrees for newcomers (Chauvel 1998). While there is not enough longitudinal data available to establish this with great accuracy in the case of cultural managers, the elevation of the level of educational attainment is clear in the younger generations. Considering the dates of creation of specialized training programmes – essentially after 1990 – few individuals born before 1965 have enrolled in them (except for those who resumed their studies); they then become increasingly numerous. The share of 'arts and performing arts professionals' with over two years of higher education rose from 13 per cent in 1982–4 to 30 per cent in 2007–9 (from 6–16 per cent for the population at large).[52] The proportions and their increase over the last few years are noticeably higher in the case of cultural managers. To mention one example only, while 60 per cent of directors, programmers and producers in the broadcasting and performing arts sectors aged 35 and over have completed at least two years of higher education, there are nearly 80 per cent in the under 35 category, including 56.7 per cent with three years of higher education and beyond.[53] This gap elicits subjective perceptions, both among the oldest, who often regret that 'technique' prevails over passion for their younger counterparts, and among the latter, who view as indispensable an educational capital that their elders do not have.

Jeanne told me about the 'clash of generations between guys who are 50–60 and us young graduates [...]. They go 'you guys are cute, you have your master's degree, but you can't manage a project', because they got their training doing something else and they carved their own place in culture. Then again maybe it's the times we live in now, you have to train for everything, so my impression is that you need to have a technical background to be able to work in culture'.

*Interview with a woman born in 1986, father a teacher in an agricultural high school, mother a schoolteacher, baccalauréat in economics, bachelor's in history, master's in Latin American studies*

Ultimately, growing competition upon entry, the rise of training programmes and, to some extent, the attractiveness of these programmes and of cultural management occupations have a mutually reinforcing effect. Even though access to cultural employment was already highly selective, there is an increasingly widespread requirement for a degree, leading those who seek to work in the field to make considerable investments in training. These investments in turn reinforce the competition for access to specialized programmes, which are, as a result, often highly selective despite their number. As we have seen, the large supply contributes to creating a demand that is all the higher because it may come from students with very varied backgrounds, among whom are many from literary disciplines seeking to convert a devalued educational capital on the job market. Although this varies from one programme to another, they are often extremely selective: master's programmes routinely receive several hundreds of applications for 20 to 30 places. This selectiveness in turn produces two effects. First, as it directly relates to the hierarchy of programmes within the higher education system, it makes them more desirable, or contributes to making them appear as 'serious' options even where they might have appeared as 'bohemian' choices (as in institutes of political studies). Then, at least for the most recognized and prized of them, selectiveness further likens academic selection to professional selection, even adopting the latter's form. Admission juries generally include members who work within the sector and treat the process partly like a job interview. The selection of applicants is in many respects an evaluation of their 'employability': their experiences, practical knowledge of the cultural world and introduction into professional networks are all assessed. In the frequent cases where selection is particularly intense, young graduates have more chances of finding a job, as their degree is often a decisive addition to their initial capital (in terms of education, relations, personal experience, etc.). While we do not have enough reliable data on this, and those who find a job often have to accept a modest salary and a precarious status, the few surveys on school-to-work transition available suggest that these selective programmes have a rather high 'placement rate' (Martin 2008). A previous study also reported good results (Lecoutre 1995). These good results, or the programmes' reputations based on these numbers, make them even more attractive to prospective students, and so this continuous loop has placed cultural management as a credible career option.

## Notes

1 European Commission, *Culture, cultural industries and employment*, 1998, cited in Feist 2000: 25. On the UK, see Casey 1995; O'Brien and Feist 1995; Rolfe 1995.
2 Recensements de la population 1962, 1968, 1975, 1982, 1990, 1999, 2008: fichiers détail individus, tabulation sur mesure [fichier électronique], INSEE [producteur], Centre Maurice Halbwachs (CMH) [diffuseur]. As the official classification of occupations in France has changed over time, we grouped occupations into clusters in order to maximize the coherence of our datasets. This process is described in the methodological appendix. Gaps between figures from 1975 and 1982 should however be interpreted with caution, insofar as they may be partly attributed to the changes in the classification of occupations despite our efforts to limit their effects.
3 For further information I refer the reader to the comprehensive summary on trends in employment in cultural professions from 1991–2011 published by the statistics department of the French Ministry for Culture after I wrote this book. See Gouyon and Patureau 2014.
4 Eurostat, *Cultural statistics*, 2011, p. 67.
5 In a study more broadly aimed at documenting the decline of the traditional forms of intellectual activity, Jean-Claude Passeron showed that employment in the entire performing arts sector decreased between 1954 and 1962, particularly for artistic occupations (actors especially). Overall, he notes that 'artistic occupations progress less quickly than the population of the branch in which they are included as a whole [and] in particular progress less quickly (or even regress where male populations are concerned) in the same branches where intellectual occupations strongly progress' (Passeron 1965: appendix 3 8–10).
6 There were 10,000 professional journalists in 1975, 13,500 in 1980, 22,000 in 1985, 26,000 in 1990 and around 30,000 in the early 2000s (Neveu 2000).
7 We inferred these figures from the contents of briefs regularly published by the *Observatoire de l'emploi culturel* of the French ministry of culture. They are compiled by sector of activity, not by professional group. The number of employed salaried workers in the cultural sector (regardless of job category) is established on the basis of INSEE's employment survey. We subtracted employees in the fields of media and architecture from the overall figure. Due to the sampling, these figures must be treated with caution.

8  Source: DARES, 'Dynamiques de l'emploi', secondary analysis of INSEE employment surveys. See also DARES, *Les familles professionnelles. Portraits statistiques 1982–2009*, Paris, 2011 (secondary analysis of INSEE employment surveys, U0Z-Professionnels de la communication et de l'information et U1Z-Professionnels des arts et des spectacles).

9  Respectively by 2.55, 2.27 and 2.15, i.e. by 2.46 for all those employed.

10 These schemes include joint financing by the central government and various local authorities, incentives to develop self-financing and private fundraising as well as recourse to EU budgets and more generally the rise of project financing.

11 The latter became the *Journal of Arts Management and Law* in 1982 and was later again renamed *Journal of Arts Management, Law, and Society* in 1992.

12 Existing studies generally focus on specific occupations and sectors but do not include global perspectives on the transformation of cultural management (Octobre 1999; Charle 2008; Goetschel and Yon 2008). On the other hand, a handful of scholars have discussed the rise of cultural intermediary functions in very broad terms, without distinguishing those that relate to management in the cultural sector in the stricter sense (Charle 1992).

13 Like *Hexaméron*, the 'magazine of cultural investment' (1985) and later *Profession culture* (1992). The development of specialized training programmes is examined in the second sub-section of this chapter.

14 Nearly 20 per cent of jobs in the cultural sector (not counting the press, architecture and broadcasting trade) and over 40 per cent of cultural occupations (journalists, translators and architects not included) as of 2007. Source: *Chiffres clés 2011*, 'Professions culturelles et emploi', ministère de la Culture.

15 Source: DARES, *Les familles professionnelles*.

16 DEPS, ministère de la Culture, 'Les demandeurs d'emploi dans les professions culturelles en mars 1998 d'après le fichier de l'ANPE', *Notes de l'observatoire de l'emploi culturel*, 19, 1999.

17 The overall number went from 129,700 to 176,600 individuals. Sources: DARES, demandeurs d'emploi des catégories A, B et C.

18 Sources: DARES. The job application rate is the ratio between the number of job seekers and the total number of those in employment and the unemployed in an occupational branch; it gives an indication of the level of unemployment in said branch. Among skilled occupations, only information and communication professionals have a similar level (17 per cent).

19 In the overall labour force the turnover rate is 49 per cent; it is below 200 per cent in all the other branches. Sources: DARES, *Les familles professionnelles*.

20 As of 1990, the proportion of fixed-term contracts was 16 per cent in cultural occupations (10 per cent in the labour force as a whole); as of 1998 it had reached 33 per cent (15 per cent) (Menger 2005b: 158).

21 Including 48 per cent in the performing arts. The proportion among the labour force at large at the time was 15 per cent (*Chiffres clés 2011*, 'Professions culturelles et emploi', p. 250).

22 Sources: DARES, *Les familles professionnelles*. Again, significant internal disparities must be pointed out: a fifth of salaried employees received under 3,000€ after tax over the year 2007 whereas another fifth received over 30,000€; these proportions are respectively 6 per cent and 12 per cent among the labour force at large. See 'Une typologie de l'emploi dans le secteur culturel en 2007', *Culture chiffres*, mars 2011.

23 In 1990, there were 21 per cent of part-time workers among all holders of cultural occupations; in 1998 they were 28 per cent (Menger 2005b: 158).

24 On 'portfolio working' among graduates from arts and creative programmes in the UK, see Pollard 2013: 54–5.

25 Sources: DARES, *Les familles professionnelles*.

26 This is partly the case for jobs in local government, where the number of contract workers has decreased and positions in cultural departments have tended to be filled by civil
servants.

27 The *Répertoire opérationnel des métiers et emplois* (ROME), which is used in France
for job listings and the referencing of training programmes, comprises a section entitled *Production et administration spectacle, cinéma et audiovisuel* (code L1302),
which includes some 20 different occupations, but excludes promotion and diffusion
activities, which fall under code L1303 *Promotion d'artistes et de spectacles* along
with fashion, sport and literature. There is another section for *Gestion de patrimoine
culturel* (cultural heritage management, K1602). Cultural mediation activities are split
between two categories (*Intervention socioculturelle*, K1206 and *Animation d'activités
culturelles ou ludiques*, G1202), which essentially refer to sociocultural activities in
a wide array of settings – some are specifically cultural (directors of cultural centres)
but most have little do with the sector (neighbourhood development committees, rural
community centres, activities for seniors, etc.).

28 They include subsidized associations, public institutions, private businesses, etc. As of
2007 there were around 65,000 employers, including 25,000 for the performing arts
only (Gouyon 2010).

29 While it is difficult to measure the increasing weight of degree level in access to cultural management occupations accurately, for lack of available statistics, it has been
evidenced by several indicators which I discuss later in the book.

30 In the second half of the 2000s, there were an estimated 110,000 holders of cultural
occupations, including 75,000 working in the cultural sector.

31 On the relationship between transformations in higher education and the rise of cultural
work, see Ashton and Noonan 2013 on the British case.

32 The population of higher education students practically doubled between 1980 and
2009, the year of our study – from 1,184,000–2,134,000 individuals (source: INSEE).
However, variations can be observed between the types of institution and study tracks;
the increase was particularly pronounced for engineering schools (+127 per cent
between 1990 and 2011), business schools (+174 per cent between 1990 and 2011) and
the *sections de techniciens supérieurs* (senior technicians). The trend was not linear
for non-selective university tracks: following a very sharp increase after 1980 and the
policy aiming at bringing 80 per cent of students in the same age group to *baccalauréat*
level, there was a slight dip (especially in the general tracks, including the humanities
and literature) and subsequently a return near the 1995 maximum (1,338,000) in the
late 2000s (1,306,000).

33 Over 40 per cent of students enrolled at bachelor's level in the general tracks in the
2000s.

34 The introduction of new forms of 'useful knowledge' was developed in the 1960s, as
Fabienne Pavis showed with the case of management (Pavis 2010). The creation of professionally oriented postgraduate programmes called *Diplômes d'études supérieures
spécialisées* (DESS) dates back to 1974.

35 http://www.artsadministration.org/

36 Resolution of the Council and the Ministers for Culture meeting within the Council of
7 June 1991 on the training of arts administrators, Official Journal C 188, 19 July 1991.

37 http://www.encatc.org. For a partial list of these centers dating back to the early 2000s,
see ENCATC, 2003.

38 For an overview in the early 1990s, see Evrard 1990; Jamet 1991 and Coll. 1992.

39 A complete and up-to-date overview can be found on websites on cultural employment and training programmes such as http://www.profilculture.com/. and http://
www.jobculture.fr

40 Such concerns were, for instance, voiced during the 1992 workshop on training and
employment in culture (Coll. 1992).

41 The regions of Ile-de-France and Rhône-Alpes are particularly well endowed, having respectively 30 per cent and 16.5 per cent of all master's programmes.
42 In 2006, there were for instance two master's programmes focusing on different cultural sectors at the University of Brest (publishing and performing arts management); the business school in the same town offered a master's programme on the 'management of cultural products and leisure activities'; there were three generalist cultural administration programmes at the University of Dijon and a master's on the management of cultural enterprises at the local business school; six master's programmes at the University of Paris I, each with its own disciplinary or sectoral niche.
43 Except when mentioned otherwise, the figures cited in this paragraph are taken from Martin 2008.
44 57 per cent in universities, 13 per cent in institutes of technology (IUT) and 12 per cent in professional institutes (IUP).
45 According to available data, around 80 per cent of university programmes preparing for cultural occupations are in the humanities, social sciences, the arts and literature (Jamet 1991: 45; Mathieu 2012: 134).
46 The programme offered in Avignon, for instance, benefits from all the activity surrounding the famous theatre festival held in the city.
47 This was partly suggested to me by Stéphane Dorin.
48 About 10 cultural master's programmes and 12 options are offered by management schools that are members of the *Conférence des grandes écoles*. Half of their students have an academic background outside of economics and management (Martin 2008).
49 The Institutes of Political Studies ('Sciences Po') are selective departments offering a multi-disciplinary training in law, economics and political science. With the exception of Sciences Po Rennes, they all offer a programme in cultural management.
50 The popular weekly magazine *Télérama* has inserts and articles on the subject (www.telerama.fr). See for instance exemple *Télérama*, Spécial formations « Métiers du patrimoine: La gestion culturelle », mars 2009.
51 While there is no accurate statistical data available on this point, it is worth noting that the share of people working in the same company for over ten years has increased among arts and performing arts professionals (from 31–6 per cent between 1982–4 and 2007–9), even as it remained unchanged in the population at large (42 per cent). This category includes artists, who have a high turnover rate: the increase is therefore probably much higher than these numbers suggest when it comes to administrative positions. Source: DARES, *Les familles professionnelles*.
52 Source: DARES, *Les familles professionnelles*.
53 Source: INSEE, *Recensement général de la population*, 2008.

# 2 Who wants to be a cultural manager?

In order to be converted into vocations, the new trends in cultural employment, the rise of cultural management occupations and of the corresponding specialized training programmes must fit the dispositions of agents who are likely to transform these objective and collective conditions into subjective and individual aspirations. Examination of the social features of these agents gives us some insight into these dispositions, and enables us to situate the social world of those aspiring to make a career out of culture. To this end, I will begin by presenting the most salient features of the applicants – namely the large proportion of women, their often privileged social backgrounds and their generally high level of educational and cultural capital. This first stage of my analysis will require separating variables that only fully make sense when related to each other. Likewise, identifying general trends should not lead us to underestimate the heterogeneity of the applicants' social and educational trajectories, which reflect the diversity of possible reasons for this career choice and the diversity of the professional positions targeted. Following this, I go on to examine the main distinctions between the applicants' profiles.

## A largely feminine vocation

An outstanding feature of the aspiring cultural managers, in comparison to those pursuing other high education degrees, is the exceptional proportion of women among them: 85 per cent among the applicants and 80 per cent among those enrolled in cultural management master's programmes.[1] Similar rates are observed in other national contexts.[2] This proportion far exceeds that of the student population at large (56.5 per cent of women in 2004), and is only matched in paramedic and social work schools (83 per cent). Not to mention the scientific tracks, where women are traditionally in the minority, proportions are systematically lower in programmes preparing for work in related professional worlds. In 2006–7, women accounted for 56 per cent of the student enrollment in artistic and cultural institutions affiliated with the Ministry of Culture and Communication, with significant gaps between sectors.[3] Although journalism has been experiencing a process of feminization for several decades,[4] there aren't more women than men in journalism schools.[5] The proportion of women is also lower in all the programmes previously pursued by applicants to cultural management master's programmes; it reaches 75 per cent in the literary *classes préparatoires aux grandes écoles*.[6] In universities, at master's level, it is in the disciplines that provide the most recruits to cultural management programmes that the share of young women is highest, but it remains lower than in cultural management: 75 per cent in literature and the arts, 68 per cent in the humanities and social science, 66 per cent in law and political science.[7]

How are we to explain the fact that cultural management jobs attract women in such high proportions? The gendered identities of professional positions ('a man's job' vs. 'a woman's job') often explain positive (by projection) and negative career choices (resulting from the exclusion of activities reputed to be suited to the opposite sex) (Perrot 1987). This only partly applies to cultural management. These positions are too recent or not well enough established to have a gendered identity assigned to them, and crucially they are far from being held by women as often as one might think. For instance the positions of directors, programmers and producers in the broadcasting and performing arts sectors, positions which are coveted by many, are mostly held by men (two-thirds),[8] a proportion similar to that of US theatre and orchestra directors in the 1980s (DiMaggio, 1987). The continuing domination of men is not limited to executive positions, which we know to be often held by men even in sectors with high proportions of women: indeed, women are also in the minority when it comes to cultural occupations at large (43 per cent in 2007). Only the occupations of art teacher outside of educational institutions (59 per cent), and especially of translator as well as executive and technician in documentation and conservation are held by a majority of women (73 per cent in both cases). Women are more present in the cultural sector (48 per cent of jobs), but make up a majority only in publishing and bookstores (61 per cent), heritage (61 per cent) and cultural education (57 per cent).[9]

Instead of this resulting from a deliberate choice of traditionally female jobs or sectors, the fact that there is a vast majority of women among applicants reflects an ongoing feminization process. Since the 1980s, proportion of women executives has steadily increased in the media, broadcasting and performing arts (according to INSEE categories) and among arts and performing arts professionals (according to the clusters of professional branches of the Ministry of Labour).[10] However, this increase does not affect technical executives, 70 per cent of whom remain men, and it has been observed more recently for executive in the arts and performing arts. The trend is more pronounced in the younger generation.[11] In addition to publishing, where the proportion of women was already higher, executive status has noticeably risen in the performing arts, where parity has been reached among those under 30.[12] A similar trend has also been witnessed for some positions typical of cultural management, such as the directors of municipal cultural departments (Dressayre 2002). Again, this mirrors Paul DiMaggio's observations: he shows that there are three times as many women among theatre directors who took up their post after 1973 than among those who took up their post between 1964 and 1973 (DiMaggio 1987).

Two explanations can be put forward at this stage. The first resides in the dynamics of the educational trajectories of young women – to be more precise in the combination of disciplinary choices and of the extended duration of studies. The traditionally observed tendency of girls to enter literary curricula from high school, even when their results in the scientific disciplines are as good as their male counterparts, still applies today. This has been blamed on their self-exclusion from science-oriented professions, on the dissuasive effects of teachers' verdicts, on parental expectations and on the emphasis placed on the 'feminine' connotations of literary disciplines (Marry 2000; Lemêtre 2009). The same pattern is also observed upon access to higher education, not only because the choices made at high school level prevent girls from enrolling in scientific curricula, but also because among the holders of scientific *baccalauréats*, more girls choose literary disciplines than boys (Convert, 2006). At the later stages of higher education, choices become increasingly connected to professional career plans, as expectations in terms of employment rise. Cultural sector jobs can then appear as possible and desirable outcomes for female students, who make up a large majority in curricula such as arts, literature, languages or social science where the main career prospect is teaching but which also indirectly provide an opening to work in the cultural field. The large number of young women in cultural management programmes may thus result not so much from a direct effect of gender on the 'choice' of this sector as from a succession of past choices, informed by gender rationales at every step of the way, and at the end of which the amount and type of educational capital accumulated leads their holders to perceive cultural sector jobs as a possible aspiration.

A second explanation lies in the differences between genders in the relationships to cultural and artistic practices, and in their different effects on professional career paths. It has long been established that more women than men have a cultural practice – at least in certain fields (Bourdieu and Darbel 1991). Many recent studies have evidenced a trend towards the feminization of these practices: gaps are widening for practices that were already predominantly female (such as reading), and narrowing for chiefly male ones (such as amateur music) (Donnat 2004). Since a strong correlation has been observed between the intensity of cultural practices and the aspiration to pursue careers in the cultural field, the feminization of cultural practices may very well be among the factors of the feminization of career paths in this sector.

It is worth mentioning that the investments of men and women in these jobs differ; they do not target the same positions, and differences are particularly observed in terms of creative vs. non-creative jobs. The overall trend towards the increase in the number of applicants to artistic jobs should not lead us to overlook gender differences. These vary from one sub-sector to the next: though they make up the majority of consumers,[13] women still are in the minority among creators (even though their numbers are increasing) – not to mention the very unequal chances of reaching prominent positions Thus, the combination of women's greater likelihood to participate in cultural activities and the endurance of a gendered division of labour in which creation is a male business may explain the very large number of women among those pursuing cultural administration careers – a pattern similar to that observed for many years in librarians (Seibel 1988) and museum mediators (Peyrin 2008), which are positions typically sought by 'women of the petite bourgeoisie […] inclined to appropriate at any price […] the distinctive and therefore distinguished properties of the dominant classes and to contribute to their imperative popularization, in particular with the aid of the circumstantial symbolic power that their position in the apparatus of production or circulation of cultural goods […] may confer on their proselytizing zeal' (Bourdieu 2001: 101–2). This could be seen as a way for women to find their place in a world where their distinctive type of capital is valued, while remaining in their place, i.e. without subverting the usual gendered division of tasks.

Women are both less inclined to pursue creative artistic careers and more likely to give them up. Dancers are a case in point, as motherhood often cuts their careers short (Sorignet 2010). When artists become teachers, more men go on to be both artists and teachers whereas more women give up their artistic work (Cacouault-Bitaud 2007). These differences can be observed at an early stage, even before the beginning of artistic careers, when we look at professional aspirations. Among aspirants to cultural management careers, fewer women envision a career as an artist (32 per cent against 44 per cent of men) and more of them give up on this prospect (47.5 per cent against 40 per cent of men). Cultural management can in this sense allow artists who cannot expect to draw a sufficient and stable income from their art to avoid suffering a painful blow by reinvesting their dispositions, the network and the skills they have accumulated over the course of their artistic careers. The predominance of women among those who pursue careers in cultural management can therefore also be interpreted as a result of their greater tendency to give up on creative work and opt for a relatively smooth career transition. This is yet another case of the reproduction of the gendered division of labour, in which production is mostly assigned to men, while women tend to be entrusted with mediation and management (Cacouault-Bitaud 2007).

This raises the question of the meaning of these professional career choices within the broader perspective of gender inequality. The educational choices discussed above can be interpreted as those of 'dominated' individuals who anticipate their likely social fate (Baudelot and Establet 1992), which includes the acceptance of the often low-earning prospects that characterize cultural sector jobs, often envisioned as a secondary source of income for the future household. The great number of women in these programmes in effect contributes to sustaining a gendered division of labour in which men tend to be assigned the better paid and more powerful positions (including economically), while women are entrusted with the role of maintaining symbolic capital and social status (Bourdieu 1984; Collins 1988: 38–43). This does not mean that these career choices are to be seen as the illustration of female 'docility', leading them to follow ready-made educational and professional trajectories and, even when they succeed, to occupy secondary positions. Indeed, pursuing a career in the cultural sector, through the uncertainty it entails and correlatively the opportunity for self-assertion it offers, can also be a way to achieve emancipation from a probable and 'reasonable' fate (as the wariness towards teaching jobs seems to indicate). It may therefore illustrate the hypothesis which posits that 'girls are less expected than boys to succeed by following the canonical model of excellence based on competition, the rule of mathematics, exclusive investment in one's career [and to] have more leeway to assert their tastes' (Marry 2000: 292).[14] The very high rates of women who pursue cultural management careers should therefore not been seen as merely the reproduction of gender stereotypes, as these careers can also constitute ways to stray from well-worn paths. However, they do not constitute a challenge to existing inequalities in the gendered distribution of occupations, since the jobs accepted by these women are for the most part low-income positions. This choice is arguably neither about reproducing nor about subverting masculine domination, but much more likely a matter of coping with it.

## Higher social backgrounds

To a statistically less overwhelmingly massive but nevertheless sociologically remarkable extent, many of the would-be cultural managers have a privileged social background. Nearly half of the students (more than 45 per cent) in these master's programmes are children of executives or of holders of upper intellectual occupations,[15] a proportion far higher than that of all university students (30 per cent) and even of all master's level students (37 per cent). Yet, this proportion is lower than that of journalism students (nearly 53 per cent) (Lafarge and Marchetti 2011).[16] The students' family origins can be divided into four groups based on social hierarchy and chances of success at school (highly privileged, privileged, average and underprivileged families).[17] Under this classification, two-thirds of students in cultural management master's programmes are from privileged (16 per cent) or highly privileged families (50 per cent); the remainder are evenly distributed among the other two categories. However, the social backgrounds of students may vary fairly significantly from one programme to another.[18]

  Similar proportions are observed for applicants to the master's programmes, about whom the questionnaire results give us more detailed information. Over half of them (56 per cent) have at least one of their parents in the category of 'executives and upper intellectual occupations'; nearly 20 per cent have both their parents in that category. The proportion of fathers belonging to that category is the main factor distinguishing the applicants to cultural master's programmes from master's level students in general (see table below). Over four out of five applicants (81 per cent) have at least one parent in the 'executive', 'intermediate occupations', or 'CEO' categories, and nearly half (47 per cent) have both of their parents in those categories. Nearly three parents out of four (73.5 per cent) have a 'privileged' position (executive, intermediate occupations, CEO). One out of three mothers is an executive (33 per cent) and nearly two out of three (63 per cent) have a privileged position; around 11 per cent do not work. The presence of many schoolteachers and teachers in vocational training, and particularly among the mothers, of social and health workers, accounts for the over-representation of intermediate occupations compared to the population of master's level students at large. Likewise, the high proportion of employees among the mothers comes from the large numbers of civil service employees and health and social workers.

Table 2.1 Social backgrounds

| | Applicants | | Master's students* | |
|---|---|---|---|---|
| | Mothers | Fathers | Mothers | Fathers |
| Farmer | 2.0 | 3.2 | 2.0 | 1.5 |
| Craftsman, shopkeeper, business owner | 3.7 | 9.5 | 6.1 | 5.7 |
| *including:* | | | | |
| *Craftsman* | 0.7 | 3.9 | | |
| *Shopkeeper* | 1.9 | 3.0 | | |
| *Business owner* | 1.2 | 2.6 | | |
| Executives and upper intellectual occupations | 31.7 | 51.8 | 34.3 | 37.8 |
| *including:* | | | | |
| *Engineers and technical company executives* | 1.9 | 7.4 | | |
| *Administrative and commercial company executives* | 1.3 | 9.8 | | |
| *Information, arts and performing arts professionals* | 4.4 | 7.4 | | |
| *Teachers, scientific occupations* | 10.8 | 7.4 | | |
| *Senior public service managers* | 1.2 | 3.9 | | |
| *Self-employed occupations* | 4.7 | 9.1 | | |
| Intermediate occupations | 30.0 | 19.0 | 13.6 | 13.7 |
| *including:* | | | | |
| *Health and social workers* | 12.5 | 4.4 | | |
| *Schoolteachers* | 9.4 | 5.3 | | |
| Employees | 20.2 | 6.5 | 10.9 | 10 |
| Workers | 1.5 | 10.0 | 7.6 | 7 |
| Unemployed, retired, non-working | 10.8 | 0.0 | 11.9 | 11.9 |
| N/A | – | – | 13.6 | 12.5 |
| Total | 100 | 100 | 100 | 100 |

*Source: ministère de l'Éducation nationale, *Repères et références statistiques*, 2009, p. 191. (all university master's programmes)

In addition to their high level of employment, the applicants' parents also stand out owing to the high representation of some areas of activity. Twenty-nine per cent of applicants have at least one parent working in the education sector (including 23 per cent of teachers) – this is the case of 12.5 per cent of fathers, which is well above the proportion for all master's university level students (8 per cent). The sectors of health (20 per cent including 10 per cent of practitioners with status at least equal to intermediate occupation), social work (9 per cent) and, more predictably, of art and culture (17 per cent including 6 per cent of artists) are also highly represented. Nearly two in three applicants (62 per cent) have at least one of their parents working in one of these sectors – more often the mothers (56 per cent) than the fathers (36 per cent). However, the latter more frequently work in the artistic and cultural sectors (13 per cent, against 8 per cent of mothers).

While the presence of parents working in the artistic and cultural sectors may simply reflect a form of professional transmission, the high representation of the sectors of teaching, health and social work may be because they combine two shared characteristics. The first is that they generally require high levels of educational capital for the social position they offer – either they require a high-level degree (architects, doctors, secondary school teachers), or educational capital prevails over economic capital in the overall volume of capital possessed by the individual (social workers, nurses, primary school teachers). This dominance of educational capital is matched not only by reproduction strategies in which school is highly valued, but also by intellectual and cultural dispositions that may lead these individuals to pursue cultural occupations. The second characteristic shared by the sectors is that they are situated in 'the world of human affairs', rather than that of 'material things', to use the distinction made by Halbwachs (1972). For that reason, the cultural sector is conducive to attracting individuals who value the

*Table 2.2* Main sectors of activity of the parents

|  | Mothers (%) | Fathers (%) |
|---|---|---|
| Education | 26.5 | 12.5 |
| Teacher (except art teachers) | 19.7 | 10.9 |
| Other | 0 | 1.6 |
| Health | 17.2 | 9.7 |
| Nurse | 7.9 | 0.9 |
| Doctor | 0 | 5.6 |
| Other | 2.5 | 3.1 |
| Art and culture | 8.3 | 12.7 |
| Architect | 0.5 | 2.1 |
| Art craftsman | 0.2 | 2.5 |
| Librarian, archivist, bookseller | 1.5 | 0.2 |
| Manager | 2.2 | 2.5 |
| Artist | 3.4 | 4.0 |
| Teacher | 1.5 | 1.8 |
| Social work | 7.1 | 3.7 |
| Educator/Social worker | 2.4 | 1.2 |
| Other | 0 | 2.5 |
| Other | 43.7 | 62.2 |
| Total | 100 | 100 |

relational aspects of professional activities, and in some cases invest in that world their own dispositions for altruism.

Somewhat unsurprisingly, these professional characteristics are matched by a level of educational attainment that is slightly higher than that of parents of students in other branches. Nearly three in four applicants (72 per cent) have a parent with a higher education degree, which is only the case of half (51 per cent) of the student population at large. This is a factor in the heightened familial investment in education and culture, which in turn may contribute to the choice of training programmes that combine the academic recognition of cultural capital and an emphasis on different forms of culture, especially those acquired within the family circle (Bourdieu and Passeron 1979). Indeed, the professional positions of the parents, the sectors in which they work and their levels of educational attainment suggest that many would-be cultural managers have experienced an early and intense cultural socialization within their family. Although statements made by the applicants on their parents' cultural practices should be interpreted cautiously, they suggest that they are noticeably richer than those of the population at large, with cultural outings in the previous year for around 90 per cent of parents, and nearly half of the mothers and 36 per cent of fathers reading at least one book per month.[19] The parents' cultural practices are, of course, passed on through a well-established mechanism of reproduction that remains a crucial factor in future practices (Octobre and Jauneau 2008; Coulangeon 2013). The parents' cultural practices also produce a cumulative effect of familiarization with the cultural world and of encouragement to make new investments that contribute to make culture a conceivable or desirable *professional* environment.

The family legacy plays a much more direct role in making culture a viable career option, through the example and the relational and informational resources provided by relatives already working in the sector. This familiarization, which is not only cultural but also more directly relational, is experienced by quite a few of the applicants: at least a third have a relative whose main professional activity is (or was) in the artistic or cultural sectors; 15 per cent have at least two; and 3 per cent have both of their parents in that case. This concerns 8 per cent of fathers, 11 per cent of mothers, 11 per cent of uncles and aunts and, more rarely, grandparents. Beyond the family circle, half of the applicants have a close acquaintance whose main professional activity is (or was) in the artistic or cultural sectors.

## Educated applicants

The examination of the applicants' educational trajectories highlights three main trends: they often have high levels of educational capital; they have frequently pursued literary studies in the broader sense of the term and received training directly related to culture; yet, they display a heterogeneity that is evidenced both by the diversity of backgrounds and by the discontinuity of individual trajectories.

A high level of educational capital sociologically matches the often privileged backgrounds of the applicants. It reflects a general trend towards the elevation of the level of educational attainment – to be more precise, the majority of positions targeted are held by higher education graduates, and to be even more precise, the youngest holders of these positions have increasingly high degrees. The educational characteristics of our population provide an indication of the scope of this trend: they show the high level of attainment not only of the cultural managers in place and of those who apply to work in these positions, [20] but also of those who are looking to acquire a degree allowing them access to these jobs. They have accumulated high levels of educational capital even before applying for a cultural master's programme, primarily exemplified by the conditions in which they obtained their *baccalauréat*. Eighty per cent of applicants for cultural master's programmes graduated from high school on or ahead of schedule (against 62 per cent for the student population at large). Likewise, more among them did so with honours: 64 per cent, including 7 per cent with the highest honours (*mention très bien*), against 3.8 per cent of all university students. Lastly, 96 per cent of applicants to cultural master's programmes are holders of a general (i.e., non-vocational) *baccalauréat*, against 82 per cent of fourth-year university students and 70 per cent of all students.

The examination of the distribution by *baccalauréat* stream appears to nuance this excellence in education, as it is in reverse order compared not only to the overall distribution of graduates, but also the hierarchy that generally prevails between the three general streams: among applicants with a general *baccalauréat*, only 18 per cent come from the *série scientifique* (S), which is usually considered as the recruitment pool of the elite; a majority of the applicants (over 47 per cent) come from the *série littéraire* (L), which is often devalued; 34.5 per cent come from the *série économique et sociale* (ES).[21] The discrepancy between educational achievement and the choice of a rather undervalued stream of secondary education, which characterizes the educational trajectories of the vast majority of young women among the applicants, is embodied by the figure of the 'good literary student'. It predisposes these students to cultivate an ambivalent relationship to the educational institution and to have partly out-of-step expectations or anticipations regarding their position within the social space, leading them to accept low-paid jobs in a socially privileged environment or to experience 'white-collar precarity'.

The somewhat high representation of prestigious selective programmes in the early stages of higher education constitutes the second indicator that applicants have high levels of initial educational capital. Nearly one in four applicants have studied in a *classe préparatoire aux grandes écoles* (almost always literary) and 8 per cent have studied in an Institute of Political Studies (IEP). These are high proportions compared to the population of *baccalauréat* graduates at large, among whom in the same generation, 8 per cent of L graduates and 6 per cent of ES graduates went on to study in a *classe préparatoire*,[22] and less than 1 per cent from the three general streams enrolled in an IEP.[23] They are even higher when related to the entire student population, which includes 3 per cent of students in *classes préparatoires* and 0.35 per cent in IEPs. Comparison with the educational trajectories of students reaching the same level in the same period would be useful, but not enough data is available for that. While the proportions might be even higher in highly selective programmes such as journalism schools,[24] it is very likely that they are unequalled among the university master's programmes in related disciplinary areas.

The predominance of achieving students is confirmed by the examination of higher education results: for instance, applicants have frequently obtained their bachelor's degree with honours. Regarding the type of education pursued, and therefore the applicants' type of educational capital, we observe a majority of literary backgrounds in the broader sense of the term. This is shown in the negative by the weak proportion of applicants who studied economics or management at university (4.5 per cent) or in a business or management school (2.5 per cent), a low proportion for master's programmes that often place emphasis on management. Former law students are more frequently found among the applicants (around 7.5 per cent; they make up 15 per cent of all university students), but much less so than students in literature (11 per cent), languages (13 per cent) and communication (9 per cent). Within the humanities and social sciences, history students are the best represented (over 20 per cent, plus 10 per cent of art history students) – nearly four times as many as sociology (7.5 per cent), a less 'literary' discipline whose social and educational recruitment is lower (Chenu 2002: 53). Then come cultural programmes such as 'cultural mediation', which are less academic and more job-market-oriented (16 per cent of undergraduate students). Students who have undergone training directly related to the arts and culture before applying to a master's programme in cultural management make up just over half of the applicants, if we add undergraduates in art-oriented disciplines (art history, 10 per cent; performing arts, 10 per cent; visual arts, 5 per cent; music, 4 per cent), students from arts and architecture schools (5 per cent), and from non-academic programmes training for work in the cultural sector (5 per cent), from a few short cycle programmes (such as technician certificates, BTS in the French system) and first year master's students.

For those students, the choice of applying to a cultural master's programme is directly in line with the logic of past educational trajectories, either because it was planned in advance, or because it results from a combination of successive adjustments and ratchet effects that made it appear as a possible option at a later stage. This does not mean, however, that the other half of the applicants with no previous training in arts and culture make a random or belated choice to pursue cultural management. Rather, this divide results from the structural coexistence of two types of educational capital that may be exploited in cultural management. The first rests on the acquisition of cultural skills during schooling under a variety of forms (artistic in art schools, applied in mediation programmes, more academic for art history students). The second attests to the acquisition of generalist skills (IEP), and/or ones that are, strictly speaking, external to the cultural field (philosophy, law) that may also be exploited in cultural management if they are combined with cultural resources accumulated outside of school (through amateur artistic practice, associative activities, pre-professional experiences).

The joint presence, in equivalent proportions, of these two types of educational capital reflects an often intense investment in schooling, but also shows that recruitment in cultural occupations remains largely open. As we have seen, the development of specialized programmes has not resulted in a unification of the available training: even without non-university programmes, the applicants come from some 15 different types of bachelor's programmes and roughly as many first year master's programmes. The educational backgrounds of job applicants in this domain are also highly diversified (Mathieu 2011, 213). Their trajectories are increasingly disjointed. Thirty per cent of students who attended a bachelor's programme in a university switched disciplines at least once or pursued a double degree; many also switched disciplines upon reaching the master's level (first year). Some also followed interdisciplinary programmes and studied partly outside of universities.

From students having pursued cultural training at an early stage for whom 'making a career out of culture' is experienced and presented as a long-established and exclusive plan to holders of an educational capital that opens doors, including those of culture, or to students in literary subjects looking for a career, we now have an idea of the educational trajectories that lead to cultural management. This diversity is however nuanced by the examination of the applicants' cultural investments outside of school, which brings a modicum of homogeneity to their backgrounds.

## Well-rounded applicants

Most applicants readily claim that their choice of pursuing cultural management jobs is 'no accident', in the sense that it is associated with a personal taste for culture and intense cultural practices, which themselves result from the combined effects of gender, family background and educational capital (on this combination, see Coulangeon 2003).

The applicants have experienced an early cultural socialization thanks to their relatives, and almost all of them had some artistic training as a child. Most of them (85 per cent) received tuition or followed classes for at least one art form, and over half (60 per cent) for two or more. The majority were taught music (50 per cent learned an instrument, and 21 per cent learned how to sing), followed by dance (42 per cent), theatre (32 per cent), the visual arts (26 per cent), photography and video (12 per cent), writing (5 per cent) and circus (4 per cent). Many of the applicants still pursued these activities at the time of their application (28 per cent, against 4.5 per cent of all French citizens in the same age group receiving artistic training).[25]

Often in connection with this artistic training, artistic practices are also widespread among the applicants: 67 per cent of them have (40 per cent) or have had (27 per cent) a regular practice (at least weekly), and over 25 per cent have two different practices or more. Music and singing are the most common practices (31 per cent), followed by visual arts (20 per cent), photography and video (15.5 per cent), dance (11 per cent), writing (10 per cent) and theatre (8.5 per cent).

These practices are pursued with a far greater intensity than in the overall population of the same group and in the student body at large.

There is also a significant gap when it comes to cultural outings, which are slightly more frequent for applicants to cultural master's programmes than for the student population in general and even students in literary and artistic disciplines (except for classical music concerts). The applicants are 11 times more likely to have been to a museum or an exhibit than the students as a whole. All applicants have been on at least one cultural outing over the previous month (only 2.4 per cent have only been to the cinema); on average they report having been on three different types of outings during the month.

The share of non-readers (not a single book read over the previous 12 months) is significantly lower among the applicants (2.6 per cent) than in the student population at large (9 per cent) (Donnat 2009). Conversely, far fewer applicants (28.3 per cent against 48.1 per cent) report watching TV every day.[26]

While it may seem self-evident that applicants to cultural master's programmes have high levels of cultural capital and frequently make cultural outings, this should not lead us to overlook a characteristic that is very unevenly distributed among the social groups and sectors of activity: the strong continuity between personal dispositions and practices and professional aspirations. This continuity can be a factor accounting for 'motivation' or at least underpin the subjective experience and public expression of this motivation (in terms of making a living out of one's passion). Although they are generally related, these personal dispositions cannot be entirely reduced either to education in school or to family legacy – arguably their conversion into professional career choices reflects a form of individuation. More straightforwardly, this continuity also reflects the professional exploitation of a range of personal resources such as familiarity with the cultural world and its codes, specific skills and social capital accumulated through one's experience of the cultural field and of its agents, combined with other resources – including educational ones. 'Passion' may not be an explanatory factor in itself, but it is not incompatible with a reasoned choice.

*Table 2.3* Cultural outings over the previous thirty days

|  | Film | Museum or exhibition | Rock or jazz concert | Theatre | Classical music, opera |
|---|---|---|---|---|---|
| Applicants | 85.6% | 81.7% | 56.4% | 43.9% | 16.5% |
| Literature and arts students* | 70.6% | 50.2% | 34.5% | 28.8% | 17% |
| All students* | 64.6% | 28.3% | 22.9% | 12.2% | 7.9% |
| Odds ratio appl./all students | 3.3 | 11.3 | 4.4 | 5.6 | 2.3 |

*Source: Observatoire de la vie étudiante, *Conditions de vie des étudiants*, 2006.

## The space of applicants

The successive examination of the applicants' salient features gives us a useful overview, but one that is too compartmentalized to highlight the associations and oppositions between the polarities among which they are distributed; it is therefore insufficient to evidence typical backgrounds. For this reason we decided to conduct a more directly relational analysis, in the sense that variables are interconnected and systems of relations between individuals are characterized. We carried out a multiple correspondence analysis based on the applicants' main features.[27]

### Methodology

Based on recoded questionnaire responses (n = 654), we selected 10 active variables, divided into 44 modalities. These variables pertain to positional attributes relating to educational characteristics (*baccaularéat* stream, high school graduation age, latest diploma obtained) and social characteristics (father's occupation), as well as to the degree of cultural socialization (intensity of the parents' cultural practices, art tuition or classes, regular artistic practice), and more precisely to professional activities in the field (friends or relatives working in culture, importance of the applicants' professional experience). As they are strongly correlated with some active variables or because they contribute little to accounting for the variance, supplementary variables (gender, experience of *classes préparatoires*, internships in the cultural field, participation in a cultural organization, associative duties in another field) are not included in the construction of the factorial axes, but the associate modalities are projected. The two axes retained account for 35.4 per cent of the variance (respectively 0.197 and 0.157 of inertia). In order to make them more easily readable, we decided to display only the variables and not the individuals in the graphs.

In Figure 2.1: The space of applicants, the first (horizontal) axis represents the level of the applicants' specific capital, measured on the basis of their degree of familiarity with culture, the intensity of their practices and the extent of their previous socialization in the professional dimension of culture. Individuals are distinguished according to the art tuition or classes they have attended, their artistic practices, their parents' cultural consumption, their relations with professionals of culture and their personal experience of that world. The level of each of those variables attests to a volume of specific capital that increases towards the left of the factorial graph. The second (vertical) axis reflects the applicants' original social level and educational capital. The best endowed among them (children of executives, holders of a general *baccalauréat*, often in the scientific stream, having graduated or on ahead of schedule and studied in a *classe préparatoire*)

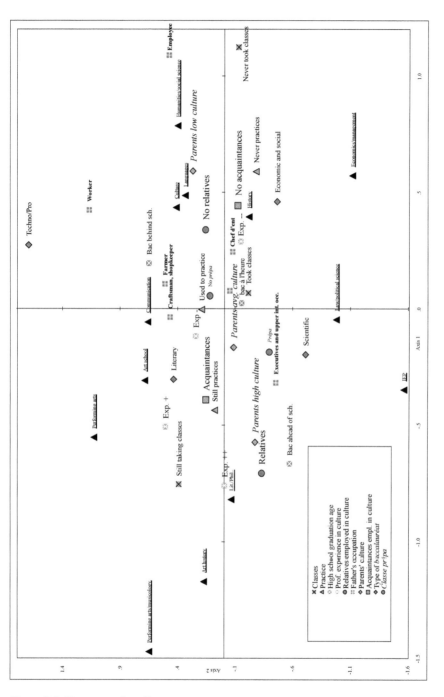

*Figure 2.1* The space of applicants

and the students who pursued more general training are found in the lower part of the graph. The children of workers or employees, the least achieving students and/or those who pursued more specialized training, especially in culture, are found in the upper part of the graph. One variable is particularly influential in the construction of both axes: the latest diploma obtained. Indeed, it serves both as an indicator of cultural socialization (the applicants' higher education backgrounds tend to be related to culture) and as an indicator of social background and of the level of educational excellence associated with that background (as the second axis shows an opposition between alumni of generalist or prestigious programmes and those of more specialized programmes with a lower social recruitment).[28]

The analysis clearly evidences the distinction between the bulk of applicants (on the left side of the factorial space) who are socially privileged, academically selected and culturally well-disposed, and other, less numerous applicants (on the right side) who are generally less endowed or whose characteristics do not combine to create efficient resources in the cultural world (such as having a father who owns a business but has no connections with professionals of culture, being trained in economics but having no artistic practice, having received academic training in the cultural field but with lesser educational achievements and little family socialization). This unequal distribution reflects a strict social and educational pre-selection, which becomes even tougher in the later stages of the individual trajectories. Insofar as these variables can be directly or indirectly used as selection criteria for admission to master's programmes and subsequently access to employment, there is every chance that this distribution will materialize in an opposition between the 'good' applicants, who are likely to be enrolled in the most selective programmes and access the positions they are coveting, and those who will have to make do with second-class programmes and lower their professional prospects as well as those whose perspectives of making it into the professional world of culture will be cut short by their failure at being admitted into a master's programme. This connection between resources and objective chances, and between the identification of their characteristics and the selection of applicants, is all the stronger as the ratio between the number of applicants and the number of available positions is particularly strained. Since from the beginning of the second master's year there are many applicants for few places, recruitments are essentially made on the left side of the space, where the number of individuals already exceeds the number of available positions. The others are left with the prospects of retrying their luck, opting for a less ambitious educational and professional path or pursuing other careers.

The multivariate analysis also confirms the distinction between the two types of educational capital previously identified (specific and generalist), and shows how this distinction more broadly matches the opposition between the two types of holders of professional positions in cultural management. This is clearly visible on the left side of the graph. The characteristic attributes of artists (previous studies in an art school or in artistic discipline at university, literary *baccalauréat*, more frequent and intense artistic learning and practices) are found primarily in the upper quadrant, which includes individuals with artistic vocations that turned to cultural management. The lower quadrant features individuals with higher social origins, high levels of educational achievement and more open academic trajectories (scientific *baccalauréat*, IEP) that have more similarities with the recruitment of executives, regardless of the sector of activity. For them culture is a choice among several possible paths. Seeing this in terms of an opposition between artists and managers would, however, be oversimplifying things, as having generalist attributes does not exclude the possibility of having strong cultural predispositions, as attested to by parental and personal practices. Rather, this reflects the aggregation of an educational capital that can be transposed from one sector to the next and serve as currency in cultural management positions and of a cultural capital acquired outside of school that makes a career in culture possible.

Although this is less clearly visible, the right side of the factorial graph, which includes the applicants less endowed with all forms of resources, displays a similar opposition in terms of the cultural specialization of previous training – reflected on the vertical axis. The lower right quadrant includes students from intermediate or privileged social categories (business owners), for whom neither past training, nor friends and relatives or personal practices predispose them to pursue cultural occupations. They make this choice at a later stage, and it is both less exclusive and more indeterminate, made often in response to opportunities such as the availability of a programme in their own university. These less motivated applicants have very few chances of success. The upper right quadrant includes students with lower social backgrounds (fathers are farmers or blue-collar workers), who have little educational capital and whose socialization and cultural practices are less intense – among them many studied in a specialized cultural programme in the first cycle of higher education. This academic specialization in culture, when supported by few extra-educational resources, stands in contrast to the generalist background of the 'well-rounded good students'. This is a choice made by individuals from the dominated classes, both weakly informed and more limited by lesser achievements in secondary school and in the early stages of higher education. They have fewer chances of finding a job in the cultural sector than is expected of a master's graduate, because they lack most of the resources (educational and social) required for succeeding. They also offer fewer opportunities to move on towards other sectors – a typical instance of the higher education system not fulfilling its promises by leading working-class students into a dead end instead of enabling their promotion (Beaud 2003). The children of blue-collar workers, among whom the highest proportion of girls is found (90 per cent), more often come from cultural programmes (36 per cent against 25 per cent of all applicants). While more of them exclusively pursue careers in the cultural sector (73 per cent against 68 per cent), they are, in effect, less likely to find a job there.

Having first mapped out the space of cultural occupations and of the specialized training programmes and subsequently identified the characteristics of the individuals who aspire to work in the cultural sector, I will now move on to consider how conditions are turned into motivations – the 'vocation work' (Suaud 1978: 9) — and interpret the career trajectories, actual and projected, to which these give rise.

## Notes

1  The gap between applicants and enrolled students can likely be ascribed to the fact that the heads of master's programmes seek to avoid an excessive or exclusive presence of women in their classes, which may result in a 'positive discrimination' of sorts for the male students, sometimes deliberately presented as such.

2  See for instance on Canada, *Graduate Survey*, Canadian Association Of Arts Administration Educators, DeGros Marsh Consulting, Ottawa, September 2005.

3  There are a majority of women in heritage (80 per cent), visual arts (63 per cent) and music and dance programmes (55 per cent), equivalent proportions of men and women in theatre and performing arts programmes (51 per cent) and in architecture schools (49 per cent), and more men in film and broadcasting schools (Zadora 2008).

4  'Women amounted for 15.3 per cent of journalists in 1965 and 20 per cent in 1974; they are 37.5 per cent in 1996.' (Neveu 2000: 181). The census figures, calculated on the basis of the number of card-carrying journalists, are slightly different, but they display a similar trend: 30 per cent of women in 1982, 38 per cent in 1990, 43 per cent in 1999, 49 per cent in 2008 (source: INSEE).

5  51 per cent of respondents in Lafarge and Marchetti 2011: 94.

6  Two-year cram schools training undergraduate students for enrollment in prestigious institutions, mainly in the *Ecole normale supérieure*.

7  Source: ministère de l'Éducation nationale, 2007.

8  Source: INSEE, 2008.

9  Source: ministère de la Culture-DEPS, *Chiffres clés 2011, professions culturelles et emploi*.

10  According to the INSEE census: 76 per cent of men in 1982, 67 per cent in 1990, 62 per cent in 1999 and 57 per cent under a new classification in 2008. The share of women among the arts and performing arts professionals has gone up from 36 per cent in 1982–4 to 40 per cent in 2007–9. Source: DARES, *Les familles professionnelles*. These numbers are yearly averages for the two periods under consideration based on *Enquête emploi* data.

11  From 1982–4 to 2007–9 the proportion of women went from 42–9 per cent among those under 30, and from 32–6 per cent among those aged between 30 and 49. It only decreased slightly for those aged 50 and over (from 37– 6 per cnt). Source: DARES, *Les familles professionnelles*.

12  Source: CEREQ, *Portraits statistiques de branche*, based on INSEE's *Enquête emploi* (all individuals in employment outside of government and local government employees), 2010.

13  See Ferrand 2004:70; Cacouault-Bitaud and Ravet 2008; regarding music, Ravet 2006; Buscatto 2003; on literature Naudier 2000; Lahire 2006: 108–9; on the visual arts Quemin 2009.

14  Here Catherine Marry draws on Ferrand, Imbert and Marry 1999. These perspectives of individual emancipation for women can be more generally reflected in the feminist leanings and claims often expressed by applicants.

15  Source: SISE database, *ministère de l'Enseignement supérieur*. The socio-occupational category under consideration is generally that of the father. See methodological appendix for more details.

16 This gap might be explained in part by the fact that journalism schools are more selective than universities. These figures are, however, subject to caution, owing to the disparity of the sources (a ministry database and the responses to a questionnaire survey).

17 This classification is used by the *Direction des études* of the Ministry of Education for primary and secondary school students. 'Highly privileged' includes 'executives and upper intellectual occupations' as well as owners of businesses with ten employees or more, schoolteachers and related occupations; 'privileged' includes the 'intermediate occupations' without the schoolteachers, as well as retired executives and holders of upper intellectual occupations; 'average' includes working and retired farmers, shopkeeper, craftsmen and employees; 'underprivileged' includes blue-collar workers, retired employees and retired blue-collar workers, other non-employed and those whose occupation is not known.

18 The proportion of students with privileged backgrounds ranges from 47–83 per cent, and is above 70 per cent in seven out of twenty master's programmes in our sample, between 60 per cent and 70 per cent in eight others, and under 60 per cent in the four remaining ones.

19 For instance, 34 per cent of women and 26 per cent of men report having read more than ten books over the previous 12 months in the 2008 survey of French cultural practices (Donnat 2009).

20 The latter's level of educational attainment is likely higher than that of the cultural managers in place. Among the applicants registered at the job fair for cultural employment, 83.1 per cent have bachelor's level or higher and 62.1 per cent have completed five years of higher education or more (Mathieu 2011).

21 Graduates from the general streams are roughly broken down as follows: S, 50 per cent, ES, 32 per cent, L, 18 per cent. On the social hierarchy of recruitment in these streams and their higher education prospects, see Convert 2003.

22 Source: « *Disparités d'accès et parcours en classe préparatoire* », *Note d'information* 08.16, ministère de l'Éducation nationale, DEPP, mars 2008.

23 This last figure is an approximation, calculated on the basis of around 260,000 *baccalauréat* holders (in general streams) per year for around 1.800 first year places in the Paris IEP and in the eight regional IEPs (i.e., around 0.7 per cent of graduates).

24 In journalism schools, alumni of *classes préparatoires* and IEPs make up respectively a third and a quarter of the student body (Lafarge and Marchetti 2011). These numbers, however, concern registered – and therefore selected – students, not applicants as in our case.

25 Source: ministère de la Culture, *enquête sur les pratiques culturelles des Français*, 2008 (age class 15–30).

26 Source: Observatoire de la vie étudiante, *Conditions de vie des étudiants*, 2006.

27 On MCA, see introduction p. XXX.

28 It is also worth mentioning that the high number of active variables (13) reinforces the statistical weight of this variable.

# 3   The meanings of a career choice

The choice of making a career in cultural management cannot be seen either as the result of necessity or, as its opposite, of the complete freedom to do anything one wishes. Two seemingly contradictory rationales are at work here: the applicants' trajectories and their discourses on these trajectories suggest that the applicants are strongly determined (in both senses of the term) but their 'career plans' remain more undetermined. This apparent contradiction can be better understood in the light of the range of future possibilities that applicants can consider. Two main references mark the boundaries of this space of anticipations, a positive and a negative one: some considered and then gave up pursuing a career as an artist, while others were going to be teachers but then sought to avoid that at all costs. This chapter will evidence the main forms of vocation resulting from the combination of objective conditions, subjective perceptions and corresponding attitudes.

## Leaving doors open

### A genuine choice

The majority of aspirants make a genuine choice to be trained and work in cultural management. The specialized master's programmes attract applicants with high levels of capital – especially educational capital; those insufficiently endowed have few chances of being admitted into a programme that meets their expectations unless they make up for their lack of educational capital by carrying out internships or accumulating enough experience, for example, in associations, to become 'credible postulants' (Mauger 2006b: 254) – young pre-professionals in search of an academic degree. These programmes are therefore anything but fall-back solutions for mediocre students, nor are they homes to dilettantes or young people who decide to extend their studies to put off looking for work. For the majority of applicants, enrolling in a master's programme in cultural management is more demanding than continuing their previous studies would have been. It is a directly 'professional' choice, in the sense that the programme serves as the last stage of preparation for seeking employment.

While some of the students develop a vague attraction for culture later on in their education, most of them report having chosen to be trained in cultural management when they began their higher education (36 per cent) or even earlier (10 per cent).

Others formulated this choice more recently, after having envisioned a career as an artist or simply in the arts and culture in general. Early choices may reflect varied, if not opposed, dispositions. While applicants often relate cultural career choices to their family background ('I've always lived in a very cultural world') and/or present it as a positive extension of their individuality (their 'project' or 'personal sensitivities'), in much rarer instances the choices may reflect the uneasy relation to the future of students with a more modest background who attempt to retain control over what they hope will be an upward trajectory.

Such is the case of Catherine, a young woman of Portuguese origin. Her father is a house painter; she was raised by her mother, a cashier, who along with one of her friends introduced her to culture – museums in particular – from the time of her childhood, with an explicit view towards narrowing the social gap between her and other children. This early exposure caused her to become interested in studying the arts; at a very early point she chose to pursue a career in cultural management, which she learned about from the guidance counsellors she often saw in high school, '...because I was really scared about the future. Browsing through the documents at the guidance centre I found that cultural mediation seemed to be the closest thing to what I wanted to do [...] Then I went to classes, to open days, etc'. As she thought that she 'lacked some things' to work in a museum, she initially pursued art history studies, which she paid for by working 20 hours a week, and then applied to 8 or 9 master's programmes in cultural mediation and management.

*Interview*

Often made early, this choice tends to be exclusive: only one in three candidates also apply for admission to a programme in an area other than cultural management. Among the third in question, 70 per cent apply for a programme in one other area, 25 per cent in two and 5 per cent in three. The range of alternatives envisioned by applicants individually is rather small. If we look at the population of applicants in general, however, we notice that the fields competing with cultural management are very diverse.[1] The most frequent field (communication) is only mentioned by under 7 per cent of applicants; all the others are mentioned by under 5 per cent of them (European studies, 4.5 per cent; journalism, 4 per cent – other fields even less). Contrary to what one might think, there is no recurring association between cultural management and any other field.

The fact that students make multiple applications to cultural management programmes shows their investment in this career path: over half of the applicants applied to at least two of these specialized programmes; 10 per cent applied to five or more.[2] They almost always report wanting to work directly after graduating (88 per cent), in the cultural sector exclusively for the vast majority (68 per cent), or in the cultural sectors and other perceived fallback sectors (a questionnaire response reads 'any sector to have a job before I find one in my branch'), often in connection to other possible training programmes, such as communication, tourism, international relations or urban planning.

The importance of the applicants' pre-professional experiences also confirms this investment. Three in four applicants have already completed at least one internship in the field of culture; half of them have done several. Half as many have experience as an intern in another field. These cultural internships appear to be (rightly) perceived as pre-requisites for admission in a master's programme. They allow the applicants to accumulate a significant amount of experience: their average duration (aggregate in case of multiple internships) is over seven months; nearly one in five applicants have interned for over a year.

Aude's choices are characteristic of a strategy aimed at maximizing her chances. This student in an institute of political science (IEP) targeted a programme that she knew to be highly selective from the beginning of her studies. She chose to make an internship in the cultural field during her third year abroad, as part of a global strategy that also informs her choice of courses (she picked those addressing cultural matters and also did an optional accountability class because she thought it would prove useful), her assignments (she wrote a dissertation on the economy of culture), and her extra-curricular activities (she created an association both out of personal interest and to add pre-professional experiences to her résumé).

*Aude, born in 1989, father special needs teacher then construction engineer, mother midwife, baccalauréat S then regional IEP, in a cultural master's programme at the time of the interview*

In addition to internships, half of the applicants report having paid work experience in the cultural sector. This was a regular job (at least ten hours a week) for nearly one in four applicants, not only during school breaks. Outside of those requiring a particular skill (in music or visual arts for arts teaching, in history or art history for 'cultural mediation' and guided tours in museums and historical landmarks), the most frequent jobs are low-skilled, and as such are typical of student jobs – often reception or assistant work. While they may, of course, serve to meet material needs, these jobs fulfil a specific function of student work: the anticipation of one's professional future (Pinto 2014: 219 ff.). In some exceptional instances, these student jobs may trigger a cultural vocation: this happened to a student who, during a selection interview, explained that her experience of working as a hostess in a theatre made her 'want to work in culture', leading her to pursue a master's in art law after her bachelor's in law.[3] Yet, in the vast majority of cases, these jobs are explicitly conceived as a means to acquire useful experience in the perspective of being introduced to the cultural world, in which their holders have already set their 'career plan'. This experience may be adjusted to the content of their studies or to the student's background (Pinto 2014: 109ff.), or to complement those with a more generalist, less directly cultural background, with a view to securing a job in that sector, and before that at increasing their chances of being admitted into the most competitive programmes, for which such work experience is clearly required. This also applies to the less skilled jobs, which even though they are arguably a means of making a virtue of necessity, they can also be perceived in strategic terms as ways for students to carve a space in an institution where they hope to later have a job more in keeping with their aspirations; to get an insider's view of how a theatre or an opera house work, and therefore to acquire specific forms of knowledge, or sometimes very explicitly to accumulate social capital by meeting professionals of culture: one applicant for example reported having taken advantage of his bartending job at a festival to meet concert promoters, band managers and heads of independent record labels.

The reasons for this career choice are, however, not univocal, nor are the applicants' levels of investment all similar. We identified the structure of their prospects regarding training and employment using a multiple correspondence analysis of the distribution of the applicants' anticipations.

**Methodology**

We selected seven active variables, divided into 18 modalities (n = 654). They pertain to the master's programme (applications exclusively in cultural management or not, perception of the programme's usefulness to find employment in the sector), the outcome of the master's (search for a job only in the cultural sector or in another sector as well, other projects such as undertaking further studies) and to professional plans and aspirations (salary expectations, search for a given type of employer or function or not, desire to work in one or several specific cultural sectors or across sectors). The two axes account for 41.2 per cent of the variance explained (with respectively 0.221 and 0.191 of inertia for the first and second axis). Aspirations pertaining to the characteristics of the job held several years after graduation feature as supplementary variables. Their projection displays a striking similarity with the modalities accounting for work aspirations immediately after graduation.

In Figure 3.1, the first (horizontal) axis distinguishes between applicants according to the degree of specificity characterizing their educational and career choices. The left of the factorial graph features those individuals with the most assertive choices: for them cultural management is an exclusive choice as far as both their training and their job search are concerned. Conversely, the right of the graph includes individuals who see culture as a choice among others, in terms of training and job search alike. As we move from the left to the right of the graph we observe the combined decline of the applicants' level of knowledge and *illusio* regarding the cultural world. The importance granted to training decreases, due

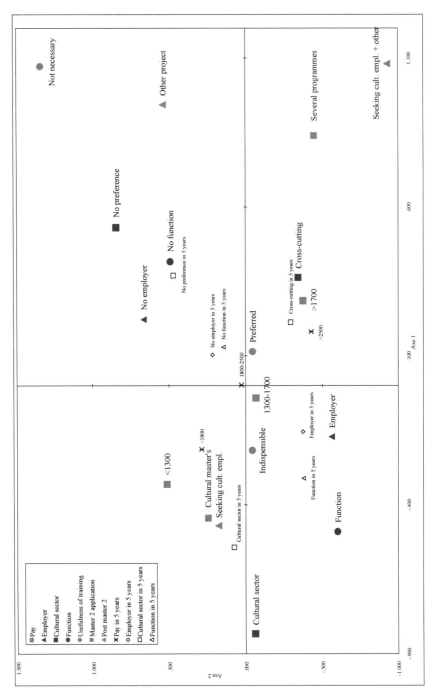

*Figure 3.1* The space of prospects

to insufficient knowledge of the employment conditions in the sector or lack of faith in the training, whereas salary expectations increase, also due to insufficient knowledge of wages usually paid in the sector and to a less distanced outlook on material rewards. The second (vertical) axis accounts for the level of precision or specification of professional aspirations in the cultural management sector. The lower part of the graph comprises applicants who express a preference for a particular type of employer, function or cultural sector. Conversely, the upper part includes applicants whose career plan is less specific or more open.

Counter-intuitively, the factorial analysis suggests that the socio-demographic and educational background of the applicants and their relation to culture have little influence on their expectations for the future. Yet, the combination of this analysis and further statistical processing (cross-tabulations and multi-nomial logistic regression) evidences three interconnected factors at play in the degree of determination of choices (first axis). The discipline of study, identified on the basis of the latest diploma obtained, is the first discriminating factor. Unsurprisingly, applicants who studied in artistic disciplines are among those for whom a career in culture is a clearly established and exclusive choice. Conversely, studies in law and political science predispose students to keeping their options more open. The statistical processing also highlights the relation between low social backgrounds and the exclusive choice of the cultural sector: as we have noted with children of blue-collar workers, this is all the more frequent when the parents have a low level of educational capital (79 per cent if neither of the parents have the *baccalauréat*, against 68 per cent of all applicants). There is also a specific effect of gender on the exclusivity of the choice. There are more men among the applicants for whom culture is one option among others. Regardless of their former studies, including when they were not specialized, women are more likely not to consider other choices (63 per cent against 55 per cent in the latter case).

It would therefore be much too simple to read the questionnaire responses literally, especially considering that both the questionnaire and the application itself probably led students to rationalize their choices, and present these career choices as carefully thought out. [4] The interviews invite us to be more nuanced. The statements made during interviews are no more or less 'true' than the questionnaire responses: the conditions in which they are made also influence their content, but to some extent they do so differently. While the questionnaire, which may be reminiscent of school tests and official interactions, can, as in the case of covering letters and selection interviews lead students to overstate the rationality and continuity of their choices, the more relaxed setting of an interview with students of the same age can give them an opportunity to recount circumstances that always involve an element of chance (encounters, trips, reputation of the programmes, hesitations), if only because they feel the need to adopt the necessary distance to avoid appearing naïve (by oversimplifying their trajectory as the relentless pursuit of an original passion) or excessively strategic (by making each step the result of a rational calculation).

To take only one example, several interviewees emphasized the key role played by trips abroad. The importance of overseas trips in the training of elites has been well documented, in terms of acquiring international capital or fostering entrepreneurship (Wagner 2007). In the case of aspiring cultural managers, they essentially produce two types of effect When trajectories are already aimed at a specific professional goal, the trips are conceived with that goal in mind, and enable the accumulation of extra-curricular capital that supports this choice by making it firmer ('it was then that I really set my mind to it', an applicant says), and because they are among the resources needed to achieve the goal. For those less secure in their choices, especially those several years into their studies, the year spent abroad is both a time for 'taking their distance from the academic game' (Lozach 2012: 72–83) and to ponder their future. This means the trips abroad can have a profound influence on the individual's life and career that retrospectively confers logic to former choices and determines future choices.

The case of Charlotte (born in 1987, mother commercial employee, father technician, international *baccalauréat*) gives a good illustration of this. After a bachelor's in Italian with no clear perspective, she went to Italy, where among other things she had various experiences in the cultural sector, including organizing small photography exhibits. She then convinced herself to resume her studies 'because with a bachelor's you can't find anything' and chose to apply to a master's in cultural management after spending some time wondering what to do. I asked myself, 'What am I going to do? What do I like?', and since I liked organizing exhibits, doing small cultural events, and I still liked photography a lot, I applied to the arts and culture master's programme'.

The year abroad was also a decisive time for Jeanne. At odds with the trend evidenced by the questionnaire results, her application to a master's programme was the culmination of a succession of non-choices rather than a deliberate choice, or even a move presented as a choice only after the fact. Asked about her academic trajectory, Jeanne is rather vague, and clearly gives the impression of having drifted along making 'unpremeditated choices'. This aimless trajectory is not what one would expect of a good student and the daughter of a couple of teachers (mother schoolteacher, father professor of economics in an agricultural high school). Yet it can probably be partly explained precisely by the fact that once she met her parents' expectations (by obtaining her *baccalauréat* ES with the highest honours), she was no longer subjected to the same (apparently) heavy pressure and faced no other substitute incentives. Her ill-prepared applications to enter a literary *classe préparatoire* were unsuccessful. She then enrolled at the faculty of history without really knowing why, beyond the fact that she hoped it would provide her with broader

perspectives than literature, which would otherwise have been her preference. Perhaps out of regret at not having been admitted into a selective
programme despite her achievements at the *baccalauréat*, or to satisfy
her parents, she submits an application every year to an institute of political science or a journalism school, but 'without really trying that hard' and
always unsuccessfully. After her bachelor's in history, she went to Spain
to enrol in a research-oriented master's programme 'to escape, sort of,
because it was the easiest way', but she soon faced her inability to conduct research at the level required. 'So I told myself, 'I really need to think
hard about what I want to do, [...] and so I thought about culture because
I had an affinity with culture'. She then applied for a master's programme
in communication and four others preparing for cultural occupations. She
gained admission into one of them, but this apparent success masked an
educational downgrading: having already completed a second year master's programme, she had to start again at the first year; the programme in
which she was accepted, hosted by a small regional university, only had
a middling reputation. At the time of our interview, she lived in Paris in her
boyfriend's apartment and was looking for work, but apparently no more
actively than she had prepared her higher education.

We should therefore neither assume that applicants are equally invested, nor
overstate the consistency of their career plan. Likewise, non-choices, choices by
default and contingent factors may play a part in trajectories that are very rarely
linear. Yet, this does not call into question our initial observation: applications
'just to see' or with undetermined anticipations are rare and in the minority; in the
vast majority of cases we are dealing with clearly asserted choices, at least regarding the general attraction to the cultural sector.

### The narratives of vocation

In addition to evidencing the social conditions of their genesis and the stages of
their development, understanding vocations requires accounting for their 'narrative
forms' (Pudal 2003: 150). Through these specific forms of self-narrative, applicants
construct the meaning of their trajectory, which may not reflect its objective truth
but can at least allow us to grasp the reasons they give (themselves) to pursue it.
Application files (including in particular motivation letters) are institutionalized
forms of narratives of vocation and, as such, this material offers a useful complement
to questionnaire data and interviews, by showing how these career choices are put
into words, if not experienced. These narratives of vocation, designed to maximize
chances of success, are undoubtedly to some extent the product of applicants'

anticipations of what they need to say. Here, I do not take them at face value or consider them as the true expression of subjective aspirations; rather my concern is to identify the recurring forms that reflect the collective rules of presentation and justification of cultural careers.

Writing about oneself requires dispositions that are unequally distributed within social space (Poliak 2002; Lahire 2008). Regardless of those at their disposal, the applicants all face the obligation of presenting themselves in the motivation letter and in the career plan that they are asked to provide in addition to their résumé. These commissioned self-narratives entail many constraints: in addition to the cultural codes underpinning the presentation of self in writing (Hua 2007) and to the formatting implicitly required in all official correspondence (Pène 1997), they are shaped by the supposed expectations of the recipients (Rémond 1999) and by standards explicitly laid out concerning the career plan – where applicants are asked to present the state of the labour market and their employment prospects upon graduation and then in the medium term. It is therefore hardly surprising that these documents have recurring features that tend to make them look somewhat similar in certain respects, considering the applicants have to follow a specific template. Yet what is required of them is not simply conforming to a pre-established model; at the same time they are asked to personalize their presentation, to make it both credible in light of their attributes and to make it stand out among the many similar applications submitted (Boltanski, Darré and Schiltz 1984). In this sense, these documents combine a very impersonal form of self-presentation with a personalized form of meeting institutional expectations, which makes them reminiscent of some welfare applications (Fassin 2000; Retière 2001). Like the latter, they are underpinned by rhetorical forms whose combinations outline postures aimed at convincing the recipient: what is at stake here is the production of a self-narrative that can command attention.

We selected 45 of the applications received by the master's programme *Politique et gestion de la culture* (Politics and management of culture) of the IEP in Strasbourg in 2010, with the intention to include the widest possible array of applicants rather than to strive for strict statistical representativeness. There were two stages in the processing of the applications: we first looked at the language used, and then at the applicants themselves. Their content was divided into ten themes constructed as variables: 1) the general posture (intellectual, academic, practical, managerial, personal, engaged, artist, idealist); 2) the types of self-description (personal qualities, academic qualities, functional qualities, passion, knowledge, practical skills); 3) expectations of the programme (acquiring professional skills, prestige, the degree, professional opportunities); 4) the relation to culture (artistic and cultural practices, tastes, personal experiences, friends and relatives); 5) professional goals (types, level of specification); 6) the representation of work in the cultural sector (informed or not, pessimistic or optimistic); 7) the discourse on culture (professional, democratization-oriented, prophetic or emphatic); 8) the relation to work (self-fulfillment, career management); 9) the international dimension; 10) self-commentaries on the applicants' trajectories.

As a complement to this thematic processing, we also reasoned in terms of individual applications, and characterized the 45 applicants on the basis of seven types of more synthetic variables matching those of the questionnaire and/or those mentioned above: 1) sociographic variables (gender, year of birth, nationality); 2) education (place of study, type of *baccalauréat*, honours, city where the *bac* was obtained, academic curriculum pursued, latest results); 3) cultural capital (artistic practices, cultural consumption, professional experience); 4) formal characteristics of the application (style, spelling, layout, letter of recommendation); 5) presentation of self (opening and ending statements, posture, self-description, self-commentary); 6) career plan (expectations of the programme, job perspectives); 7) projection of self (representation of employment, relation to work, discourse on culture, international dimension). Mostly elements from the first stage of processing will be used; the second will essentially be used to relate the authors' statements to their backgrounds.

Here, I will essentially focus on the postures adopted, i.e. the overarching register used in the presentation of the application, and on the forms of self-description – in other words, how applicants write about themselves. As one might expect considering the context of the application and the main types of resources that the applicants may put forward, the academic posture prevails in self-presentations, often centered on the academic trajectory as the main factor explaining the choice of cultural management. The applicants' qualities as students (hard-working and achieving) are not often emphasized. As was also to be expected, considering the vocational nature of the programme, there are many occurrences of the practical posture, in which experiences of concrete achievements and skills acquired or to be acquired are valued, tying in with a similar self-description that lays emphasis on technical skills or organizational abilities – it is often combined with the academic posture, serving as a complement. Conversely, the intellectual posture, characterized by scholarly references and the discussion of concepts, is rarely found, and when it occurs, it is almost always as a complement to other postures. While references to artistic experience are more frequent, they are not so much made to support an artistic posture, but rather to document a 'genuine interest in art', which in itself serves to justify the choice of pursuing artistic occupations: 'While providing a comprehensive overview of all my artistic experiences is out of the question, I considered it important to emphasize that my attraction for art is neither recent nor superfluous' [8].[5]

I will emphasize what is probably the most significant feature in these standardized presentations: the mobilization of a more personal register. This takes several forms, all meant to highlight a 'personality' that cannot be reduced to the objective landmarks of the applicant's trajectory and, in particular, to his or her diplomas, and which is shown to be the foundation of their career choice. This is a feature in common with the usual language of artistic vocation (Kris and Kurz 1981). While it probably relates to some extent to the propensity of a certain student elite to distance themselves from an academic trajectory that others would conversely call attention to (Draelants and Darchy-Koechlinn 2011), the following statements made by an applicant during an interview, immediately after mentioning her academic trajectory in a few words, is an almost ideal-typical illustration of this form of narrative of vocation focused on individuality.

> Recounting my academic background is not sufficient to encapsulate who I am. I followed a fairly standard trajectory, but there are other things. I've practiced photography and life drawing for a long time. There are other sides to my personality: I'm curious; I go and see exhibits when I travel abroad. I've always liked images, I'm interested in broadcasting. I think I have an open and curious mind, so naturally that's why I'm interested in culture and would like to work in culture.
>
> *Observation VD10, woman born in 1989,* baccalauréat *L,* classe préparatoire *in a prestigious Parisian high school then regional IEP*

Beyond the expected talking points on 'personal qualities' ('I am dynamic and motivated, available and committed' [12]) that characterize the motivation letter as a genre, the posture adopted is more largely personal, in the sense that individual sensibilities and histories are the main driving forces of the vocation narrative – as in the *Bildungsroman*, an experience that occurred during the applicant's youth or a landmark book that triggers the decisive realization.

> I've been attracted to the cultural sector since I was very young. [...] Over time, museums, theatres, concert venues have for the most part become familiar places, where I spent the most intense moments of my life' [3]. Ariane Mnouchkine wrote a wonderful foreword to Jacqueline Jomaron's book, *Le théâtre en France, du Moyen Age à nos jours* [pub. 1993], in which she relates how, in the Warsaw ghetto, a Jewish woman deprived herself of her daily ration to make puppets out of breadcrumbs and bring a modicum of joy to all those whose lives had suddenly become a nightmare. I am telling you about this story simply because it summarizes everything I chose to work in the cultural sector for. [33].

Likewise, the recurrence of the language of passion in the applicants' self-descriptions arguably reflects a standardized form of presentation rather than necessarily 'true motivation' (Baudelot and Gollac 2003: 193ff., Noël 2010).

Having resolved to work in the field I am passionate about, namely management or communication in cultural institutions such as theatres and
museums, I intend to give myself every chance of making this wish come
true' [3]. Being very often in touch with artists from different horizons;
photographers, sculptors, painters, I was lucky enough to develop a
sense of a lively culture and to see a growing passion for art blossom in
myself. [24].

This may, to some extent, reflect a youthful naivety or the clichés of the
biographical illusion (Bourdieu 1987a); not all applicants are unaware of
these pitfalls.[6] Yet, we shouldn't overlook the fact that applying for a cultural
management programme makes some things possible that would seem out of place
in other fields. These vocation narratives function as what applicants assume to be
a necessary response to the implicit requirement of a personal motivation for their
application. There is no paradox in observing that, here as in the case of artistic
occupations as well as some vocational occupations of the social sector (Bodin
2009), the adoption of an openly 'personal' posture meets the requirement of a
collective standard.

### Choosing the cultural sector rather than a given occupation

The choice of cultural management is rather rooted in the attraction to 'culture' and
the personal and professional perspectives it may offer rather than in the contents
of a specific activity or the characteristics of a specific job. The applicants have a
(genuine) professional interest in the cultural field, but few aim to work in a given
occupation, function or structure. This is a vocation to work in the cultural sector,
not in a particular job. In this respect cultural management stands out from other
vocational occupations, such as journalism, teaching, art and research, whose attractiveness comes from the corresponding practices (writing, investigating, teaching,
creating or researching). Choosing a career in culture management means wanting
to work in the cultural sector rather than performing management tasks.

While the vast majority of questionnaire respondents report wanting to look
for a job in culture immediately after graduating, they are generally vague about
the specific jobs they want to pursue. First, two thirds of them report wanting
to work in the cultural field without mentioning a particular sector (46 per cent
report wanting to work across sectors and one in five states no preference whatso-
ever). Only a third of the applicants intend to work in a particular cultural sector –
most frequently theatre and music. This may reflect personal taste (of the fan or
enthusiast), experience (having set up a troupe or managed a rock band) and skill,
attested by a specialized diploma or not (for those well acquainted with cultural
circles). The high representation of the performing arts reflects the fact that this is
a very varied sector, which accounts for much of the employment available in the

cultural field (see Chapter 1). Additionally, there are programmes specific to other sectors, such as the book and publishing trades or public reading, which could explain the scarcity of references to them in the applicants' career plans.

Then, less than half (45 per cent) of the applicants aspire to hold a function (or several) in particular immediately after graduating – and only a quarter (27 per cent) in the medium term. These functions are generally referred to in somewhat elusive terms. For this reason, and because of their wide spread, it is difficult to give a convincing statistical account of these responses. It is, however, worth noting that the most generic titles are by far the most frequently mentioned for plans immediately after graduating (n=347): *chargés de mission, de projet* or *d'action culturelle* (65), then directors (sometimes with additional mentions, 29), *chefs* (13), *responsables* (5) and the design and co-ordination (5) of cultural projects.[7]

This relative indetermination of the career choices is probably not entirely specific to cultural master's programmes, and may more generally be considered as a largely shared feature among students with literary and generalist backgrounds. In some instances it results from a lack of knowledge of the professional circles in question or from an ill thought-out 'plan'; these two flaws precisely rank among the main motives for rejecting applications. Flora, who was denied admission to the cultural master's programmes to which she applied after being 'disillusioned' in a prestigious Parisian institution where she attended a master's in sociology, gives us an illustration of this:

> So, well, culture, I couldn't really say what I meant by cultural occupations because it was still very hazy and I think it still is. [...] I didn't really know about cultural jobs, I used to always say I wanted to 'set up projects', I had this sort of ideal vision of things. I wanted to work with people around culture, it could be film, or theatre. It wasn't really a well-defined thing. [...] I felt like working on subjects that I was interested in, like theatre, film, literature... I wanted to set up projects but I didn't really know what about. I was very confused.
> *Flora, born in 1986, father doctor, mother nurse,* baccalauréat L, *literary* classe préparatoire *in a prestigious Parisian high school, bachelor's in literature then master's in sociology*

Such indetermination is, however, more surprising in the case of applicants whose socialization in the cultural world and pre-professional experiences give them a practical knowledge and a sense of placement that should logically allow them to make finer choices. This includes children of professionals of arts and culture, who more than others tend not to report a preference for a particular sector or function. The first explanation for that pertains to the characteristics of jobs in the field, whose definitions tend to remain rather fuzzy. The general vague or multi-faceted nature of the functions and of their titles is not seen as an issue, as it fits the desire of many applicants to have a 'complete picture' and do 'a bit of everything' during the early stages of their careers, in order to gain a clearer idea of the opportunities at their disposal and later make more specific choices (in such cases communication jobs are particularly targeted). In the longer term, this may also be because polyvalence is associated with high-level executive and decision-making positions (with project supervision and management, as in the following excerpt, looming on the applicants' professional horizons).

> When it comes down to it management is one of these words that can mean anything and everything. [There's] a difference between managing things a little from above and really being in the thick of it. I have more interest in doing multi-faceted things than in operating within a more restrictive field, like being just a mediator. 'Cause, you know, when you're managing a project, you're going to have financial aspects to deal with, an administrative aspect, this whole network... all kinds of partners and different contacts with artists and other project managers, and it's that pluri-polyvalent or pluri-dimensional side of things that I'm interested in [...] I'd rather be on top of... well, how should I say, juggling multiple tasks, let's say, having several things to do, several different sorts of things to deal with.
>
> *Clarisse, born in 1987, parents business executives,*
> *baccalauréat L, first year of literary classe préparatoire*
> *then regional IEP and master's in culture*

Second, the indetermination of career plans also results in part from the lack of linearity of the expected professional trajectories: instead of making regular progress throughout their career in the same job, the cultural managers will likely experience a succession of positions entailing multi-faceted functions that may vary from one post to another. In this respect, to some extent the vagueness of the 'career plans', including for some of the better-prepared applicants, reflects their realistic anticipation of future trajectories that are very difficult to foresee.[8] Last, the imprecision of their choices can also be interpreted as a conscious or unconscious strategy to increase their chances of success, by not closing any doors and thereby being able to seize more varied and numerous opportunities in a sector where finding a job is notoriously difficult.

Here, the incentives to 'professionalize' faced to an extent by all higher education graduates may prove somewhat paradoxical, as the applicants face two seemingly incompatible constraints: they have to formulate a concrete plan that must be consistent, while also adjusting their choices and expectations to whatever opportunity they encounter considering the job situation in the sector. In addition to tactical considerations, this specific sense of placement required for accessing the professional world of culture is informed by two principles of the ethos prevailing in that world. First, this regulated improvisation benefits individuals who are always ready to move on towards the next 'adventure' and have a 'strong personality', at odds with the rigidly planned career paths of others perceived as stifling. As the following self-presentation of an applicant shows, personal dispositions (open-mindedness) are combined with the supposed features of cultural careers (the presence of multiple opportunities): 'I'm a very open person. For me everything's still possible. I'd like to help disseminate culture among young people. If it doesn't work out, I can always bounce back; there's a wide array of things to do in culture'.[9] Second, a similarly regulated form of eclecticism tends to turn an exclusive cultural preference into an axiological near-impossibility as well as a professional mistake: one has to be able to be 'interested in anything' provided one 'remains consistent' and that 'the quality is there'.[10] I will elaborate on these two points later.

First, I will show how the applicants deal with these two constraints in the formulation of their professional aspirations. For these purposes I go back to the analysis of the applications, and more specifically to the 'career plan' required from the students, in order to identify the types of professional positions targeted and the reasons given to support these choices. The logic of the application demands a rationalization and a strategy of presentation aimed at making the 'plan' – and therefore the application – credible. As I have noted previously, this is not about finding out the applicants' 'true' aspirations, but rather about documenting their rationalization process and, more broadly, the rhetorical forms they employ. Yet, precisely, even in a formal and standardized exercise such as an application file, the formulation of the career plan often remains elusive, very general or fragmented. This further supports the hypothesis that imprecision does not always reflect a lack of preparation: it may be a deliberate way to accommodate the constraints that characterize strategies of access to the sector.[11]

This can first be seen in the four main ways in which applicants produce consistency as they outline their future plans. The first way consists of referring to one or several cultural sub-sectors, a country or a geographical area, drawing on past experience and sometimes distinctive skills: 'Being passionate about the Latin-American continent as well as fluent in Spanish, I would more specifically like to dedicate myself to cultural co-operation with Latin America, by setting up events or cultural projects promoting exchanges, creation and co-operation between European and Latin American cultural organizations [21]'. The second way is the reference to a generic type of organization, suggesting an activity or career path. Among the most frequently mentioned are the 'European cultural co-operation circles' [4], the 'Community framework' [25], 'French cultural institutes and centres abroad […] important actors of the cultural co-operation between the Member States [that] contribute to building an open, modern and humanist society' [24] and 'local authorities, [which] play a key part in cultural democratization' [2]. A third way of providing consistency and detail is the reference to the applicant himself or herself, defining their professional future on the basis of a 'personal plan' whose achievement will eventually lead them to 'set up [their] own structure' [6] – this personalization allows them to shift the definition of the job targeted towards that of the activity proposed (in this case, an opera festival). A similar shift is at work in the fourth way, which is more political and consists in presenting a global agenda in lieu of naming a specific position or function. In such cases individual career choices are asserted through emphasis on ambition and vision.

> I'd like to have a job that enables me to find a balance by combining culture and all sorts of issues I care about: urban planning, housing, employment, training, education, migrations, local development. To be more specific, I would for instance like to offer and implement cultural development actions in a setting where culture is not usually present; by working as a cultural policy officer in local government, specifically in a disadvantaged area, or as a development officer in an association for artistic action working with disadvantaged publics. [5]

As is exemplified here, applicants can make attempts at detailing a career plan while keeping their opportunities open. There are three main ways to do this. The first is to list alternatives, thereby outlining a general orientation and at the same time proposing numerous possible paths: 'in the medium to long term I intend to work in administration or management, either of a musical institution or of a festival' [4]. The second is to mention possible fall-back solutions, thereby displaying a knowledge of the job market that makes the applicant's aspirations appear realistic.

> Being eager [...] to travel over the course of my career, I would par-ticularly like to work [...] in a cultural institute abroad. [...] However, as the number of positions is limited, I have envisioned other alternatives. I would then be interested in the occupation of project officer, and then project manager, in the smaller units of the public or private sector, as in theatres, museums or organizations in charge of cultural events. [20]

In addition to dropping catch-all job titles such as cultural project officer, which are more connotative than denotative, the use of such lists of positions, though they may ultimately not be very meaningful, is a way to accumulate 'professional' references without excluding anything. This is the third way of keeping one's options open.

In light of my expectations, aspirations and skills, ideally I would like to hold a position either in cultural mediation, combining communication and management, or as cultural programmes manager (*chargé de l'action culturelle*), cultural development project officer (*chargé de mission en développement culturel*), or as cultural attaché abroad [35] Upon graduating, I would like to put my new skills into practice in the production of cultural events or within private or public structures, European or international organizations. My role would consist in ensuring the monitoring and co-ordination of the legal, human and financial resources involved in the process of producing a cultural project. [1] The missions I am particularly interested in […] are supporting creators in the implementation of their projects, assessing the feasibility of projects according to their features (place, duration, etc.), establishing the costs and finding the funding for projects, and defining strategies (financial strategies, partnerships, etc.). I am fascinated by the evaluation of the distance to cover between the project imagined by the artist and the implementation of that project, especially as it is a key stage in the elaboration of the work. [9]

Beyond this, the sense of keeping things open or even of deliberately avoiding any specific mentions that might be limiting are themselves rationalized, and constitute more or less deft ways of staging the search of a professional identity founded on function rather than post, on 'cross-cutting' work rather than on a specific sector, on 'project' rather than category-specific interests, on challenges rather than routine – illustrating the 'ideology of de-compartmentalization' that serves both as a professional posture and as a cultural policy orientation (Pinto 1991; Dubois 2012a: 356, 394).

I could add other cultural organizations and public administrations and make a pointless list. But my career plan consists neither in working in a specific administration, nor to have a specific job. *Rather, I am looking for a category of functions:* organizing a cultural event with limited resources or managing to reconcile divergent interests between several actors are of great interest to my eyes. [8, emphasis already in the application].

It is therefore hardly surprising that multi-positionality, or more precisely the mediator's position at the 'crossroads', is frequently highlighted. The eagerness to navigate one's way between several cultures or professional and social worlds underpins the interest in that position asserted in the applications: 'What attracts me [...] is the opportunity to have access to different spheres' [22]. The insistent yet elusive reference to a 'project' or 'network' not only reflects a vision of the social world in which dividing lines are blurred, it is also a way for applicants to state that they share the language in use in the professional sector where they aspire to work, and to use its polysemy to make their aspirations intelligible as well as extensible and adaptable.

Such is the case of an applicant who, after mentioning the position she wishes to hold, goes into further detail on her view of that job: 'Cultural mediators have a function of communication and pedagogic promotion. They contribute to the elaboration and implementation of the project, which takes different forms depending on the public(s) concerned. They enable encounters between the various parties involved in the project: organizers, artists, institutions. Mediators are resource persons [...], they must already have a network in place, which they will then tirelessly broaden in order to be able [...] to develop their projects.' [34]

## A third way between art and teaching

I wanted to work in the music field, not to be a musician, not to be a teacher [...], and then I kind of discovered everything that you could do, and that was it.'

> Marie, born in 1987, father secondary school teacher,
> mother librarian, literary baccalauréat with a music option,
> then bachelor's and master's in musicology and
> master's in cultural management

The choice of pursuing cultural management occupations is made in the light of the other options – likely or possible, envisioned or conceivable, desirable or not. Two of these other options have a particular place insofar as they are structuring references and used by landmarks for the applicants making their choices. Teaching is a likely future for many of the applicants. Yet they have a primarily negative view of it, and define their aspirations by opposition to teaching. By contrast, an artistic career is a desirable but often unreachable horizon, serving as a positive reference – although it should not be merely seen as a failed dream for which cultural management acts as compensation.

*Teaching as a foil*

Disaffection with teaching is currently widely shared among graduates in the process of choosing their career. This disaffection concerns many countries in Europe, and has become a policy issue at the EU level (IBF 2013). In France, it is in particular evidenced by the very sharp decrease in the number of candidates to the open competitions for positions in secondary education, regardless of discipline (−52 per cent during the 2000s for external public education *concours*).[12] There are general reasons for this shift away from teaching, resulting in an often diagnosed 'crisis of teaching vocations' (Périer 2004): the declining prestige of the profession has been felt all the more intensely as at the same time their levels of social and educational recruitment have risen (Farges 2011); working conditions have worsened (or at least the popular representations thereof); the reform in the training of teachers launched in the late 2000s (the so-called masterization) and the sharp decrease in the number of positions offered have had further disincentivizing effects.[13]

While it is not unique to them, this trend is particularly notable in applications to cultural programmes, even though the social worlds of culture and education appear to be close in terms of the agents' characteristics and the types of capital valued. Very few of them include teaching among their possible choices; only 1.5 per cent simultaneously apply for training in that field. It is worth mentioning that the possibility of pursuing teaching mostly concerns applicants liable to combine art teaching and their artistic activity. Still, a variety of factors, such as the very high proportion of young women as well as students with backgrounds in literature and the humanities and the high proportions of teachers among the parents, combine to make teaching the choice expected of many of the applicants. In addition to the general trend mentioned above, the trajectories leading to cultural occupations steer students away for more specific reasons, as teaching routinely serves as a foil for them.

Teaching may act as a foil because the world of cultural occupations partly defined itself (as cultural policies did, at least in France) by asserting its difference from education (Dubois 2012a: 237; Urfalino 1993). In addition to the dispositions of the aspiring cultural managers, this distance from teaching therefore relates to this divide between the worlds of culture and education in France – a divide that informs and is in turn reinforced by the logic of career choices.

Just as it regularly happens that teachers eager to change career paths are attracted by cultural occupations, many aspiring cultural managers have at one point considered a career in teaching, before giving up on it to pursue what is generally presented as a more motivated option. As one applicant says: 'Initially I wanted to become a teacher. And then after I did various internships, I realized that I wanted to bring culture across in a *more playful* way'.[14] The notion of playfulness in a sense epitomizes the distance taken from teaching, whose mention contributes to defining some properties of the choice of culture in the negative. Teaching is perceived as the repetition of an always identical activity while culture is thought to be a permanent path of discovery: 'I was afraid it'd be intellectually limiting and that I wouldn't learn anything anymore, it wouldn't bring me anything anymore [...] afraid I wouldn't go forward anymore'.[15] Beyond the activity itself, the comparison also applies to the career path, defined by permanence and constraint ('there's not much of an opportunity for change once you're caught in teaching'[16]). In other words, teaching poses the risk of stagnation and routine while culture allows for movement and keeping opportunities always open. Beyond the preference for one or the other professional world, the distinction between teaching and culture reflects much broader oppositions (security vs. risk, closure vs. openness, repetition vs. creation) that outline lifestyles perceived to be mutually exclusive.[17]

The use of teaching as a foil is also particularly widespread because it allows applicants to emphasize their attachment to freedom and risk in contrast to the comfort of a path that is already mapped out (Bourdieu 2000). Indeed, in many cases, opting for culture against teaching is a means for the applicants to escape what they perceive as their fate, or at least to persuade themselves that they are free in their own choices. 'I had the feeling that I hadn't chosen what I was doing, having gone to a *prépa* [*classe préparatoire*] and ending up studying literature at the university. And telling myself I was going to do the CAPES exam like all those girls who attended a *prépa* and find myself teaching in high school, to me it was *im-po-ssible*. So actually I ruled out teaching.'[18] Unlike those women who perceive their access to the profession of teaching either as 'the accomplishment of an often early "vocation" that merely amounts to the internalization of a probable future, or as the necessary culmination of their schooling' (Chapoulie 1987: 449), in this case it seems that refusing to teach helps aspiring cultural managers to assert the authenticity of their vocation, for which they use educational capital but do not let themselves be confined by that capital. This form of transgression of their likely trajectory is one of the common features between the aspiring cultural managers and those who pursue an artistic vocation (Sorignet 2010: 60).

### The artistic vocation as a reference

In a sector that revolves around the figure of the creator, the choice of devoting oneself to organizational tasks can be seen as a second choice, whereby one's activity at the service of artists makes up for having given up on a career as an artist that was out of reach. While there may be some truth in this hypothesis, depicting the applicants as failed artists would be grossly oversimplifying things; indeed, the relations between artistic vocations and the choice of cultural careers are much more complex.

Although it constitutes a minority, the proportion of students who pursue careers in cultural management after having given up on an artistic career is not altogether insignificant (12.5 per cent). This is the case of Salomé, whose parents chose a scientific *baccalauréat* for her (albeit with an optional course in visual arts) and who quit a regional fine arts school after a few months. She then studied art history and worked as an artist, hoping to make a career out of her art.[19] She moved to several places, including abroad, and as the years went by, ultimately turned to cultural mediation. 'I used to think I could make it with my paintings; I'm a failed artist [laughs].' It would be useful to be able to make a better assessment of how intensely that career was pursued (i.e. whether it amounted to a romantic day-dream or if the student enrolled in a specialized training programme or made first attempts) and to pinpoint how and why it was abandoned. Our research suggests that in most cases this earlier career choice was not a vague childhood dream and that often recent and sometimes important experiences played a part.

When this is the case, renouncement may reflect an exclusive and particularly demanding conception of the artistic vocation. One needs to 'have faith' and be certain of the internal drive that guides this choice, as doubt in one's chances of success and in the sincerity of the calling may lead the artist to give up – as in the religious vocation. This is what an applicant explained during a selection inter-view. He received a master's degree in art history, while simultaneously being trained as an actor in one of the most renowned private schools.

If I can reconcile my activity as an actor with management, then why not; but to be honest I've written off my vocation as an actor. One day my teacher at the theatre school asked me if I could do something other than theatre. I took some time to think about it, because I'm interested in a lot of things. And finally I told her that yes, I could see myself doing something else. So she told me 'then do something else. If you want to become an actor, you have to feel that this is the only thing you can do'. And since I'm interested in other things, well, I've written off my vocation as an actor.

*Observation VD21, man born in 1987*

This mythical vision of the artistic vocation is not the only reason for giving up; in other cases the experience of the everyday life of artists may be a factor. At any rate, these two forms of the rationalization of the relation between artistic vocation and the choice of cultural management each shed light in their own way on the meaning agents confer on their trajectory. Here, the personal or familial experience of the art world strictly speaking may support one's choice of pur-suing cultural management, both positively and negatively, because it is about doing 'something different' and opening up to organizational, political and social dimensions that tend to be ignored by the 'artists'. A young woman, the daughter of two artists, a dancer who has pursued training in arts and cultural occupations since the beginning of her higher education, exemplifies this twofold relationship. In her case it works as a way of managing her family's legacy; an artistic heritage that inherits the inheritor, to paraphrase Marx's famous phrase, but that is selec-tively used by the inheritor to define 'what really interests' her – in other words to make the best of her dispositions and resources without being bound by them, which is also a way to gain emancipation from the parental model.

I've always been immersed in an artistic, culturally open environment, due to my parents' jobs, my national origins and classical dancing (...) My parents are artists. I've always wanted to be in a creative environment in everything I do. I've studied dancing, I've been in that world a lot, but it's too specialized. I need things to be more open, I need to open myself up to the social and political issues of culture. What I'm interested in is not being in touch with artists. I found out what I'm interested in thanks to my internship [in an institution that organizes dance shows]: it's how cultural projects fit within their environment. I realized that I responded to cultural projects with a strong social dimension.

*Observation VD19, woman born in 1989*

A slightly older man is considering cultural management after having started a career in music, not because of a professional failure or because he is looking for a more stable job, but as a 'lifestyle choice', consisting of preferring 'opportunities' and a sedentary life to the stage, for which 'you have to be kind of obsessive' and ultimately 'you don't have a lot of time for yourself'.

His overall demeanor sharply contrasts with that of most applicants. He is not as well-dressed, speaks hesitantly, and seems rather depressed and stressed out, when applicants generally attempt to project self-confidence, enthusiasm and a laid-back attitude. 'My academic studies have been a bit disjointed. At first I did a lot of music, a lot of concerts [in various jazz bands], and then I began studying again, in musicology. [...] Now I'd like to become more invested in the organization of concerts and make it my job. Mostly I'm quite big on music, but my tastes go beyond that. It's also a lifestyle choice. I realized that irregularity, being on tour all the time, a musician's career didn't suit me. You don't have a lot of time for yourself, you're always with people. And then it was also kind of by accident, I found out through my experiences that making musicians play can be more gratifying than playing yourself. To be a musician, you have to be kind of obsessive, always working on your instrument, only think about it... I felt like taking some distance, to have other opportunities.'

*Observation VD23, man born in 1984*

The relation between artistic vocation and the choice of cultural management cannot, however, be limited to a more or less forced career shift. We might also consider that they are two forms of the translation of cultural aspirations into professional aspirations, taking shape at different moments in individual trajectories. In other words, rather than seeing the artistic vocation and its vagaries as the reason leading individuals to seek out a career in cultural management, we can identify identical rationales and factors favouring these two choices, based on partly shared dispositions, especially developed during familial socialization. These are specifically cultural dispositions such as practising an artistic activity or attending concerts or art galleries. They are more broadly speaking social ones: turning to non-conventional jobs, valuing personal self-fulfillment, placing less emphasis on material wealth (Coulangeon 2004; Sapiro 2007a; Sorignet 2010). Chronologically, they are expressed first under the romantic form of a yearning for art, lasting for the duration of that temporary state of weightlessness experienced during high school or the first year of academic studies, 'a socially neutral time where the shared feeling of an adolescent temporality is forged, and where one has the impression of having their whole future ahead of them, in the way that those who do not really have to worry about the future do' (Muel-Dreyfus 1983: 166, see also Mauger 1994), as familial, economic and professional constraints are suspended. As personal experiences and parental or educational incentives (Verger 1982; Lemêtre 2009) reshape the 'space of possibles',[20] and as graduation nears, the same dispositions may be expressed in a related but outwardly less risky and more 'serious' choice, that of cultural management. This choice is then not so much the result of renouncement as the translation of the artistic vocation under a more 'reasonable' form, i.e. one that is adjusted to the constraints that were previously put aside temporarily.

Lastly, and this is worth some emphasis, the choices of pursuing artistic activities and cultural management are combined as often as the latter follows the former. The applicants who still plan to pursue a career as an artist are indeed roughly as numerous (15 per cent) as those who have given up on the prospect. Nearly a quarter of them are men, a proportion that is slightly higher than among the entire population of applicants (15 per cent). This higher proportion of men is generally explained by the gendered division of labour mentioned earlier, and more precisely reflects the high proportion of more 'masculine' jobs among the occupations targeted by the artists-applicants (including music, particularly popular music). The artistic occupations targeted are distributed as follows: writer, scriptwriter (24 per cent of the respondents); musician (24 per cent); actor (14 per cent); film or stage director and choreographer (13 per cent); visual artist, painter, illustrator (13 per cent); photographer (9 per cent); dancer (5 per cent).[21] They are 'serious contenders' in higher proportions – at least for admission to a cultural master's programme, since in comparison to the applicants at large, they have accumulated more pre-professional experience (active participation in cultural associations, internships, paid professional experience), and they more often have friends and relatives working in the fields of art or culture. For them, the acquisition of skills or at least of a diploma in management, funding, curating or public relations comes as a complement to their artistic skills. Unsurprisingly, they have studied far more often than other applicants in art and architecture schools (14 per cent against 4 per cent), and at university, they have more frequently followed performing arts and visual arts curricula. Likewise, they have more often received artistic teaching or tuition and far more often continue to do so (41 per cent against 25 per cent), particularly in highly institutionalized settings (conservatories), or in a school or academic setting. If we add the fact that a diploma is not always required to access an artistic occupation (Mauger 2006b) – this is for instance not the case in the field of popular music – it is understandable that cultural management training programmes are rarely in competition with artistic programmes (only 3 per cent of applicants apply to both). However, those who envisage an artistic career more frequently apply for a master's in another field (42 per cent against 34 per cent). Given that their initial amounts of educational capital tend to be lower (more hold-ers of literary *baccalauréats*, who often graduated behind schedule and without honours) and that they subsequently study at lower levels (fewer students enrolled in selective programmes), they appear to develop a double academic strategy, con-sisting of obtaining a degree to support their perspectives of diversification and acquiring skills they can use to complement their artistic skills, especially in man-agement, organization and law.

The combination of artistic and administrative activities takes two main forms. The first is the projection into a double career of artist and manager. In this case cultural management is an activity pursued in parallel with a more uncertain artis-tic practice, offering a modicum of security in the same world. This is the ration-alization of a case frequently encountered in the cultural sector – for example of actors who add para-artistic activities to their initial vocation (Menger 1994). Applicants may to some extent conceive this double career as a plan, even though it also reflects a form of anticipation of material necessity.

Photography's a passion for me. At one time I thought about turning it into a career, but I thought it was also possible to do it alongside a profes-sional activity. So I'd like to move towards the organization, management side of things. Actually *I aspire to do both: creating and managing.*
Observation VD9, man born in 1987, studied law – emphasis mine

I play a few concerts [as a pianist and organist] but I can't make a living out of that. [...] I try to do a variety of internships to see all the jobs you can do. [...] I'd like to create my own business, to be an agent for artists and to play at the same time.
*Observation VL7, woman born in 1986, studied musicology and then enrolled in a master's in music management*

Cultural management can also be combined with artistic practice following a rationale of functional diversification, whereby artistic and para-artistic activities are not only juxtaposed out of economic necessity but actually relate to each other. The occurrence of such combinations in professional projections reflects a trend towards the growing integration of functions of production, organization and diffusion. This is for instance the case in independent rap or popular forms of electronic music, when an artist considers branching out to perform managerial tasks in order to 'extend his control over the production chain and the diffusion of artworks and develop a global vision of that process' (Jouvenet 2003: 102). In such instances, pluri-activity does not only consist in adding up activities to ensure a more stable income (managing and creating); the combination of functions is required by the organization of artistic activity (managing one's creation). The application to a cultural management programme then relates to the acquisition of a second (administrative, financial, institutional) skill considered as necessary to one's artistic activity, reflecting a transformation of the capital specific to the artistic field (Mauger 2006b: 237 ff.), which is considered to include a 'managerial' component that used to be experienced as an external constraint by former generations and is now internalized as 'part of the job', since 'art's a market'. One of the applicants, a visual artist turning to management, argues: 'It's not substitution, it's not about living vicariously through the artists [...] It's not like I'm giving up for good. It's just that you need a network that I don't have at all. I need to know how things work administratively, how to apply for funding and all that. Besides, art's a market, no question. There's not much room for young creators'.[22] Likewise, Charlotte, who does photography, still hesitates between a career change, para-artistic activities and putting her new managerial skills to use in her activities as an artist.

I've always been attracted to art, but let's say it's hard to commit yourself to studying art because you're always a bit scared that nothing's going to come out of it. [...] That's also why I did [this master's], because it's supposed to be work-oriented [...] The internship's very formative, it's a little bit more reassuring [...] because then it will be easier to look for clients [...] I know how it works on the other end, I know a little bit about all the aspects, how to organize a cultural event, it's also going to come in handy when I feel like exhibiting my work in an actual venue.

*Charlotte, born in 1987, mother business employee, father technician, international baccalauréat, bachelor's in Italian then master's in culture*

At odds with the stereotype of the 'failed artist' often attached to para-artistic occupations, we witness a partly new pattern whereby artists rationalize their creative activity by complementing it with the skills allowing them to ensure its practical and economic conditions.

# The social rationales of a career choice

While some of the social foundations of the choice of cultural careers and of its meanings are shared by all the would-be cultural managers, overall the rationales behind this choice are no more unambiguous than the population of applicants is homogeneous. These rationales may partly relate to the specificities of the cultural world and of cultural occupations, but they are not exclusively rooted in that world. The examination of four typical cases will allow us to account for this variety of rationales and document the broader trends – also at work in other fields among the educated middle classes and part of the upper classes – that inform this career choice. While the absence of similar research and data on other national contexts prevents me from generalizing my empirical results, the polarities they reveal could nevertheless be used for comparative purposes. The prospects of upward social mobility offered by cultural intermediary occupations, of which they were a symbol, have been largely thwarted by classical forms of socio-professional reproduction and by the strategies of those better endowed in educational and social capital to fend off downclassing. The collective dreams of social promotion through culture of working-class and lower middle-class children have given way to the individual aspirations of self-fulfillment of upper-class contenders who do not fit the social standards expected from their milieu or training.

## *Dreams of social mobility*

The upward social mobility strategies implemented by working-class graduates have in the past resulted in the social diversification of some cultural occupations.[23] They had also been conducive to the emergence of a key component of the 'new petite bourgeoisie' which in the 1960s and 1970s made up the bulk of those who occupied the then new cultural intermediary positions (Bourdieu 1984: 365–72). This social diversification process has now been halted if not reversed, as objective chances of social promotion through access to more indeterminate positions have decreased. The proportion of children of blue-collar workers and farmers has been steadily decreasing in the fields of media, arts and performing arts, dropping from 22.5 per cent in 1982 to 19.3 per cent in 1992 and to 17 per cent ten years later, while concurrently increasing in the executive and upper intellectual categories in which these occupations are included (respectively 19.2 per cent in 1982 and 23 per cent in 1992 and 2002).[24]

Such backgrounds are now strongly in the minority, even among aspirants. Only 12 per cent of applicants to master's programmes in cultural management have a working-class background (here, I use this term to refer to blue-collar workers, employees and farmers), against 20 per cent of all master's students.[25] To some extent, this also applies to children of holders of intermediary occupations: although they are present in higher proportions (22 per cent, i.e. roughly the same share as in the labour force), they are mostly found among the most educated of these occupations (as is evidenced by the majority of schoolteachers among them). The proportions are similar among the population of enrolled students, but the working-class applicants tend to enrol in programmes offered by second-rank universities[26] with more uncertain job prospects.

Yet, aspirations to achieve social advancement through cultural employment have not disappeared. Catherine, who I already mentioned, is a case in point. She grew-up in a working-class suburb of Paris. Her father and both of her grandparents worked in construction, her mother was a cashier, and her grandmothers were cleaning ladies. Her investment in school was hindered by the jobs she took since high school, working 15 to 20 hours a week, to pay for her studies. She received the *baccalauréat* on her second attempt, and subsequently had to retake the first year in her bachelor's of art history. After graduating, she enrolled in a second-rate cultural master's programme. Having received an initiation into culture thanks to her mother, who took her to museums, she decided fairly quickly that she wanted to pursue this path, explicitly for purposes of upward social mobility.

> This 'I want to work in culture' thing, it was about not wanting to do any of that! I didn't want to be a cashier, I didn't want to be a cleaning lady, I didn't want to be a mason. [...] The fact of choosing something cultural when you come from the projects, culture is like music, museums or that kind of thing, it's also something that socially allows you... to elevate yourself, kind of [...] to not stay where I am... erm, where I was.

In keeping with what is usually observed, the educational trajectories of the working-class applicants are weaker than those of the other applicants (in terms of *baccalauréat* results, of enrollment in selective programmes and conversely in less prestigious programmes and short-cycle university programmes). They also have different types of educational capital. Unlike their counterparts from the middle- and upper-classes, whose more generalist training prepares them better to access executive positions and, if need be, to seek work in other sectors, the working-class applicants tend to specialize at an earlier point in their academic trajectory. They sometimes do so directly after graduating from high school, in programmes preparing for cultural occupations and cultural mediation that begin at bachelor level.[27] This also applies at master's level, as working-class applicants twice as often specialize in culture in the first year as the others (42 per cent, against 21 per cent of middle-class applicants and 21 per cent of upper-class applicants). In some respects, this early specialization, conceived as a means to increase the applicant chances of finding a job, can often end up being a trap. First, it makes a career shift to a different sector more difficult (which is already indicated by the fact that fewer working-class applicants apply to master's programmes in other fields). Second, it prevents them from accessing the executive positions that would ensure them real upward social mobility.[28]

These educational trajectories and professional projections are arguably characteristic of what Jean-Claude Chamboredon calls the *espérance rêveuse* (the dreams and hopes) of children from working-class and lower middle-class back-grounds (Chamboredon 1991). What may seem like unrealistic aspirations from these students can be analyzed as the result of three types of disconnect: from their background, from the higher education system and from the professional world in which they aspire to work. As they enter higher education they are steered away from the 'reasonable' career choices promoted by their relatives and peer groups. Studying cultural mediation at bachelor's level thwarts their prospects of academic achievement and reinforces their disconnect from their original social circles, without being directly rewarding from a professional standpoint. Indeed, this comparatively lower educational capital does not reach its full potential on the job market due to a triple deficit. First, applicants lack exposure to culture outside of the educational framework, having less frequent or less legitimate cultural practices (i.e. more television, less reading). Yet, this 'personal' culture is particularly expected in a world where it is customary to assert one's distance from schooling and one's attachment to the institutional and legitimate forms of culture. Secondly, they lack professional experience, having more rarely had a job in cultural domains (30 per cent against 36 per cent); when they have, the experience is less frequently significant. Pursuing cultural programmes at an early stage in their higher education leads them to carry out numerous and often long internships; yet, it is likely that, in part because they occur at an early point in their trajectory, they consist chiefly in performing subordinate tasks or are carried out in structures enjoying little recognition (like small independent businesses). Lastly, they lack social capital, as they less frequently have relatives in the worlds of art and culture. This is a known decisive factor of educational downgrading, hindering the social advancement of working-class graduates (Peugny 2009).

For these applicants, applying for a master's can be a means to avoid a harsh form of downgrading resulting from excessively early entry into the labour force, and to somehow make up for an average educational trajectory by extending their schooling with a programme reputed to be selective. Yet, these applicants are quite likely to see their social and educational origins catch up with them later on, either by having more difficulty in finding a job or having to content themselves with less prestigious and well-paid positions (in less well-endowed structures) or less valued functions (being in direct contact with the public rather than the artists and partners). The relative vagueness surrounding cultural occupations only conceals the hierarchy of positions for those who nurture dreams of upward mobility. Therein arguably lies an additional explanation of the vocation to work in the cultural sector rather than to hold a specific occupation discussed earlier: to aspire to be 'part of that world' is to hope to get close to those who have prestigious positions even though one has objectively few chances of being in their place one day; these social advancement strategies are not so much based on the conquest of positions as on the accumulation of a symbolic capital through proximity with prestigious institutions and individuals.

These dreams of upward social mobility should not be seen merely as the quest of individual salvation through culture. Indeed, it is precisely those working-class students who consider that they have gained 'access to culture' and hope to make a career out of it who are the most eager to ascribe a collective meaning to this choice by referring to cultural democratization projects – if only to assert their fidelity to their origins. Again, Catherine illustrates this best, by explicitly mentioning her personal experience of discovering museums as the basis for her career plan.

> Most of my friends didn't go, right, it was a really weird thing to do. And I for one didn't understand why people didn't love museums and I told myself, 'well, in order to enjoy museums you have to know them ever since you were a kid', so I told myself, 'well, that's it, I really want to reach out to the younger public'. So that's where it came from. The love of museums came from my mother taking me to them, and then the fact that I wanted to make others love them came from that.

This is also the case of Sofiane, whose Moroccan immigrant parents invested a lot into their children's education. After an economic *baccalauréat* (he had previously hesitated with the literary stream), he unsuccessfully applied to a decorative arts school. He declined to enrol in the visual arts department where he had been admitted, perceiving it as not practice-oriented enough and too focused on art history, which he described as 'a bit too much of a pompous art'. He ultimately enrolled in an economic and social administration programme (*administration économique et sociale*, AES), partly because he knew he would be there with friends from high school, and then in the first year of a master's in political science. He read a lot, went to the library on a regular basis, and drew. His cultural universe, revolving around science fiction, heroic fantasy and manga, is on the fringes of highbrow culture. He attributes his 'artistic side' which he nurtures to encounters with people who have resonated with him or helped him, his aunt who draws, a high school friend who pursued visual arts studies, French and visual arts teachers.

> And I tell myself that not everyone was necessarily as lucky as I was… 'cause for me reading, really you can't imagine what it's like! It does me sooo much good, I think it's awesome! And so I wanted to bring reading, and I also do theatre, so bring reading and theatre into my neighbourhood, since I come from a ZEP [educational priority zone: an underprivileged school district receiving specific attention from the government], my neighbourhood's in a sensitive urban area, so not necessarily where you get the most cultural things, you know. […] I feel like giving the opportunity that I had to somebody else, it really is that, if I want to leave a small trace, it's about passing on to somebody else what I had myself. […] I'd really like other people to have that chance too. It really is what drives me.

Sofiane was not admitted into a cultural master's programme, and eventually turned to the open competitions for public service positions.

The increasing scarcity and difficulty of upward social mobility trajectories through culture means that one of the social foundations of belief in cultural democratization is crumbling. The shift from a political relationship to culture considered as an area of social emancipation to more technical or managerial relationships results from generational factors relating to the socialization settings informing involvement in the field (the mobilizations of 1968 and their aftermath; then the professional process that began in the 1980s and the following economic redefinition of cultural issues). This shift is likely also due to the fact that the social recruitment of cultural occupations leaves increasingly little room for upwardly mobile trajectories.

### Professional reproduction

While 'the decades of rapid growth had been the opportunity to witness the emergence of an elite that came out of nowhere [...] the contemporary situation in which there are more applicants than positions freed by retirements' (Chauvel 2006: 57) is conducive to the return of the 'inheritors'. This trend has been spurred on by the combination of rising educational standards and increasing scarcity of job offers liable to meet graduates' expectations. It is difficult to assess the scope of this return with great accuracy where cultural occupations are concerned. Studies of cultural occupations providing detailed data on social recruitment now date back to a few decades (Seibel 1988), and scholars analyzing them from the perspective of shifts in social space remain rare (de Saint-Martin 1996). More recent studies have not addressed this aspect, even though the generational changes they evidence, particularly regarding the increasingly managerial skills and conceptions of the job, could be usefully related to changes in social backgrounds.[29] The sample sizes of the national employment surveys (INSEE's *enquêtes emploi*) that we subjected to additional processing are too small to yield useful results at a fine level of aggregation of occupations; yet, in the negative and for the generic category of media, arts and performing arts professionals, they confirm the continuous decrease in the proportion of working-class backgrounds.

While we lack sufficient data to establish this systematically, all signs suggest that the intergenerational transmission of professional positions has increased over the past few decades. If we stick to the applicants that make up our study's population, it is worth recalling that around 17 per cent of them have parents working in the cultural sector. Although they remain largely in the minority, this proportion is ten times higher than the estimated share for all jobs. Having parents working in the cultural field and endowed with the dispositions and practices that come with it (frequent cultural outings, reading, discussions, etc.) is not only a direct factor of professional heredity; it also works as a factor in an intense cultural socialization that in turns encourages the pursuit of careers in the sector. 'My dad's an artist, my mother works in the cultural press. Ever since I was a kid, I've been used to that world, going to concerts, visiting exhibitions, going to a festival to hand out booklets…'[30] As this applicant shows, cultural dispositions of a specific kind are also passed on, through the early acquisition of familiarity with culture and practical experiences (handing out booklets) that constitute first instances of the shift from the world of consumers to the world of the producers. These applicants have much more frequently than others considered a career as an artist which they have now given up on, which gives further credit to the hypothesis of a cultural socialization leading to two successive forms of aspiration (to be an artist, and subsequently to be a cultural manager) against the oversimplifying view of the applicants as failed artists. In a world connected to public events whose organization sometimes entails an informal and collective dimension, transmission creates a heightened continuum between individual and private practices (going to the theatre) and professional discovery (going backstage).

My father's a photographer and he helped set up the *Rencontres de la photographie* [the most renowned photography festival in France]. My mother works in a festival. So I've been immersed in that since I was a little kid, I've seen people work, helped any way I could. Also I did dancing, piano, theatre. It was also my family background that made it possible. So I've always wanted to work in culture.[31]

The parents' social capital is an added benefit, facilitating contacts in the cultural field, encounters and internships, especially as more of these applicants come from Paris, where a large part of the cultural jobs are found, and live there.[32] 'I know the field, my father works in a cultural institution; and through my contacts I was able to meet people who work at the Musée d'Orsay'.[33] In addition to their parents, and in part thanks to them, these applicants also much more frequently have close acquaintances in cultural circles. It logically follows that their professional experience of culture is much more frequent and significant than that of the other applicants. Their dispositions, early skills and relational resources make it more likely that they will find a job in a world where a degree is increasingly required, but must also be complemented by 'personality', experiences and a 'network'.[34] Additionally, these applicants do have the required degree and are often better endowed in educational capital than the others (having more often graduated from high school ahead or on schedule, with honours, in general study, and more often been selected in a *classe préparatoire*).

Only a longitudinal study conducted over several generations would allow us to establish this with precision, but arguably this transmission does not so much reflect the continuity of a long line as the extension of recently acquired familial positions. I have already noted that many of the jobs in the field were created at the time when the parents of today's applicants entered the labour force. The older cultural occupations are rather based on the transmission of economic capital (as in the case of art dealers), and as such less in line with the typical prospects of the newly trained cultural managers. My hypothesis is that this professional reproduction applies to a large extent to the children of those who in the previous generation had the first cultural jobs and thereby moved up the social ladder to reach a level that the new generation is trying to a maintain. Today's aspirants are probably the inheritors of the 'new petite bourgeoisie' rather than a new generation of its working-class component.

In addition to contributing to raising the social barriers to entry, this heredity accentuates the institutionalization of the professional positions of cultural management – positions that are now reproduced (or passed on) more than invented. Together with the decline in upward social mobility trajectories, this is another factor transforming the type of investment of the agents concerned in their professional activity. One is likely to be less predisposed to experiencing this activity as a 'mission' – particularly one of cultural proselytism – when the parents' legacy makes it considered 'normal' to occupy a similar position, than when this position is conquered as a means to escape one's original position through culture.

### A devalued literary capital and a reinvested educational capital

The trend towards higher and more restricted social backgrounds does not only result from a mechanism of inter-generational transmission of professional positions; it is also influenced by the strategies used by upper class children to fight downclassing. As they seek to avoid the risk of downward social mobility or tone down its effects, they leave less room for those who target the same positions in a perspective of upward mobility. A similar process happened with teaching since the stabilization of mass unemployment: upper class children – again, mostly girls – were drawn to teaching, which in former generations used to constitute a vehicle for promotion for working-class children (Geay 2002; Charles and Cibois 2010).

In order to test this hypothesis of a strategy to fight social and educational downgrading, we have singled out those among the applicants who were high-achieving female students in literary subjects with upper-class backgrounds: young women with at least one upper-class parent, holders of a general *baccalauréat* obtained on schedule and with honours, who did not enrol in an institute of political science (IEP) or in a school (of any kind) and who studied literature, languages, philosophy, history, art history, visual arts, performing arts, musicology, communication or culture at bachelor's level – a group that makes up 15 per cent of the overall population of applicants. This group can indeed be considered as characteristic of applicants both strongly endowed with social, cultural, educational and, for some, economic capital and facing the likely inability to obtain positions matching this capital. In terms of cultural practices and professional experience, the backgrounds of its members do not differ much from the broader population of applicants (some features usually observed are sometimes heightened). Assessed on the basis of their artistic education and of the presence of family members working in the cultural sector, their cultural socialization is slightly higher and their tastes tend to favour legitimate art forms somewhat more. They have less often anticipated a career in cultural management,[35] probably because the cultural resources accumulated during socialization in the family and in school were converted into a professional horizon once their studies had ended and the time to choose a career path had arrived. Such is the case of Clara, the daughter of a 'well-off' physician. After studying for two years in a literary *classe prépara-toire* in a prominent Parisian high school, earning a bachelor in literature and then unsuccessfully turning to sociology (she was unable to secure funding for her PhD), she started envisioning a career in the cultural field at a rather late stage – a return to her roots, or rather a professional conversion of her original cultural capital.

> I told myself I couldn't do a PhD because I wouldn't get funding and we were told so often that there was no future in sociology, so I was trying to find a way out and I thought about culture because it's true, it was some-thing… I grew up in an environment where cultural activities were quite encouraged, my parents, my family, ever since I was a little kid we've been going to exhibitions, I play music, I play the flute, I was able to do theatre. So yeah, I've travelled quite a bit with my parents, I've seen cit-ies, museums. I was already in a conducive environment that allowed me to get access to all that culture, and then I thought that actually my literature studies could also be a way to move on to that programme and turn towards cultural jobs.
>
> Clara, born in 1986, father physician, mother nurse, literary
> classe préparatoire *in a prestigious Parisian high school,*
> *bachelor's in literature then master's in sociology*

Whereas at other times, similar trajectories are likely to lead to a teaching career, here it predisposes Clara to reject it. This is why it is necessary to consider paths of access to different sectors, which requires going back to the social logics of attraction to indeterminate positions analyzed by Bourdieu in his sociology of the new petite bourgeoisie. While upward social mobility for working class graduates is now much more difficult, the conditions for the social maintenance of upper class children have changed drastically. Due to the generalization of the longer duration of studies, to the transformations that impacted the role of edu-cational capital and the different forms it takes (e.g. the decline of literature and the humanities), these children (especially girls), who now face more competitive selection in school and more often fall through the cracks, often seek to capitalize on their family inheritance by maximizing a form of educational capital that is devalued (particularly in literature).

In this context, cultural management programmes constitute both a way to avoid teaching (now a devalued occupation), which used to be one of the main career paths chosen by students in the humanities, an outlet for cashing in on the cul-tural dispositions inherited from family socialization and, if not clear professional career perspectives, at least holding out the hope of finding one's place in a world that enjoys a certain degree of social prestige. This is made easier by the fact that the weak codification of cultural occupations and of the paths to access them often creates intermediate situations well suited to avoid experiencing failure, which might happen brutally when seeking more established positions; in other words, they are lifelines for individuals who face the risk of educational and social downgrading, and because they are women with upper class backgrounds, are less affected than others by restrictions pertaining to job stability and income. The social and symbolic capital that they can expect to gain by having an occupation in the cultural sector compensates this risk.

### *Self-assertion*

While strategies to achieve upward mobility or fight downclassing primarily reflect a quest for social salvation through culture, other ambitions are also at stake. Like some trajectories that are not characterized by a prospect of upward or downward social mobility, these strategies may also involve a 'personal' factor, where social conditions combine to enable a career choice based on self-assertion. This factor can be found in virtually all applicants, but it tends to matter more for students whose training did not specifically prepare them to work in the cultural world and initially offered them more varied prospects, generally more stable and financially rewarding than cultural jobs. I chose to focus on a group of applicants sharing these features, namely alumni of institutes of political studies (IEP), for whom culture is a relatively marginal choice among a wide array of possibilities (administrative competitions, journalism, finance, management, etc.). In their case this unlikely choice, not directly resulting from their educational trajectory, gives us a particularly illuminating showcase of the personal factor that informs career choices.

First, a few indications on these applicants, although it bears noting that my intention here is not propose a comprehensive sociology of this group of students (additionally, the hypothesis of self-assertion should not lead us to overlook differences in their trajectories), but rather to use their sociological features to test this hypothesis. IEP students are significantly younger and comprise more male students, often from socially and educationally privileged backgrounds. They are unsurprisingly high-achieving students, having often graduated from high school ahead of schedule and with honours. They have more often followed scientific tracks rather than the literary ones during their secondary education. Many have studied in a *classe préparatoire* (58 per cent, against under 25 per cent of all applicants), where literary dispositions are valued.

In keeping with the major ruling principle (*nomos*) of IEPs, which consists of keeping all options open (Lozach 2012), these applicants are less exclusive in pursuing cultural management. They more often apply for master's programmes in other areas and leave the possibility of seeking employment elsewhere open. This diversification is partly an effect of the institutional constraints that inform their choices.[36] At least for the best endowed among them, it results from the self-confidence conferred by their versatile training and often by the combination of high social and educational resources. This confidence in themselves and in their future leads them to consider that no option should be ruled out in principle. Self-assertion in such cases lies in the feeling of freedom that leads them to think that everything is possible, even choices that may not be entirely transgressive but break from the expected standard choices: while pursuing an artistic vocation is a transgression of the likely trajectory for upper-class children (Sorignet 2010: 68), cultural management is a half-transgression of sorts in light of the institution's standards – first because it encompasses activities that fit those standards (management), and then because this choice is envisioned rather than actively pursued.

There are least two main outcomes for these applicants. The half-hearted applications of those who develop a belated interest in culture, among many other things, lack most of what could support and justify their motivation and have very few chances of success. The more well-founded applications of students better endowed with all forms of capital and whose cultural experience comes in addition to a number of assets that prepare them for a successful career, are dominated by the importance of their resources, which (especially for men) may ultimately *obligate* them (in the sense of *noblesse oblige*) to make a choice that meets the social expectations associated with these resources more adequately. Cultural management then constitutes more of a possibility, envisioned and subsequently dismissed to the benefit of a more expected choice, as if to tell themselves that they made a 'real choice', since they could have pursued a different path that would have been desirable in other respects.

Keeping opportunities open is expected from IEP students; the frequency of frustrated artistic vocations is more surprising. That they received more art tuition and followed more classes in the past, often within the institutional framework of a course at the conservatory or in an art school is the result of their social background. Yet, the fact that more of them still follow art classes suggests that there is something beyond complying with parental expectations during childhood and adolescence at stake here. This investment, in both senses of the term, is confirmed by the fact that more among them have had an artistic practice and especially that more of them still play an instrument or write. These applicants have more frequently turned this investment into a career choice than the others, but these artistic vocations appear to have been frustrated at an early stage, as more among them gave up on the artistic career they once envisioned, and proportionally fewer of them had an artistic practice in a professional setting.

For those who experienced this frustrated vocation, the choice of cultural management appears as a means of returning to a pursuit that they put on hold during the 'serious' studies they made to indulge their parents. It can in such cases be a way for them to 'reconnect' with themselves in the name of an ideal of self-achievement. Logically enough these applicants particularly exhibit a tendency to expose their 'personality', as an aforementioned applicant who starts her presentation by claiming that 'recounting [her] academic background is not sufficient to encapsulate who [she is]' and goes on by listing the 'other sides' of her personality' or another whose presentation revolves around her 'personal project'.

I chose this programme in light of my personal project. [...] I do theatre, I do music, I wear many hats. [...] I can't see myself working in something I'm not interested in. What I'm interested in is culture. [...]. I've had my heart set on working in culture for several years. [...] Having gone to the theatre since I was a young child, when I came to Sciences Po, I asked myself how I could work in the cultural field without necessarily being an artist. [...] I'm also interested in opening up to other countries, exchanging, creativity, meeting people... So working in culture combines all my areas of interest.

*Observation VD22, woman born in 1989, regional IEP*

My hypothesis is that the individuals who pursue this personal quest feel out of step with the social model or the peer group of their initial training and with the professional prospects they typically offer (administrative competitions, management...). This may be result of a somewhat random accession to the IEP or of a low social background, which is rare in these institutes. The following two portraits illustrate both cases.[37]

At the time of the interview, Clara is a student in the master's programme in cultural management offered by the IEP in which she studied, having chosen this particular institution with a view to being enrolled in this specific programme. Yet Sciences Po was not her initial choice. At the high school, she prepared a literary *baccalauréat* with a specialization in art history and graduated with the highest honours. After an unsuccessful application to the École du Louvre, she planned to enter a *classe préparatoire* and subsequently study art history at university. She had conversely ruled out studying in an art school, in order to avoid following in her parents' footsteps and, even more, to avoid being a student in their class, as they both teach fine arts in a large provincial city. Influenced by teachers, an acquaintance and many fellow high schoolers, she submitted an application for direct admission into two IEPs that automatically admit students who obtain the *baccalauréat* with the highest honours. She hesitated between the IEP and a *classe préparatoire* and eventually chose the former 'to see what it was like' – she would spend the remainder of her studies there. Yet she felt out of place: 'Early in the first year, I told myself "Oh my God, where am I?"'. The IEP's curriculum was utterly at odds with her 'professional desire'. She was uneasy with the strong mathematical bent in the teaching of economics, but also had trouble with other subjects. Fed up with competing with other high-achieving students and having less time to devote to her cultural practices, which she had until then pursued with great intensity, she seriously considered quitting to make another attempt to get into the École du Louvre. While she eventually decided to stay, with the prospect of the third year of studies abroad and the master's in cultural management on the horizon, she did not fully play the social game of the institution. 'I went to the integration weekend [...] and after that I quickly removed myself from all that. I didn't join any of the student associations... So of course I went along with the mass movement at first, and then I quit doing all that.' She does not even participate in the arts associations. She is also one of the very few students that does not take part in the landmark events that most students look forward to, such as the annual gala: 'I didn't go with the flow'. She has made few friends. 'I didn't buy into this whole Sciences Po hypocrisy – "we're all buddies and we all get along fine"'. She felt people looked at her 'like an alien', because she had made a 'choice that isn't easy to defend, compared with very different trajectories, much more career-oriented', in line with the institution's standards, shared by the majority of students. This sense of being out of step is even visible in the way she dresses; people make fun of her outfits for being too flashy. She felt more at ease during her year abroad, where she attended sociology and anthropology classes, including some addressing artistic and cultural issues. Instead of sharing a flat with other students and being 'in the Erasmus mould', she moved in with older artists and resumed her intense cultural practices and frequent outings. Upon returning to France, she picked the less prestigious track, being the one that includes the least economics and law classes (the dominant disciplines in IEPs), and was eventually admitted into the master's in cultural management she had initially targeted. In addition to her personal practices, she possessed most of the resources that proved her determination, having carried out several internships in various cultural institutions and written a dissertation on museums. She considers the prospect of working in culture as self-evident, even though she does not have a very precise idea of her future job. Well, the thing is, I've been immersed in that world since I was a small kid. [...] So what am I interested in within that world? I've always known it, I've always experienced it, so of course it feels innate. But what drives me is the idea of making a living out of my passion, right. It's being able to combine creation and project management. It's doing something I enjoy, that's part of my passions; ultimately it's a matter of having a pleasant job and being happy to go to work in the morning [laughs]!

Aurélie's background is very different from, and in some respects symmetrically opposite to, Clara's. At the time of the interview, she is a fourth-year student still weighing career choices; cultural management is only one of several possible paths. She spontaneously mentions her family background as we begin the interview – she is the only daughter of two blue-collar workers. Her unexpected success at the Sciences Po entrance competition (she has a literary *baccalauréat* with a *mention assez bien* – honours – and says she was lucky at the *concours*) gave a particular meaning to her studies: 'for a worker, having your daughter getting into Sciences Po is like hitting the jackpot'. This social background put her at odds with the other students from the start. She says she is not comfortable; some students call her 'the prole'. She socializes mostly with classmates whose social origins are relatively low (children of mid-level executives or schoolteachers), but still higher than hers. She attended the first integration parties, but soon stopped going, tired of those who 'think they know everything', including what it's like to be unemployed or to live life with a small income, which they only know 'from books' at best. She is an avid reader herself, essentially of political and social critique essays. She hardly discusses her cultural practices beyond reading, to which her father initiated her. In addition to her working-class origins, she was raised in a small village, which did not facilitate cultural socialization. Her possible choice of pursuing a cultural career was inspired by an experience as journalist: as she was investigating street art, she came across a group that she joined as an intern working on communication. Now she hesitates between culture, social economy and labour law. I don't know if I really want to get into the performing arts as a communications or marketing officer or some administrative position, 'cause I'm not able to walk on a tightrope, right! But I… I don't know. Also I think it's too far removed from reality. [...] That's why for instance in addition to the cultural master's I'm considering, I've been looking more and more into labour law. But not at all labour law as In labour Inspector, or lawyer in the industrial tribunals, more like unions, legal counsel, or even lobbying' The 'reality' she refers to is the reality of her social origins, on the basis of which such hesitations are often settled. When friends and relatives are politicized and unionized, the possibility of returning to one's roots is constructed politically. This is not entirely the case for Aurélie; her career prospects, in the cultural sector and others, are informed by a vaguely anarchist political bent indicated by her choice of reading material, her socialization in radical left circles during her year abroad and expressed through a disdain towards marketing and trade. Culture, labour law and social economy appear as three of the possible forms of a yet to be formulated critique of capitalism.

As culture serves as a vehicle for the – albeit sometimes sublimated or negated – expression of the principles of vision and division of social space and of the ways to define one's role in that space (Bourdieu 1984), the choice of pursuing a cultural occupation is perhaps a clearer reflection than others of the aesthetic, ethical and political preferences defining relationships to the social world. This will be the focus of the final section of this book.

## Notes

1  We recoded former academic trajectories in 18 groups: Arts; Business and marketing; Communication, public relations; European studies; Health and social work; Humanitarian aid; International relations, co-operation; Journalism, press and media; Languages; Law; Literature; Management and human resources; Preparation for teaching exams, education sector; Public administration, preparation for civil service entrance exams, Research in the humanities and social science; Tourism; Urban studies and planning; Other.

2  While multiple applications are an indicators of a strong investment, applications to a single programme cannot be seen as reflecting a lesser investment: they may relate to geographic mobility constraints or, in the case of students having completed the first year of the same programme, the near-certainty of being selected.

3  Observation VD27, woman born in 1986. Observations listed in this manner were conducted in Strasbourg in June 2011. The reference includes the researcher's initials and the order of the interviews observed (here, Vincent Dubois, 27nd interview).

4  The applicants fill in responses to the questionnaire at the same time as they are submitting their application; for this reason they are probably inclined to seek consistency in their responses, for themselves, their relatives and the selection jury. Additionally, the questionnaire was sent together with the applications, and it is likely that some respondents picked the 'right' answers in terms of selection, even though we did mention that responses were anonymous and not connected to the application.

5  The numbers in brackets refer to the applications in our corpus.

6  'Culture has been a part of my life since I was very young', an applicant says before adding 'even though this is a mundane thing to say'. Observation VL4, woman born in 1988, second-year master's programme in a regional IEP and work-based management school.

7  These findings are consistent with those of a study at a job fair for cultural employment, showing that the titles of the first three positions sought (out of 15) are generic and open: Project design and co-ordination (30.1 per cent), Communication and marketing (16.8 per cent), Polyvalent position (12.9 per cent). These are also the positions for which the ratio between the number of applications and the number of job offers is the most unfavourable (Mathieu 2011: 211).

8  My thanks to Olivier Roueff for calling my attention on this point.

9  Observation VD11, woman born in 1985, bachelor's in history in a prestigious Parisian university, first-year master's in political science in a large regional university.

10  Here, the phrases in quotation marks refer to comments frequently made by applicants and professionals of culture.

11  It is worth noting that we have sought to provide the most comprehensive account of the diversity of these formulations, without disregarding those that do no fit this hypothesis. We also constantly made sure to avoid the pitfall of compiling a collection of 'bloopers', mocking the students' mistakes, naivety or bombastic prose. In the same spirit, we left the syntax as is, but corrected spelling errors.

12  Direction de l'évaluation, de la prospective et de la performance, ministère de l'Éducation nationale, « Les concours de recrutement de personnels enseignants du second degré dans l'enseignement public et privé », *Note d'information*, 24, 2011.

13  –46 per cent of positions offered in the external public competitions for secondary education between 2000 and 2010. Sources: *ibid.*

14  Emphasis mine. Observation VD13, woman born in 1989, bachelor's in history in a small regional university, then first year in a master's of culture and heritage management in the same university.

15  Charlotte, born in 1987, mother business employee, father technician, international *baccalauréat*, bachelor's in Italian then master's in culture. It is worth noting that even though they are also rare, research and higher education – activities of intellectual creation (*auctor*), not only of pedagogic repetition (*lector*) – are more often found among the possible associations. Over 5 per cent of applicants also apply to a research-oriented second year of master's (3.3 per cent in the humanities and social science, 1.8 per cent in literature). Notoriously, it is the scarcity of employment prospects rather than lack of motivation that steers students away from research.

16  Ariane, born in 1986, father electrician, mother social worker, *baccalauréat ES* then DUT *carrières sociales* and IUP *développement territorial*.

17  On the way involvement, challenges and interest are valued in cultural labour, see Hesmondhalgh and Baker 2010: 127–32.

18  Flora, born in 1986, father doctor, mother nurse, literary *baccalauréat*, literary *classe préparatoire* in a prestigious Parisian high school, bachelor's in literature and master's in sociology.

19  Salomé, born in 1986, father administrative executive in a training centre, mother dressmaker.

20  i.e. the possibilities among their likely future as they are subjectively perceived by individuals.

21  The total slightly exceeds 100 because some applicants mention several artistic occupations.

22  Observation VL5, woman born in 1987, bachelor's in visual arts then first-year master's in arts and cultural occupations.

23  This is the case of librarians, whose social recruitment used to be traditionally high, and among whom a growing number of working-class agents started coming in beginning in the mid 1970s (Seibel 1988). Despite this increasing social inclusion, chances of accessing positions are still highly unequal depending on social origin.

24  Over the same period the proportion of children of employees increased very slightly (around 12% in the media, arts and performing arts and 14.5% of executives and holders of upper intellectual occupations as of 2002). Source: INSEE, *Enquête emploi*, with additional statistical processing by the author. See the methodological appendix for more detail on this processing.

25  Source: ministère de l'Éducation nationale, *Repères et références statistiques*, 2009. These categories make up between 55 per cent and 60 per cent of the labour force.

26  Source: SISE database, ministère de l'Enseignement supérieur.

27  This choice of pursuing potentially short vocational training programmes (three years) is reminiscent of the popularity of BTS (technician certificates) for the working-class students studied by Sophie Orange (Orange 2010).

28  We lack the data to systematically identify the effect of social origin on employment opportunities. Yet this factor is clearly highlighted in Marc Lecoutre's study (Lecoutre 1995).

29  See Octobre 1999 and the special issue 'Le renouvellement des générations', *Bulletin des bibliothèques de France*, 2005, 50 (3).

30  Observation VD11, woman born in 1985, bachelor's in history in a prestigious Parisian university, first-year master's in political science in a large regional university.

31  Observation VD26, woman born in 1989, bachelor's and first-year master's in political science in a large regional university.

32  The concentration in the Paris area is particularly pronounced in the sectors of film and video, radio and TV broadcasting (two employees out of three). It is also notable, albeit to a lesser extent, in the fields of heritage conservation (55 per cent) and publishing and bookselling (42 per cent) (Cléron and Patureau 2009, statistics from 2006).

33  Observation VD6, woman born in 1989, regional IEP.

34  Cultural management programmes themselves play an important role in the accumulation of a social capital useful to find a job (Lecoutre 2006), which in itself doesn't mean that the social capital acquired in the family plays a decreasing role as the author suggests.

35  58 per cent of them report having made this choice 'this year or last year', against 43 per cent of the other applicants.

36  IEPs are five-year degree courses, following which students may obtain a national master's degree in addition to the one awarded by the IEP. It is therefore in their best interests to enrol in a master's programme offered by an IEP, and preferably the one where they have studied: students from a given IEP who wish to enrol in the same institution's master's programme in cultural management cannot apply in an equivalent master's programme in another IEP. Yet, they have no guarantee that they will be accepted in that programme, which is why they submit applications in other areas.

37  These portraits are based on interviews conducted by Ugo Lozach within the framework of his research on IEP students.

# 4 Intermediate dispositions and adjustment strategies

Cultural managers readily present themselves as intermediaries: they act as brokers between creators and their financial or logistical backers, mediators between the artworks and the public and conciliators between artistic, administrative and economic interests. Being situated at the crossroads of different rationales and different worlds, they are also intermediaries because of their social positions – between the middle and upper classes. These roles and positions are matched by dispositions that are no easier to characterize globally and homogeneously than the trajectories with which they are associated. Indeed, a salient feature of this socio-professional world is that it attracts individuals whose preferences, starting with cultural tastes, vary widely. However, they are united by a relationship to culture in which legitimism and eclecticism have a mutual influence. These cultural dispositions are part of a broader relationship to the world combining anti-conformism and individual strategies of adjustment to the social order. While this is partly attributable to the young age of the applicants, it relates more generally and durably to the reasons for pursuing such professional positions and the way in which they are envisioned.

## Between cultural legitimism and eclecticism

If the choice of pursuing a career in cultural management is informed by a taste for 'culture', it is worth investigating the type(s) of culture to which the applicants are attracted. Studying their tastes and practices, and the way they can be converted into professional preferences and references allows us to a get a better grasp of the strictly cultural workings of the choice of cultural management, and establish the foundations of the orientations and prescriptions formulated by these future intermediaries (in all senses of the term) of culture.

There are two main sets of factors distinguishing the applicants. The first pertains to the intensity of their cultural investment, assessed through the quantity of cultural consumption and practices and the number of cultural interests reported (represented in the first horizontal axis of the multiple correspondence analysis presented below). The left side of the space mapped on the factorial graph includes avid readers, who often go to the theatre, to museums and concerts, watch little television and enjoy numerous cultural genres; the intensity of the practices and the number of cultural interests decrease on the right side of the graph. While it is hardly surprising that applicants whose previous studies had no specifically cultural content (economics, management, communication) tend to be on the right side of the graph, it is more unexpected to find that this is also the case of those who studied in cultural mediation programmes. We have seen that many of these students have a working-class background with little exposure to culture; the cultural orientation of their academic curriculum does not appear to make up for the deficit of cultural capital inherited from their parents.

The second principle of opposition (represented on the vertical axis) distributes applicants according to their preference for contemporary forms of culture and creation (on the upper part of the graph) or for heritage and more classical forms of culture (on the lower part of the graph). There is a clear distinction between the (relatively few) applicants who have studied history or art history and report an exclusive taste or preference for classical and heritage-oriented forms of culture. The two main axes combine to evidence two complementary principles of opposition, outlined by the diagonal lines of the space of tastes and practices. The combination of intense investment with a preference for creation forms the basis of an opposition between 'artists' (in the upper left quadrant) and the applicants who have no personal artistic practice (lower right quadrant). The combination of a strong investment with a partly more classical orientation reflects an opposition between the more 'legitimist' (in the lower left quadrant) and those whose relationships to culture are more distant and whose tastes are more lowbrow (upper right quadrant).[1]

**Methodology**

Based on recoded questionnaire responses (n = 654), we selected 17 active variables, divided into 41 modalities, to account for the artistic and cultural practices and tastes of the applicants. Three dichotomous variables account for their dispositions to make art: practicing an artistic activity or not, receiving art tuition/attending an art class or not, considering an artistic career or not (in red on the factorial map). Four variables account for cultural consumption: frequency of reading, frequency of TV watching, diversity of cultural outings over the past month and cultural media reading (in green on the factorial map). The other ten variables, based on recoded responses to an open-ended question, account for cultural tastes: diversity, degree of legitimacy and contemporaneity of the genres mentioned (in blue on the map), mentions of different cultural genres or lack thereof. The axes retained have an inertia of 0.138 (first axis) and 0.101 (second axis), i.e. 23.9 per cent of the variance explained.

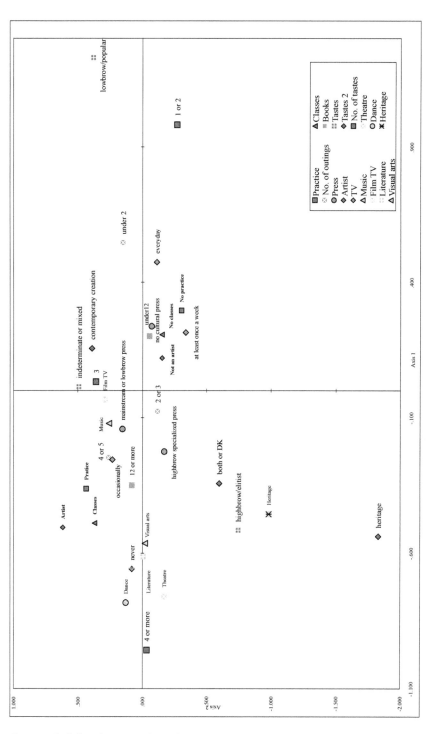

*Figure 4.1* Cultural tastes and practices

This analysis not only allowed us to establish polarities in the cultural orientations of applicants, but it was also particularly useful in putting into perspective preferences within the global space in which cultural tastes and practices are distributed. First, it is again worth noting the weak representation of preferences for heritage, both in terms of tastes and practices reported and of their professional extensions. Under 10 per cent of applicants have tastes that may be referred to as 'heritage-oriented' or 'classical': either they report being exclusively interested in heritage in the stricter sense (historical monuments, archeology), or they express a preference for works of the classical repertoire (for instance in music) without also mentioning more contemporary forms. As a sector of activity, heritage clearly belongs in the nebulous world of cultural management, but it also has its own training programmes (such as the *École du Louvre* and the *Institut national du patrimoine* [National heritage institute]) and channels of recruitment (the open competitions or *concours* for curatorial positions). Unlike students looking to work in the performing arts, for which there are no equivalent programmes or recruitment paths, these heritage-oriented students are seldom found in multi-skill cultural management programmes.

Also noticeable is the under-representation of lowbrow tastes. While these tastes are represented, they are rarely mentioned exclusively (only for 6.5 per cent of respondents). Cross-analysis of tastes and distastes provides us with more detailed data.[2] Only 1.4 per cent of applicants fit the strict definition of a lowbrow set of references – i.e. they report having tastes situated exclusively in the lower levels of the cultural hierarchy, sometimes mentioning a single genre ('rap music'), more often several ('RnB, pop music, musicals, breakdance', 'vampire movies, Ancient Egypt, American TV shows, sci-fi novels, brass bands') while also expressing their distaste of more established genres (including opera, classical music, contemporary dance and art). If we consider individuals with lowbrow tastes and varied distastes the proportion increases but remains very small (3.5 per cent).

This allegiance to a lowbrow cultural world is made by a broad range of individuals, from those who believe themselves to be culturally incompetent ('I don't have the codes'), to others making attempts at counter-cultural inversion (using underground culture's ability to assimilate varied registers) or yet others pursuing strategies of cultural progression (i.e. starting with manga to end up getting into Molière). Three individuals in our sample illustrate those cases. François, born in 1985, has a distant relationship with highbrow culture, whose ambivalence arguably relates to his social background (his father was a plumber and his mother a librarian). After a bachelor's in geography and a second-year master's in history, he enrolled in a master's in cultural management, where he was studying at the time of our interview. François never goes to the theatre, preferring 'festive' nights out, particularly in the small provincial town where he grew up. He only visits museums during tourist trips. 'I go there to look [he smiles]. I don't have the codes to understand'. While contemporary art makes him 'feel nothing', he admires street artists. Yet he does report affinities with more legitimate forms of culture, including cinema, whose role in possible cultural shifts has been well documented

(Duval 2015). He has only recently developed an interest in art-house cinema; in particular his interest in Ken Loach's films reflects his 'social' and 'critical' sensibilities. This introduction through politics to a cultural world enjoying more recognition than the one he was familiar with then led him to enjoy the work of directors who combine critical and public success (Von Trier, Fellini…). Sofiane, on the other hand, has much lower social origins (father railway worker, stay-at-home mother) and comes from a family of North African immigrants. He applied unsuccessfully to a cultural master's programme. He strongly criticizes 'square' conceptions of culture that exclude the most popular genres – and exclude him. 'I get the sense that today, you have ONE definition of culture and that's it. I think that's completely wrong […] I for one know that I have this culture of manga [but] nobody knows that France is a great manga country. People underestimate that culture, even though if you were to talk of culture in terms of numbers instead of classicism, it's way bigger'. Drawing general observations from his personal experience, he refers to his disheartening exposure to the classics to advocate a cultural strategy that begins with 'what people like'.

> You know, you get this kid to come over, to interest him in reading a manga, to bring him to come to the library, well then you'll be able to show him some Molière, to show him that there are parallels in stories, in tales. Start with what people like and then you bring them to the works of reference, instead of trying to cram Molière into an eleven-year-old kid's head. Really, that's terrible! I remember seeing *Scapin* [by Molière] when I was 11, and I got nothing out of it! […] I was really into reading sci-fi. Then I moved on to Barjavel, and then I read some Boris Vian. When they speak to dead people, it's not necessarily very real, and then I read some Nietzsche… it opened some doors for me. And now I get the sense that they're trying to do the opposite, they're trying to force people to get from there to here. Not to build bridges between the two, between what people like and what they're being taught. That's my little plan for the future, you'll see when I'm President I'll change all of that [he laughs].

Marion, born in 1987, has higher social origins and benefited from more cultural socialization through her family. She was brought up mostly by her mother, a schoolteacher; her father, who worked in advertising, died young. After a literary *baccalauréat*, she did a bachelor's in modern literature in a provincial university, a first-year master's in modern literature abroad, and finally another first-year master's in communication in Paris. She was a student in a cultural management master's programme at the time of the interview. Even down to her physical appearance (body piercings, tattoos), she asserts the tastes she inherited from a 'very rock'n'roll' mother and indirectly from her father, an 'early punk'.

Her own history with culture has quickly led her to consider – in more assertive and documented fashion than Sofiane (among other things she makes references to cultural studies and Michel de Certeau) – that one gets a richer cultural experience by starting from popular or 'underground' cultural forms rather than by adopting what she considers to be a closed-minded, legitimist view of culture.

I did a little bit of theatre, in clubs, in the village when I was in a high school. I took theatre as an optional course too [...] but we did only Beckett the whole year, and... it didn't work out for me, no way! Well, I really didn't get into it so... eventually I gave up on the course. [...] I'm crazy, crazy about music, well I love music, going to shows, I'm always up to discover new stuff. I binge on music. [...] I get the sense that the guardians of highbrow culture have trouble factoring popular culture in their view of culture, and on the other hand, those who are a little bit hipper, kind of underground, subversive, and all that... they have no problem saying that, yeah, a Picasso painting is culture, right. I get the sense that it only goes one way, right.

Despite the diversity of individuals belonging to a lowbrow cultural world, they remain largely in the minority. This might seem surprising considering that due to the applicants' young age they could be influenced by a 'youth' culture partly associated with a low level of legitimacy (which partly applies to popular music). Yet it makes more sense if we take into account their social background and their generally high levels of cultural capital. These features do not entirely neutralize the effect of age, but they drive the applicants away from the most lowbrow genres and towards recent forms in the process of gaining legitimacy or mixed interests – or in some cases the culture promoted at school. The low representation of individuals favouring mostly popular and lowbrow cultural forms also matches the definition of cultural management as a sector of professional activity, which distinguishes itself as superior to the most commercial cultural production and to the semi- or infra-cultural community activities (*animation socioculturelle*). It is likely that the applicants have internalized this distinction; either because it fits their pre-existing dispositions, or because they adjust their answers accordingly.

For the most part the cultural universe of applicants to cultural management master's programmes is bound by classical and heritage-oriented forms of culture on the one hand and popular or commercial culture on the other. Most individuals are concentrated between the centre, the upper parts (contemporary creation) and the left (intense practices) of the factorial space, and share a relationship to culture that combines forms of cultural legitimism and eclecticism in seemingly contradictory fashion.

Over a third of respondents have legitimist profiles – the most frequent, ahead of middlebrow profiles (a quarter) or those combining several levels of legitimacy (a little under a third). This legitimism can also be observed in the negative, as the most popular genres make up a majority of the distastes reported.[3] This legitimism is however moderate, or, like the Bach clavier piece that might illustrate it, 'well-tempered'. It is essentially characterized by the preference for widely recognized cultural forms, i.e. also ones that are widely known, and reflects somewhat conventional tastes more than a predilection for genres and artworks that are distinctive through their rarity. Among the book titles mentioned, there is a great deal of standard school reading material, from older classics (Balzac) to (mostly) twentieth-century works (Marguerite Duras) alongside references of middlebrow and mainstream culture (Amélie Nothomb; Paolo Coelho). Conversely, the cultural forms that applicants claim not to like are for the majority contemporary productions, popular or highbrow (55 per cent); under 4 per cent specifically assert their distance from classical references.[4] While respondents sometimes mention examples from former artistic avant-gardes that now enjoy recognition ('Japanese cinema', 'Russian avant-gardism'; the 'Dadaist and surrealist period'), references to a single field of limited production are rare. Additionally, there is a widely shared defiance towards artistic avant-gardes and contemporary art, expressed by individuals who move in circles where they are generally valued.

Jeanne studied art history and attended the *École du Louvre* but remains very wary of contemporary art and artistic avant-gardes in general. 'I have a hard time with all things contemporary art. The fact that the artist says it's contemporary art is enough to justify in itself the fact that his production is considered to be art. I find it really problematic, because I don't think putting a chair against a wall saying it is art… [she frowns] OK, so it's art and you accept it and you understand it, and you even buy it in the museums. […] And then you're forced to like it. That's what I call the *Télérama* [culture magazine] syndrome [she laughs]. *Télérama* will always [lavish praise on] a black-and-white super 8 Polish movie, and they will for sure if it's about lesbians. Well, I mean, it's not that a movie like that can't be interesting, but what I find exasperating is that position where everything that fits the image people have of the avant-garde is necessarily good.'

*Jeanne, born in 1985, parents psychologists, literary* baccalauréat, *bachelor's in art history and archaeology in a provincial university then* École du Louvre *and political science. She was studying a cultural master's programme at the time of our interview*

That Jeanne would mention *Télérama*, a widely circulated (over 600,000 copies per month) cultural weekly magazine that is a staple of the 'educated public', as an example of avant-gardist excess reflects this largely shared form of fairly conventional legitimism that ultimately reflects the middlebrow cultural model that characterizes roughly a quarter of the applicants. Yet, it is mostly by relating this legitimism to the eclecticism that attenuates it that we may fully understand it. Amounting to nearly a third of the applicants, the profiles combining several levels of legitimacy are nearly as frequent as the strictly legitimist profiles. Their cultural openness is further exemplified by the fact that applicants mention a fairly high number of preferred genres (five on average) and that over a quarter of them do not report disliking a single genre. Openness and eclecticism are clearly emphasized in questionnaire responses, which read 'all kinds of cultural activities', 'music (all genres except reggae and '"violent" metal' or describe a particularly broad range of tastes: 'modern art, all kinds of cinema (from US action movies to art-house films), discovering other cultures' rituals, traditions and myths, food from other continents, Indian dance and salsa, the great French classics'. Additionally, numerous respondents explicitly mention that they do not rule out any genre from their possible tastes and interests, or make comments on the question to that effect.

> That's a funny question. There is no cultural genre in particular that I don't like all (well, maybe videogames if we're talking about cultural practices).

> I cannot answer this question, I have very eclectic tastes and I'm interested in everything.

> I'm open to virtually everything maybe except for some contemporary music composers.

> There are no cultural genres that I don't like at all, I simply have less affinity and interest in Japanese and Chinese cinema.

> There's no cultural genre that I hate on principle, maybe I find it a little bit hard to appreciate metal music.

> Beyond the anthropological or sociological interest in all forms of cultural expression, I'm quite impervious to Celtic music, military action movies and reality shows.

That applicants being open to a wide array of genres doesn't mean that no distinctions are made between levels of legitimacy. Their forays into genres enjoying less legitimacy never extend beyond the boundaries of a certain definition of 'good taste', which for instance excludes 'blockbusters and action movies, pop, RnB'. Specific genres, such as metal and rap, which are known to be enjoyed by individuals with less educational capital and cultural openness (Bryson 1996), are very often mentioned as examples of distastes, despite the applicants' young age and the degree of recognition enjoyed by these musical genres. It would be an oversimplification to see in this mix of eclecticism and legitimism the confirmation of the rise of the cultural 'omnivores' among the more educated classes: the integration of lowbrow genres into the space of what is culturally thinkable and utterable for applicants remains selective, and does not amount to the disappearance of genre boundaries and levels of legitimacy. As Philippe Coulangeon points out, having eclectic tastes, when it takes the form of a selective foray into domains far removed from the canonical definition of cultural legitimacy, reflects a particular form of aesthetic refinement which, ultimately, is probably hardly less distinctive than exclusively dealing with highbrow culture (Coulangeon 2013).

In addition to being an elaborate distinction strategy, the combination of legitimism and eclecticism should also be read as an effect of the internalization and/or projection of the standards of the professional world of which they aspire to be a part. These standards precisely include the cultural 'quality' that cultural managers are supposed to safeguard. At the same time they are also increasingly asked to promote 'openness', especially since the 1980s, as the diversification of cultural offerings has become an objective of cultural policy (Dubois 2012a: 393ff.). Rather than the hypothetical generalization of a 'regime of cultural justice' making illegitimate any form of hierarchizing of cultural values (Glevarec 2005), the introduction of a (relative) relativism in the relationship to culture expressed by applicants is also a way for them to comply with the ethos of the professional world they seek to enter. Sometimes this merely consists of parroting the official line on cultural openness in order to avoid being perceived as excessively elitist. This is the case of one female applicant whose smart, conservative attire and linguistic hypercorrection indicated her upper-class background. She appears at a selection interview for a cultural master's programme after having studied museology and history, and then research in art history at the *École du Louvre*: 'People [living in the projects] are far from idiots. You shouldn't have an elitist view, you have to be able to see their culture as well'.[5] This display of conformity does not preclude the political or moral promotion of cultural diversity or the individual emphasis on curiosity as a personal quality, which is precisely at work in the cultural world. The three levels – professional, political/moral and personal – have a mutually reinforcing effect, creating dispositions for a degree of openness to different cultural registers. Because they combine these three factors, aspirants to cultural occupations are particularly good illustrations of the thesis of an 'ostentatious openness to diversity' (Fridman and Ollivier 2004), not because this openness has now become a shared value, but because it matches social and professional aspirations.

In addition to being a professional standard and an attitude reflecting social and political dispositions, cultural openness also meets a practical imperative of placement for applicants. As I noted in the analysis of their professional aspirations (see p. XXX), in a weakly formalized and highly competitive professional world, they need to keep their options as open as possible. At odds with the specialist's or the fan's exclusive restriction to a specific genre or niche, having a wide diversity of interests and knowledge is thought to increase one's chances of fitting into more varied cultural domains offering more opportunities.[6]

Geared towards contemporary creation rather than the classical repertoire or heritage – although it does not entirely overlook the latter –the range of tastes and possible orientations of future cultural managers cover a very wide spectrum, only excluding the most strictly commercial cultural forms, which are explicitly rejected by the majority of the applicants, and popular forms – either folkloric or rooted in rural or working-class traditions – which are only exceptionally mentioned (Dubois, Méon and Pierru 2013: 17–22). Their relationships to culture range from elite conservatism to underground radicalism. However, a majority of them tend to occupy an in-between space, preferring a genre without ruling out others, favouring established cultural forms but making forays into the avant-garde or popular culture; like the mediators they aspire to become, they combine strategies that might appear opposed, such as legitimism and populism, but are in practice often mixed (Passeron 2013). As with the posture of openness that they embody, which reflects a mix of personal dispositions, professional strategies and moral attitudes, this cultural compromise is part of a broader relationship to the social world that reconciles individual success and belief in collective values and combines anti-conformism with adjustment to the status quo.

## Reinventing the artist's life

In the second half of the nineteenth century, the 'invention of the artist's life' established a connection, in a state of social weightlessness, between the selective inheritance of upper-class properties and the constitution of a social identity constructed as a rejection of the bourgeois condition (Bourdieu 1987b). The investment in positions such as those of cultural management operates as a contemporary form of reinvention of the artist's life, readjusted in function of the distribution of educational capital and of the state of the labour market, which currently determine the meaning and the objective opportunities of the placement of children from the educated middle and upper classes. This reinvented artist's life is rationalized, as it is exempted from the radical uncertainty of artistic careers and complies with logistical, organizational and economical imperatives. Those who pursue it may therefore envision work with an outlook that is both realistic (in the sense that they target a 'serious job') and enchanted (as the job may be fulfilling). Because they include dispositions for 'artistic critique' in the practical organization of labour, these trajectories are among the social foundations of 'new spirit of capitalism' (Boltanski and Chiapello 2005). The individuals who follow them tend to approach politics differently, outside of established forms, which relates to professional positions that are likewise defined by their distance from the well-worn paths of conventional occupations and activity sectors.

### Re-enchanting work

In the 1970s, the gap between the students' aspirations and their opportunities, due to educational inflation, resulted in a sense of collective disillusionment towards work, then made possible by a context in which access to employment was not a real problem (Bourdieu 1978, 1984). Both this gap and the sense of disillusionment it elicited contributed to the rise of post-1968 critiques arguing that work made it impossible to achieve the ideal of self-fulfillment they defended (Baudelot and Gollac 2003; Boltanski and Chiapello 2005). This gap is now even wider, due to the combination of the further massification of higher education after the mid-1980s and the sharp deterioration of the job market – particularly for newcomers. However, I argue that at least under certain conditions, this gap is now less a motive for refusing to work or criticizing it collectively, but is rather increasingly experienced as a prompt to achieve self-fulfillment through work or even thanks to work.

The population under study here illustrates this hypothesis well. Jobs in the artistic and cultural sectors are usually considered as ideals of satisfaction at work (Baudelot and Gollac 2003: 146, 162; Menger 2003: 52–3), in the sense that they allow rewards in multiple forms, whose diversity and combinations are not limited to the binary opposition between monetary and symbolic gratifications (Bense Ferreira Alves and Leblanc 2013). When considering aspiring cultural managers, it is therefore less important to define the amount of these rewards, the way they use them or their disillusions towards them (Sinigaglia 2011a) than to investigate their belief in the potency of rewards, which make them more likely to meet social expectations pertaining to self-fulfillment in and through their work. I have already in part shown the extent of this belief in my discussion of the narratives of vocation, with the central role played by the language of passion and self-fulfillment. As I noted earlier, this form of personalization relates to a collective standard in force in the professional world that they aspire to enter. More broadly, it also reflects a relationship to work in which the boundaries between personal and professional life become blurred. This is likely the result of the increasing replacement of the 'work ethic' defined by Max Weber as a constitutive feature of the development of capitalism (Weber 2002) by the blend of the personal and the professional that characterizes its contemporary forms (Boltanski and Chiapello 2005). More precisely, this relationship to work is specific to individuals whose characteristics (a majority of women with rather high social backgrounds, high cultural capital and few secure prospects for the future) lead them to see this blurring of the lines between the personal and the professional as desirable, and to find in cultural sector jobs a way to achieve it and extend the indetermination of their youth. It is in this light that the frequent statements in which professional career choices are presented as a direct extension of personal life and identity should be understood: 'My goal is to transform my personal desires and interests into a professional career plan',[7] 'I tell myself that [culture] is the work sector where I'll be most able to be myself'.[8]

Because they want to 'be themselves' at work and look for a job that 'fits them', applicants express expectations for their professional career that mirror their self-described dispositions and/or qualities. Those who claim to have soft skills, which are generally associated with feminine dispositions and high levels of cultural capital, emphasize the quality of human relationships and interactions at work (teamwork, atmosphere). Those who have internalized values of autonomy and initiative, and present them as personal qualities, are eager to have freedom in the way they organize their work and independence in their choices (many want, for instance, to be able to develop their own projects or to put together the programme of a festival or venue themselves).[9] As they possess two types of cultural capital (through their family and their studies), they are inclined to keep accumulating knowledge after completing their education. They use their adaptability and versatility to develop skills expected in future professional experiences. Dispositions toward openness, particularly regarding culture, translate into a search for new horizons that is held up as an objective in their future career. While finer analysis would be necessary in order to show how the respective work-related expectations are weighted according to individual characteristics, the above constitutes the shared basis of the applicants' relationships to work. Below, Clarisse combines these features in a virtually ideal-typical manner:

Born in 1987, Clarisse is the daughter of a couple of marketing executives; her mother previously worked as a lawyer. She was a good student: after graduating high school (literary *baccalauréat*), she was accepted into a literary *classe préparatoire*, then studied in a regional Institute of Political Studies before being admitted into a highly selective cultural master's programme. Right after her master's, she was offered a one-year work contract in an international co-operation organization, where she manages a youth cultural education programme. During the interview, she uses her current work experience as the basis for describing her expectations toward the professional career she has just started. There are conditions that you can't measure financially that suit me [very well]. From a purely relational point of view, you know, when you go to work everyday and you feel good in a team where there's a good atmosphere, well, it changes a lot of things. I'm very happy, especially with the people with whom I'm in touch for my job. Time-wise, we organize our week sort of as we want to, as long as we put in the hours. So because of all these factors that have no direct connection to money, I like it [...]. It's the participative aspect of it, you see, developing your personality, and while you're at it discovering new horizons, be they artistic or cultural [...], from the intercultural point of view, discovering, say, a new culture or a new country, a new language, other people coming from different horizons [...]. It's about expanding your skills, your knowledge and your sensibility through artistic fields, through themes, you think about identity, you think about what difference is [...] You discover your own skills and you also think globally with other people, other cultures. It's this combination of knowledge, skills, reflection, discovery of the other and self-discovery [that] I actually find super rewarding.

*Interview*

These projections are not as naïve or utopic as they may seem: they are associated with realistic, far less positive perspectives regarding employment conditions. This association can be the consequence of 'values' (such as wariness of material success) or of the preference towards a 'cluster of non-monetary gratifications – psychological and social gratifications, appealing working conditions, few routine tasks, etc. – [which] makes it possible to compensate on the short- or long-term for the loss of income' (Menger 2003: 52; see also Abbing 2002). It should, however, be related to the trajectories and dispositions on which adhesion to these values and the expression of this preference are based, and which also makes holding such occupations an elective choice. It is also necessary to consider the logic behind the anticipations of the types of gratification that can be expected in these jobs. In this perspective, this relationship to work of aspiring cultural managers, combining high expectations in terms of self-fulfillment and low expectations in terms of wage and employment conditions can be understood as the product of personal social characteristics and histories (including gender, social background and education), which together constitute the basis of career choices in the cultural sector and the lack of concern for material considerations. It also operates as a form of rationalization of this 'choice', which to some extent consists of accepting the likelihood of precarity, as if to make a virtue of necessity or to persuade others (and/or themselves) that they have picked a path they are entirely comfortable with.

Applicants expect to be paid relatively little, including several years into their career: 1,500€ a month on average upon graduating, which is a rather high assessment, but under 2,200€ after five years, which attests to the acceptance of relatively low salaries over the long term.[10] François, who hopes to 'be himself' in the cultural sector, illustrates this acceptance: 'You're not going to make 3,000€ a month working in culture'.[11] As Emma Pollard shows in the case of creative students in the UK, graduates even consider accepting unpaid work 'to establish a foothold' on the job market (Pollard 2013: 55–6).

Beyond money, applicants are often aware of the difficulty in finding a job and of precarity in the sector.

'There are few jobs', says François, 'and most of them are in Paris. A lot of them are badly paid, many are subsidized contracts, so you have to fit the criteria for subsidized contracts. There are many part-time jobs. So you really have to have an idea of the sector.' Catherine also emphasizes the need to be realistic. 'There's a lot of competition [she laughs]! There are very few positions and many applicants. [...] If you take a similar position in finance or things like that, in culture the pay will always be less, even with five years of higher education. Right now I'm expecting to start on minimum wage, you know? When you're in culture you don't expect to make huge amounts of money. I do hope to make a good

living, but I'm not fooling myself about the pay. [...] I think it's difficult to be too demanding, I can't say "if I don't have a raise in six months I'm out of here", because then they'll just tell me "well, that's no problem, there are ten other people waiting for your job"'
*Catherine, woman born in 1985, father house painter, mother cashier, literary* baccalauréat, *bachelor's in art history then cultural master's*

The flipside of this enchanted relationship to work consists in accepting the prospect of under-employment and at least temporary precarity. Precarious or part-time contracts are the lot of young graduates in many sectors (on the media, see Marchetti 2012: 151ff.); they must cope with them insofar as these employment conditions have become the norm for newcomers in the job market. However, the prospect of having a less than decent job, which is often the case in the cultural sector (see Chapter 1), does not stop after the first few years. While the existence of a form of close-knit community between the educated often attenuates the painful character of the subjective experience of unemployment or precariousness disguised as bohemia (Rambach 2001: 219–21), the fact remains that the extension of the indeterminate time of youth and fulfillment in work come at the cost of often long-term uncertainty, which becomes less acceptable with time. [12]

The acceptance of poor employment conditions takes a variety of forms according to the applicants' backgrounds. For young women whose families are well-endowed with economic capital and who may count on their partner to meet their financial needs, which frees them from the constraint of finding a well-paid job, this consists in emancipation from financial concerns, as in the case of Deirdre: 'If I don't find something that pays well, that's okay, I'm kind of free since my boyfriend works in a bank'.[13] Those with a working-class or lower middle-class background, used to more modest living standards, have low expectations in terms of pay for different reasons but also have a less relaxed relationship to money (as they face more of an incentive to 'make the most' of their studies). Not considering the pay as a priority can in their case be understood in relation to the educational and social distance they have covered, which can in itself be an unexpected personal success – this applies for example to a cashier's daughter who was admitted into a cultural master's programme, had several experiences in prestigious institutions, and now competes with 'girls who studied in Sciences Po'.[14]

This blend of realist enchantment and of non-resigned acceptance may thus reflect varied reasons and translate into varied ways. In any case, it characterizes the prevailing relationship to work of cultural managers, which is part of a broader relationship to the social world that combines critical dispositions and adjustment to the social order.

*The new spirit of capitalism embodied*

The encounter between art and management is without fail an opportunity to reformulate the 'artistic critique', which refuses economic rationalization in the name of the specificity of art (Chiapello 1998). Yet it also introduces references to artistic creation in new principles of economic organization, so that 'artistic critique' has become part of the modes of justification of this renewed capitalism. Cultural management and by extension the current forms of economic and administrative organization of culture are in this sense vehicles of the 'new spirit of capitalism' (Boltanski and Chiapello 2005). So are the inclusion of activities that are specific to the artistic field in the 'creative industries' and the now ubiquitous reference to 'creative economy', defined through the role played by innovation, knowledge, creativity and ideas as factors of growth (see Bouquillion 2012 for a comprehensive critical synthesis, and Garnham 2005 on the British case).

Some of the values defining the 'new spirit of capitalism', including self-reliance, creativity, mobility or the search for inter-personal contacts, structure the dispositions and aspirations of those who pursue careers in cultural management. The concepts of 'project' and 'network', which are central to neo-capitalism, have for a long time structured the discourse, the references and the organization of cultural activities. They feature in the names of professional positions and training programmes on 'project management'. There have been innumerable calls, particularly at the European level, for 'networking', which is purported to better meet the 'actors' needs' than the institutions in a 'constantly changing' world.[15]

Where Boltanski and Chiapello lay emphasis primarily on these values and how they relate to critique based on the contents of the managerial literature, I adopt a different perspective focusing on the social features that may be conducive to supporting these values and critical principles, by conducting a sociological analysis of the agents associated with them. Aspiring cultural managers are a case in point, because artistic critique is part and parcel of their strategy to enter and adjust to the world of work and the social and economic order at large. I argue that they are among the groups that embody the new spirit of capitalism, due to their trajectories and the related ways of being, thinking and acting, but also *through* these trajectories themselves. The aspiring cultural managers adopt a critical posture towards the economic system in place, if only through the lesser value they assign to material wealth as evidenced by their career choice. Yet, at the same time, they partake in the posture of 'realism', reasserting that even culture must be funded and managed. They combine a critique of the capitalistic rationales of trade and profit and the appropriation – if only partial and distanced – of marketing and management techniques.

The adoption of a distanced approach to the imperatives of financial profit, in some cases leading to the development of a 'reverse economy' pitting economic success against artistic success, constitutes the *nomos* that historically defined the cultural field as a specific social space with its own principles (Bourdieu 1996a). The schemes of perception of those who aspire to secure a position in the field, including in functions of mediation and management, remain influenced by this founding principle, or at least refer to it. In spite of transformations in the economy of the cultural field (such as the growing weight of large corporations and financial rationales in publishing – see Reynaud 1999), and in spite of several decades of policies promoting the 'reconciliation of economy and culture' and more recently 'economic development through culture' (Matz 2012), the refusal to consider culture under the sole angle of economic profit remains a structuring element in the applicants' representations and projections. 'I don't see myself working in a world where money is the name of the game, so not in the corporate music business', is a fairly typical statement, made by an applicant who wishes to work in music and organize film screenings with live music.[16] The rejection of the imperative of profit is made possible by the public funding of culture in France. This explains why students tend to favour the subsidized cultural sector over the cultural industries. Other economic and policy settings certainly discourage such attitudes. In the British case, students in the creative sector 'are produced and produce themselves as neoliberal subjects', internalize the necessity of 'employability' and adjustment to the job market, which does not predispose to critical attitudes towards capitalist economy (Allen, Quinn, Hollingworth and Rose 2013). Cuts in public budgets for culture and the promotion of the 'entrepreneurial' cultural worker as a model in Europe, through policy recommendations and renewed training programmes are factors in the decline of critical attitudes towards a money-driven socio-economic system.

This ongoing process is also observable in France, where it leads to new compromises. Private sponsoring, for instance, a symbol of the selflessness of the 'corporate citizen' (Rozier 2001), is seen in an increasingly positive light by the applicants, both because public funding is stagnant or decreasing and, because like public funding, it is a means to at least appear to break from a purely profit-oriented logic. Marketing techniques are for their part increasingly accepted because they are used for purposes of improving attendance and building audience loyalty in structures that have no commercial vocation – they serve as heteronomous means for autonomous ends (the 'cause of culture', 'broadening the audience').

The distance towards the market economy varies in form and intensity, from the simple reluctance to numbers inherited from a literary training to a politically constructed discourse inspired by experience of activism. Overall, however, few would-be cultural managers express a radical opposition to profit-oriented economic rationales, the likes of which are popular in critical independent publishing, where it is directly combined with a political engagement (Noël 2012a: 262–9, 2012b). For instance, during her interview, Jeanne makes lengthy statements criticizing the way in which 'society in general is more and more governed by economics […] and the market value has become the leading value', but then she goes on to explain in very pragmatic terms that she expects her master's programme to provide her with 'practical, accounting, legal and HR management skills'.[17] Students may decry marketing classes for not paying heed to the 'specificities of culture', but then again they also explain that they come to learn 'techniques' and 'operational' skills that will make them directly 'employable' (which include marketing). It appears that for them, although they do not entirely disown their anti-economist stances, the conversion of personal 'passions' into professional perspectives requires the inclusion of principles and techniques imported from the worlds of management and trade to their set of references and skills. An applicant with a 'passion for cinema and the performing arts' who 'wanted to make a living out of [her] passion' explains: 'Initially, I was reluctant about all the aspects pertaining to numbers, management, administration, because I had a more literary background. And then I progressively took an interest in that. I told myself I could also work in that field, but with a different approach'.[18] They develop a relationship to economics that functions as a relationship to useful, serious things, liable to lend credibility to a career plan and to help them project themselves as professionals. The tension between the rejection of the market economy related to the choice of a cultural career and the importation of economic management techniques is crystallized in these practical conversions to practical skills. Beyond the dialectics of critique and responses to this critique, these conversions – albeit often painful and incomplete – are the locus for the incorporation of the 'new spirit of capitalism' through the development of social dispositions whereby the importation of the 'artist critique' in the economic organization is the very thing that underpins support to this organization.

Master's programmes in cultural management contribute to such conversions. This is sometimes an explicit goal, as in a book reflecting on teaching methods in arts management in the US, entitled *Disciplining the Arts: Teaching Entrepreneurship* (Beckman 2010). Beyond teaching contents and methods, in a less straightforward way, these master programmes bring together students with backgrounds in art who have come to acquire the tools of managerial rationality, and others with more generalist or managerial backgrounds who are interested in culture. We would need to know about the encounter between these students from different backgrounds and their associated habitus in more detail and, more broadly, to show how this conversion works in practice (Abraham 2007). There may be exceptions, but overall this does not translate into an opposition between the two groups divided into separate factions; conversely, it results in a mutual learning process, a form of anticipation of future professional relationships (where tensions may of course still arise). Training also provides an opportunity for students to expand their 'network', make individual contacts and enjoy the group dynamic – it is a time of adjustment between artistic/cultural rationales and economic/organizational ones, and a space of socialization where the cultural managers, who are 'dual beings' like the art dealers studied by Bourdieu, acquire and consolidate their hybrid dispositions (Bourdieu 1996a).

More broadly, these programmes can be seen as a means to accommodate the tension between utilitarianism and selflessness that characterizes both the applicants' trajectories and the higher education system, between professionalization and finding a job quickly as the sole finality and 'studying for studying's sake' with (provisionally) no concern for necessity. Without reproducing the old models of student bohemia or studying for the sake of it, they nuance the utilitarianism that now prevails in higher education by combining a professional finality (ultimately, they prepare students for jobs), the interest for the domain under study and a degree of distance from the strictly material criteria of success, in particular in terms of salary levels upon graduating, with more emphasis on self-fulfillment and on carrying out personal projects. In the process they offer a compromise in the 'conflict of the faculties', which pits a critical conception of knowledge as universal and research-oriented against a pragmatic and applied approach, closer to secular, economic and political powers (Bourdieu 1990: 36ff.; Le Gall and Soulié 2009). This compromise is also a factor in the emergence or reinforcement of dispositions combining critique and economic necessity among students. Again, this compromise may be challenged by the ongoing promotion of an entrepreneurial market-driven model, which could lead to the decline of critique, and a more straightforward imposition of economic necessity.

### A different form of political awareness

In their own way, the future cultural managers reinvent the artist's life by envisioning work under the angle of self-fulfillment and creativity and by promoting a definition of the economy that includes them through a realistic adjustment of the artist critique. In doing so they are also reinventing a form of 'artistic' relationship to politics. This relationship does not fit the usual patterns of the artist's engagement; in keeping with their broader relationship to the social world, it combines anti-conformism and individual strategies of adjustment to the social order.

Political preferences are far from homogeneous among the applicants, but many lean towards various strands of the left. However, just as their educational investment comes with a critique of educational institutions and as their search for 'management tools' is combined with a critique of purely managerial views, the politicization of the applicants is nuanced by their distancing from established political forms. Unsurprisingly, very few of them are members of political organizations: a little over 3 per cent report having been a member of one of them during the five previous years. It is unfortunately impossible to relate this proportion to the share of political activists in the population at large, or among the same age group, but it is very likely higher. If only due to their level of educational attainment, of the high social backgrounds of the majority and of their frequent experience in humanities courses that are more conducive to political socialization than other disciplines (Michon 2008), they are probably less de-politicized than most individuals of their age.

While applicants may readily express defiance towards political parties, they are not necessarily uninterested in politics; rather, they tend to envision politics outside of the institutionalized structures. This political posture is associated with a closeness to the artistic field, which may lead some of the applicants to reproduce repertoires used by artists to intervene in politics (Balasinski and Mathieu 2006; Roussel 2010). In such cases they are doing politics by proxy, so to speak, by organizing events (festivals, concerts, exhibits…) that blend arts and politics and giving artists a platform to express themselves politically instead of speaking out themselves. Some may however organize cultural events of this kind as a direct extension of their political engagement – this applies for instance to Marion, a feminist activist:

I'd like to try to set up a kind of festival, not necessarily a festival, but a place for... a place of creation for, hmm... for women artists, because it's difficult, and I thought maybe – it seems a bit remote, I guess – but a festival of erotic and pornographic films for women, 'cause male pornography is just unbearable, in my opinion anyway, so the idea was to give women a chance to speak, because in general they're objects of sexuality, and it's about letting them have their say, so the idea would be to create... yeah, maybe a festival, or a space for creation or diffusion....

*Marion, born in 1987, mother schoolteacher, studied modern*
*literature then communication, studying in a master's*
*programme in cultural management at the time of the interview*

Such projects fit within the much more mixed register of 'doing politics differently', which more broadly attracts individuals who share similar social, cultural and age characteristics (CURAPP 1998; Arnaud and Guionnet 2005; Agrikoliansky 2005). This involves at least operating outside of established organizations, partially doing away with the professionalization of political activities and its most institutionalized forms (such as electoral competition), promoting other forms of organization (networks, associations, weakly hierarchized structures) and other practices (forums, grassroots work) as well as addressing themes often neglected by professionals of politics and parties (Collovald 2001). The 'artistic critique' then applies to the functioning of the political field, valuing flexibility in contrast with bureaucratic structures and group participation in contrast with authority. This register is neither new nor specific to the generation of the applicants, having developed in the late 1960s (Hatzfeld 2005). Yet now its meaning differs from the one it had for the generations that initially promoted it, due to the succession of political transformations that occurred after May 1968[19] and to the historical developments of its components and various phases.[20]

What is worth noting – even though it may not be an entirely new development – is that this relationship to politics, from its most committed and strongly anti-institutional variant (libertarian activism) to the more common version, which is more detached and alternates with a greater conventional register (intermittent voting), directly relates to individual projections. The interaction between political engagement and professional activity has been documented in the case of artists.[21] Here, I wish to emphasize the affinities that develop between professional career choices and political leanings. Radical left artists exemplify this, in the same way as the members of the 'new petite bourgeoisie' of the 1960s and 1970s tend to favour positions in the social and cultural sectors: they may no longer be new, but they remain at least partially compatible with their political ethos (Luck 2010). Professional choices are probably very rarely over-determined by political leanings; rather, a range of personal characteristics (social background, structure of the capitals possessed, social trajectory) determines both political and professional orientations (Bourdieu 1984). As the current state of French politics is probably less conducive to forms of identification based on political affiliation than for previous generations, and as the state of the labour market causes much uncertainty regarding the future of the new entrants, it makes sense than the connection between political and professional choices consists not so much of a strictly political choice of occupation, but rather in a way of perceiving politics that is influenced by career projections. When they broach political subjects, the applicants do so in a thematic manner, which often very directly relates to a possible professional horizon. While, like their elders, they have a preference for doing politics 'differently', it does not so much reflect a collective utopia as the search for a career that could allow them to repurpose political dispositions.

By way of an example, Ariane (born in 1986), is the daughter of a blue-collar worker (who was himself the son of a Communist worker) and of a social worker, whose parents were both very 'secular republican' schoolteachers. She does not describe her own parents as strongly politicized, but claims to be 'addicted to politics' herself. She is passionate about political debates, and while she is not a member, says she 'might be closer to the PS [Parti Socialiste]'. Because she was 'always divided between the world of culture and the world of politics', she decided to pursue a career in the implementation of local cultural policies. Having been denied admission to the cultural management master's programme that would have prepared her for this career, she now targets jobs in local development – more precisely participatory democracy – which is another way for her to combine politics and work. François was born in 1985 to a plumber father and a librarian mother. Although like Ariane he was involved in the social movements that occurred since he began his studies, he now expresses doubts about the 'effectiveness of demonstrations'. If he were to get politically involved again, 'it would be more in alternative things, 'because political parties, well...'. However, this is currently not an issue, as he is now pursuing 'this personal, individualist thing'. He once thought about working in sustainable development, but now dismisses it because it 'still follows a capitalist logic', and is instead interested in 'degrowth, non-consumption, all that stuff'. He came to culture through cinema and music 'with a social vocation' (hip-hop and punk). His shift towards culture remains hesitant: his plans are still foggy and he hasn't given up on the idea of working in humanitarian aid, a way of 'doing politics differently' (Dauvin and Siméant 2002), combining activism and the search for professional salvation.

This could also give us some insight into the reference to 'cultural democratization' that is very frequently made by applicants to explain their choice of cultural management. Historically constructed by artists and intellectuals as a means of doing politics against the established political representatives by 'going to the people', cultural democratization has become a job, or at least a professional reference, with the development of state cultural policies (Dubois 2012b). Making this reference today, as the future cultural managers do, means both conforming to a belief that, although it has been questioned, still structures the legitimation of these policies and of the positions and institutions associated with it (subsidized public cultural institutions and their staff), and giving a modicum of political meaning to a career choice that can be experienced as a 'mission'. This is also one of the ways in which these young graduates speak and think politically, and the vantage point from which they approach social inequalities, citizenship and the role of the state – generally with a legitimist institutional view of culture nuanced by eclecticism, more rarely extolling the virtues of 'cultural difference', radical self-management or counter-culture. Unlike their elders, who having often come to cultural action through political activism subsequently turned their political and cultural commitment into a job, the newcomers pursue professional integration strategies which, depending on the case, allow them to import and express previously shaped political dispositions, or, as most often happens, come with the appropriation of the political language used in the world in which they aspire to work.

## Notes

1  On the changing relations between these types of culture in students' tastes, see Grisprud Hovden and Moe 2011 on Norway.
2  After the question 'What cultural genres fit your personal tastes most?', the applicants were asked 'Conversely, what cultural genres do you not like at all?' For more detail on the construction of these cultural profiles, see the methodological appendix.
3  60 per cent, against 13 per cent of highbrow genres among those eliciting negative comments, 1 per cent of middlebrow genres and 26 per cent of responses referring to genres with varying levels of legitimacy.
4  Around 16 per cent make negative mentions of both classical and contemporary references; a quarter of respondents do not report disliking a single genre.
5  Observation VD8, woman born in 1988.
6  Such professional placement strategies contributed to broadening the subsidized cultural field in the early 1980s in France (Dubois 2012a: 399).
7  Observation VD8, woman born in 1988, master's in museology and history, then in art history at the École du Louvre.
8  François, born in 1985, father plumber, mother librarian, bachelor's in geography then second-year master's in history, studying in a cultural management master's programme at the time of the interview.
9  This can also be making a virtue out of necessity, when self-employment compensates for the lack of job offers. On self-employment among creative graduates in the UK, see Pollard 2013: 52–4.
10  The median monthly income in France was around 1,500€ in 2009, the year this research was conducted.
11  François, born in 1985, father plumber, mother librarian, bachelor's in geography then second-year master's in history, studying in a cultural management master's programme at the time of the interview.
12  This is a paradox of cultural occupations: while the satisfaction expected from them leads individuals to pursue them, and to accept – at least partly knowingly – often poor employment conditions, these poor conditions precisely often later spoil enjoyment of work (Hesmondhalgh and Baker 2010: 148–51, 157–8) and lead individuals to seek out jobs in other fields, outside of the cultural sector in which they had placed so many hopes (Sinigaglia 2014b).
13  Deirdre, woman born in 1985, father administrative executive, mother lawyer then high school teacher, scientific *baccalauréat*, studied art history in the USA.

14  Catherine, woman born in 1985, father house painter, mother cashier, literary *baccalauréat*, bachelor's in art history then cultural master's.

15  Among many similar examples, see *Networking culture – The role of European cultural networks*, Council of Europe, Strasbourg, 1999.

16  VL Observation 14, man born in 1989, studied economic and social administration in a provincial town.

17  Jeanne, born in 1985, parents psychologists, literary *baccalauréat*, bachelor's in art history and archaeology in a provincial university then École du Louvre and political science. She studied in a cultural master's programme at the time of our interview.

18  Observation VD1, woman born in 1986, *licence professionnelle* and first-year master's in performing arts.

19  To briefly name some of them: the rise and decline of leftist utopias, the reshufflings in the socialist party, the hopes and disillusions of the left in power, the decline of the Communist party, the success of neo-liberalism, alter-globalism, etc.

20  Leftism, counter-culture and neo-liberalism for the 'generation 68' studied by Mauger (Mauger 1994).

21  Olivier Roueff established that the affinity between musical and political radicalism partly reflected practices and organizational forms in which professional placement strategies played a part (Roueff 2001), whereas Jérémy Sinigaglia showed that the maintenance of professional exchange networks in the performing arts featured among the conditions favouring the mobilization of the *intermittents du spectacle*, and, in return, reinforced professionally useful relationships (Sinigaglia 2014a).

# Conclusion

Pursuing a career in cultural management can be a response to a wide range of demands that sometimes contradict each other. Applicants may seek to maintain a sense of their own freedom by investing personal dispositions into their career choice, thereby reinforcing the idea that they chose their own path. In some cases they try to soften the effects of downclassing or keep their aspirations of upward social mobility alive. They need to find a place in the labour market and social space with resources that are partly out of step with the most frequent and immediate requirements of economic and social life, like the graduates from literary disciplines whose knowledge has become 'useless'; they must also find a way not to disown the dispositions associated with this mismatch, such as bohemia and a propensity for critique, while meeting the conditions to fulfil the social and material necessity of having a job.

The indetermination of cultural occupations attracts individuals with varied social and educational trajectories, associated with strategies ranging from the realistic repurposing of artistic dispositions to the 'dream of social flight' of graduates who, having studied longer, have higher expectations but cannot meet the requirements necessary to fulfil them (Bourdieu 1984). This indetermination also allows for projections into the future that lay emphasis on trying and discovering new things. More prosaically, in lieu of the alternative between success and failure that characterizes access to the most established occupations, soft transitions between intermediary positions are conducive to downplaying precarity by being more rewarding; such forms of temporary half-success allow the holders of cultural occupations to keep hoping for greater successes to come.

Cultural occupations are also perceived to provide relief from the harshness of the social world by those who pursue them because of the multiple forms of gratification they allow. Putting aside monetary rewards, which are here second to other priorities, these include the social prestige conferred by the cultural world, meeting artists and journalists, having varied and often collective activities, seeing one's work yielding concrete and publically visible results, enjoying a degree of freedom in the organization of one's work, having the opportunity to leave one's personal mark, the perspective of continuing to learn, the moral satisfaction of helping out (the artists, the public) or to work for a common good (such as the creation and spreading of artworks). These multiple forms of gratification may be combined; crucially, they can also be compensated (meaning that achieving some of them can make up for lacking others), thereby allowing a projection into the future where it is always possible to hope for contentment in one's position, both in terms of work and in terms of one's place social space.

Whether these hopes are actually fulfilled, for whom and under what conditions, is an entirely different story, and one that warrants further research. By focusing on how careers in cultural management begin, I have largely left aside what follows logically and chronologically. The study of the individuals who invest in such careers and of what they invest in them could be fruitfully extended by analyzing the conditions for actually accessing these positions. In this study, we evidenced the combination of a strict social and educational selection beginning with the applications to specialized training programmes; it is likely that a similar selection is at work after the aspiring cultural managers graduate (Lafarge 2008). Instead of replacing the selection based on capitals pertaining to social and family background by a selection based on the diploma, which would allow the social openness of recruitments, the increasing requirement of a degree works as an additional filter. Indeed, as is observed elsewhere, there is every reason to think that educational capital (conferred by prestigious degrees) and social capital (by relations in cultural circles) are mostly accumulated by those who have the most to begin with, if only because of the effects of selection upon admission.

This drastic selection produces effects that suggest at least partly calling into question a purely economic vision in terms of the 'inflation of degrees' (Passeron 1982) and of inadequacy between labour supply and demand. The strong rise of cultural management training programmes may not constitute a response to a pre-established need for labour of corresponding scope, but the success enjoyed by these programmes has led to higher requirements for selection upon admission. Accordingly, graduates are strongly endowed in resources of all types, and often already introduced to the professional world in which they aspire to work. This explains why their employment rates are better than might be assumed in light of the 'overproduction' of graduates in a sector where few positions are available for the taking. Considering their resources and the characteristics of employment in the cultural sector, access to the first job is less of a problem than the employment conditions, the risk of under-employment and stabilization in employment. Having contributed to the professionalization of occupations in cultural management, the development of specialized training programmes may well conversely be a factor in the destabilization of employment in the sector by producing a highly invested labour force, often working as interns or under short-term contracts, blurring the boundaries between work and volunteering (Simonet 2010).

Further research could investigate the effects of these initial conditions and paths of access to employment on subjective relationships to work and its constraints (Bourdieu 1996b). Unlike the dilettantism observed by Bourdieu in the late 1960s, the enchanted relationship to labour of the aspiring cultural managers and the instability of their employment conditions might combine, and encourage a very intense investment in their work. In some cases, such an overinvestment can serve as the basis for a form of exploitation that is especially effective because it appears voluntary, at least for the new entrants. It would then be worth documenting the evolution of this relationship to work over time and of the succession of positions that make up a career. Insofar as cultural management is not strictly divided into clearly identified occupations and statuses, we must do away with the linear view of careers that applies to established positions and, together with the succession of positions, identify the activities performed as part of each of them (as functions are often multifaceted and involve a wide range of tasks).[1] Only then can we retrace the successive shifts that make up careers, from one function to another (from relations with the public to programming), from one type of institution to another (from a drama company to a subsidized theatre) or from one sector to another (from classical music to contemporary dance). Mapping out careers in this way would allow us to identify the space of the positions that define cultural management, a prerequisite for a morphological study of this professional group that remains largely to be done.

Beyond the case of cultural management, the analytical approach used to study them in this book should also lend itself to further developments. I will first recall the defining features of the ideal-type of vocation that served as the starting point for this study, distinguishing vocational career choices from other professional paths. The combination of *illusio* with a reflexive relationship to their own determinations leads applicants to pursue a strategy of professional and social placement, if not to formulate a coherent 'plan'. Their distinctive relationship to work then leads them to see their occupation as a means or at least an opportunity for self-fulfillment. These individual projections come with the belief that their future activity will serve a higher cause or values. I identify these factors not so much to identify vocations as to account for the reasons, modalities and meanings of these particular forms of projection into one's social and professional future.

In order to do this we need to situate the vocational occupations pursued within the space of thinkable and possible aspirations, and relate objective changes to the preference systems that determine choices. On that basis, we will be able to establish what makes certain occupations attractive and who (i.e. which categories of social agents) may be attracted to them. Yet, for a vocation to be awakened or strengthened, it requires the prescriptions or at least confirmations formulated in the spaces of socialization of these agents – the family, the peer group or the school. This is where the vocation work truly comes in: it consists in sublimating the social conditions of vocation into an elective choice. Even if it is also that, the resulting narrative of vocation cannot be reduced to the rationalization of a career choice; it reflects a broader relationship to the social world that the formulation of this choice provides an opportunity to express.

In this book I applied this general agenda to a specific type of vocation that particularly resides in the imprecise definition of the positions targeted, contrasting with more traditional and established vocational occupations such as a doctor or professor. In this regard, cultural management is comparable with other previously mentioned career choices, such as humanitarian work (Dauvin and Siméant 2002), European professions (Michon 2009, 2012), communication and social economy (Darbus and Hély 2010). In all these cases, the relative fuzziness of the positions allows for keeping opportunities open and seeking out gratifications other than financial at work; in variable combinations they also display at least one of the three main sociographic features of applicants to cultural management master's programmes (high proportion of women, high social backgrounds, high levels of educational attainment). As in their own way they also work as responses to the contemporary problems of social reproduction at a time of mass unemployment and massification of education, particularly in the middle class, these career choices may warrant further examination of the hypothesis of crisis-induced vocations formulated in the opening pages of this book.

## Note

1 I owe this suggestion to Olivier Roueff. See also Hesmondhalgh and Baker 2010: 139–41 on 'the decline of the career' in cultural labour.

# Appendix

Before I move on to more technical considerations on the collection and processing of the data used in this research, the reader should probably be aware of some personal information shedding light on my relationship to my object of study. This relationship is a very close one indeed: at the same age as the applicants studied in this book, I had myself temporarily considered pursuing a career in cultural management and enrolled in a specialized training programme in the event that my project of writing a doctoral thesis, and in the longer term teaching and doing research, would not have been feasible. That cultural management was a possibility for me at the time had nothing to do with chance, as I shared some of the social and educational features found among the applicants (being the holder of a literary *baccalauréat*, having received a multidisciplinary training and been actively involved in cultural activities since I was a teenager, to name a few). Thus, despite the gain in objectivity and hindsight resulting from the distance allowed by the tools of sociology and from the changes having occurred in higher education, in the cultural field and in my own position, a form of empathy may have influenced and, at any rate, largely facilitated the interpretation of these educational and professional 'choices'.

Eventually pursuing a career in research did not lead me very far from that world, as during my doctoral study on cultural policies, I had numerous dealings with cultural managers. Since the beginning of my thesis I taught in specialized training programmes on a regular basis, in universities, public institutions training cultural executives and civil service schools. Later, as higher education reform following the Bologna process was being implemented, I created a master's programme on *Politique et gestion de la culture* (cultural policy and management) at the institute of political studies (IEP) of Strasbourg. While these activities constitute an extension of my scholarly work on cultural matters, the opposite is also true: this research is partly the outcome of the conversion of an investment in teaching into a scientific interest. Despite this relationship I have not adopted a so-called applied approach, focusing for instance on the adjustment of training programmes to 'needs' in the sector or on the evaluation of the employment rates of graduates; yet it does have an effect on the way I address problems, including in terms of critical distance. I have largely taken advantage of my position as an occasional insider, even though I cannot claim that it supported an ethnographic posture. Meetings with teaching staff, the recruitments of outside lecturers, selection juries, classes, the supervision of internships and theses, graduation ceremonies, student parties, etc. have been, if not always opportunities for participatory observation, at least practical experiences that nourished my sociological investigations, and on a more practical basis gave me access to material and information that would have been more difficult to access for a total outsider.

While I drew on this insider knowledge, it is because I both lacked systematic information on the features of this population under study and in order to counterbalance the proximity related to my personal experience by using statistical data that I chose to rely primarily on a quantitative methodology. I will now address more strictly technical questions.

In light of the lack of available data, the first step of this research consisted in submitting a first test questionnaire to applicants to the master's programme in Strasbourg in June 2008 (n = 107), allowing us to revise the questions and to precode some of those left open. We then selected the programmes, the applicants of which would be sent the final questionnaire. In order to avoid the excessive dispersion of the population in a very diverse sector, we combined five criteria allowing us to identify the core cultural management programmes. 1) We only considered programmes offered by universities, which make up the majority in the field, thereby leaving out cultural curricula in business schools and programmes on the management of art teaching institutions of the Ministry of Culture, as well as private schools. 2) We focused on second-year master's level programmes who recruit all or some of their students at that level, which applies to the majority of them. 3) The exclusive specialization of programmes in the cultural field, excluding those in the sample for which culture is only a component or an option (for instance, a master's in local development comprising a course on culture). 4) As a complement, we only included generalist programmes in the cultural field, leaving aside programes focused on a single sector (such as theatre or publishing), to maintain the cohesion of our sample. 5) For the same reasons, we also left aside programmes whose content strictly focuses on a single discipline (like cultural law).

Based on previous knowledge of the programmes, directories, university websites and specialized websites, we came up with an exhaustive list of 22 master's programmes fitting these criteria. Nineteen participated in this research; two were unable to do so due to the organization of their recruitment process, and one never responded. The latter programmes are, however, not entirely absent, as multiple applications are listed in the questionnaire.

*The following programmes participated in this research:*

Master 2 Administration des institutions culturelles, Université
    Aix-Marseille 3 (IUP Arles)
Master 2 Métiers des arts et de la culture, Université Lyon 2
Master 2 Conception et direction de projet culturel, Université Paris 3
Master 2 Conduite de projets culturels – connaissance des publics,
    Université Paris 10

Master 2 Développement culturel et direction de projets, Université Lyon 2
Master 2 Direction de projets culturels, IEP Grenoble
Master 2 Expertise des professions et institutions de la culture, Université
    de Nantes
Master 2 Expertise et médiation culturelle, Université de Metz
Master 2 Ingénierie de projets culturels, Université Bordeaux 3
Master 2 Management des organisations culturelles, Université Paris 9
Master 2 Management des organisations et manifestations culturelles,
    Université Aix-Marseille 3
Master 2 Management du spectacle vivant, Université de Brest
Master 2 Métiers de la culture, Université Lille 3
Master 2 Politique et gestion de la culture, IEP Strasbourg
Master 2 Politiques et gestion de la culture en Europe, Université Paris 8
Master 2 Projets culturels dans l'espace public, Université Paris 1
Master 2 Sociologie politique des représentations et expertises culturelles,
    IEP Toulouse
Master 2 Stratégie des échanges culturels internationaux, IEP Lyon
Master 2 Stratégie du développement culturel, Université d'Avignon

Each of these programmes encouraged applicants to respond to the questionnaire online in ways that they chose themselves (by sending an email during the application process, mentioning it on the master's webpage, or asking to print the last page of the questionnaire as a proof of response in the application file). Combining the administration of the questionnaire and submission of the application had the benefit of increasing the number of responses. At the same time, it created the risk of confusion between the two – applicants might, for example, have sought to write answers putting themselves in a positive light (i.e regarding their professional experience or cultural practices). Yet, the fact that the questionnaire was anonymous, and that we emphasized that there was no 'right' answer, guaranteed the applicants that their application file wouldn't be cross-examined, and considering that the majority of questions were both precise and factual, that possible bias was no more likely to be an issue than in any other self-administered questionnaire. From the knowledge we had of the applicants otherwise (from application files, interviews and conversations with the students), we inferred that this distorting effect was likely to be very weak. Nevertheless, questionnaire results are always the product of a specific investigatory relationship, and attention was paid to the conditions of their administration in their interpretation.

We processed over 1,500 responses between February and July 2009. Having cleaned up the sample (by removing duplicate, incomplete, nonsensical and irrelevant responses), we retained the responses of 787 individuals. In order to process the most homogeneous possible population, we decided to focus on individuals who were still students. The sample extends beyond students in 'initial training' in the administrative sense of the term, as we also included individuals having worked or interrupted their studies for a short time only. The purpose of this was to retain in the population under study young people in retraining and account for the diversity of former trajectories, without only considering the most direct and uneventful ones. The selection was based on the following criteria: individuals born in or after 1982 (i.e. aged 27 and under as of 2009), having registered in higher education at least once during the three previous years and not accumulated more than two consecutive years of professional activity. On this basis we removed 96 individuals – adults resuming their studies or in lifelong training. We also left out 36 individuals of foreign nationality who had not registered in a French higher education institution within seven years of their application, for reasons of comparability of educational trajectories. Overall, 133 individuals were removed, and the final sample was made up of 654. As each of them simultaneously applied to several programmes among the 22 that fit our criteria, this amounted to a total of 1,470 applications.

Establishing a response rate is impossible considering we have no data available on the original population (consisting of all the applicants), and it would be especially difficult due to multiple applications. Yet an approximation of this rate can be provided on the basis of the 12 master's programmes for which we have the total number of applications received (figures provided by the directors of these programmes). They make up over two thirds (67.2 per cent) of the applications reported by the questionnaire respondents. These 12 programmes received 2,006 applications, 1,257 of which were identified in questionnaire responses (i.e. 62.7 per cent). The average response rate per programme is 64.6 per cent, with significant variations (from slightly over a quarter of the applicants in two programmes to almost all of them in three others). It is likely that the propensity to respond varied according to the incentives given by the master's programmes at the time the questionnaires were submitted. This bias is largely compensated by the frequency of multiple applications, which often allowed us to find out about applicants to programmes that gave few incentives to respond thanks to others who gave more.

The questions we asked the applicants pertained to three main themes.

1  *The characteristics of the applicants:*

 i   their basic features (gender, date and place of birth, nationality, place of residence);
 ii  their family background (nationality, occupation, highest degree and cultural activities of both parents);
 iii their educational background (*baccalauréat* stream and results, courses and programmes attended in higher education, degrees obtained); their international capital (foreign languages, stays abroad);
 iv  their professional and personal experiences (jobs and internships inside and outside the cultural sector, participation in non-profit organizations, unions, political parties).

2   *Their relationship to culture:*

    i   the distribution and intensity of their cultural consumption and practices (going to the cinema, theatre, museums, exhibitions, concerts; reading books; watching TV);

    ii   their cultural preferences and tastes (see below);

    iii   their artistic training (discipline, type, duration, certification);

    iv   their artistic activities, past and present (type, duration, intensity);

    v   their participation in cultural organizations;

    vi   their relatives and friends working in the cultural sector.

3   *Their future plans:*

    i   regarding education and training (past effective or considered applications and projects; present and possible future applications and projects; opinion regarding training requirements to access employment);

    ii   regarding their professional career in the short term and in the long term (work in the cultural sector, in other sectors; types of position and organization envisaged; preference for a specific cultural sector; salary expectations; possibility of an artistic career).

Listing the entire coding operations that we performed would be tedious and of little use. By way of an example, and because this is a matter of frequent debate, I will only discuss our coding of cultural tastes here. We adopted a relational approach to reported tastes and distastes, probed mainly on the basis of two open-ended questions: 'What cultural genres fit your personal tastes most?' and 'Conversely, what cultural genres do you not like at all?'. In each case we counted the number of genres cited, and subsequently recoded and divided responses in three ways. First, they were divided into major sectors (dichotomous variables: music/theatre/film, TV/dance/literature/heritage and architecture/visual arts/ other); then, on the basis of their affiliation with classical or heritage culture or contemporary creation (or their being mixed or indeterminate from that perspective); and finally according to their degree of legitimacy. For the latter coding, the more complex one, we chose to reason in terms of leanings in order to process the responses in the way that would reflect them better. We would, for example, classify a response listing 'contemporary art, comics, art-house cinema, Japanese theatre' as preferred genres and 'rap, action movies' as distastes under 'very legitimate', because positive references are essentially found among the most recognized forms, and the negative references are exclusively picked among the least legitimate genres. Coding it under 'varying degrees of legitimacy' might have been justifiable because of the reference to comics, but would have failed to reflect the general leanings evidenced in the response; additionally the response as a whole suggested that the applicant probably referred to the most 'artistic' forms of comics. This appeared to us as a sounder method than merely recording the diversity of tastes, which would have resulted in the vast majority of responses being coded under 'varying degrees of legitimacy', with very little informational gain, unless we distinguished between multiple profiles in terms of 'dissonance' or 'consonance', which would have been methodologically problematic and did not fit our research goals (Lahire 2004).

In addition to the original results drawn from the questionnaires, this research relied on secondary analysis of data from two main sources: the syntheses on cultural employment of institutions such as the Ministry of Culture and DARES and the INSEE's *enquête emploi* and census (fichiers détail individus, tabulation sur mesure [fichier électronique], INSEE [producteur], Centre Maurice Halbwachs (CMH) [diffuseur]). We only used the results of the *enquête emploi* pertaining to the years 1982, 1992 and 2002, in order to limit the effects of the changes in the classification and the methodology of the research (after 2003 all years were covered). Due to our sampling method, and in order to ensure the significance of our findings, we conducted the analysis on all occupations falling under the socio-occupational category of media, arts and performing arts (codes 351 to 3,535, CS 35). In order to limit generational effects, only individuals in employment were considered (working population aged 15 and older). The numbers of individuals falling under CS 35 investigated within the framework of this research are respectively 380 in 1982, 565 in 1992 and 624 in 2002. We were unable to achieve a finer analysis of the social backgrounds of individuals holding jobs listed more precisely in the classification of occupations due to their low numbers. For instance, as of 2002, the sample only comprised 45 executives in media, publishing, broadcasting and the performing arts (3,521), 21 artistic executives in the performing arts (3,522) and 37 technical executives in the performing arts and broadcasting (3,523). Similarly, we did not use data from the Formation, Qualification Professionnelle (FQP) surveys because they include too few individuals that are part of populations relevant to this research (for example, only 83 media, arts and performing arts professionals – CS 35 – investigated in 1993), even though they provide much more detailed indicators of social background. The socio-occupational category of the father (detailed except for farmers, PCS 1982) is filled on the basis of the occupation held 'at the time when the [individual] stopped attending school or going to the university on a regular basis'.

We also constructed a continuous dataset out of the INSEE census data from the years 1962, 1968, 1975, 1982, 1990, 1999 and 2008 based on the current definition of category 35 'media, arts and performing arts occupations'. The classifications of 1982 and 2003 are identical in terms of categories but differ within these categories. For censuses from the years prior to the 1982 change of classification, we used the group 93 'artists' as a basis, excluding architects, urban planners, as well as technicians and workers,[1] and adding a few occupations falling under the group 91 'intellectual occupations' ('museum curator', 'librarian', 'man of letters, expert in various areas', 'journalist') in order to ensure as much consistency as possible with the following classification. For reasons of comparability, we took into account only individuals in employment (the occupation of those unemployed is not always precisely filled).

In order to compare and put into perspective the questionnaire results, we also used data retrieved from the 'Système d'information et de suivi des étudiants'

(SISE) database of the Ministry of Education, allowing us to establish the characteristics of students registered in 20 master's programmes relevant to our research from 2005 to 2009 on the basis of a few core indicators (age, sex, type of *baccalauréat*, parents' occupations, etc.).[2] The reprocessing of this data allowed us to give a few elements of comparison between the population of applicants and the students already enrolled in those programmes.

For the final stage we collected three types of qualitative material. We put together a corpus of 45 application files (CVs, letters of motivation and career plans) for one of the programmes in our sample, which enabled us to systematize the analysis of the applicants' modes of self-presentation and of the narratives of vocation, following a method that is documented in the relevant chapter. As a complement, we carried out systematic observations of selection interviews for the master's programme *Politique et gestion de la culture* in June 2011. Fifty of these were conducted following a common template by Victor Lepaux, who was present among the members of the jury but did not participate in the interviews, and by myself – I was both asking questions and taking notes, for the dual purpose of accumulating material for this research and participating in the selection process. Lastly, 20 interviews were conducted with successful or unsuccessful applicants, who were asked to retrace their trajectories and their educational choices, and with students in cultural management master's programmes. They were selected on the basis of the questionnaire results, with a view towards ensuring the representation of a variety of backgrounds rather than striving for statistical representativeness.

I quickly realized that conducting these interviews myself would be impossible. The difference in age and status would have, in all liklihood, led the interviewees to speak less freely about their experiences, the reasons for their career choice, to overstate the consistency of their trajectories and downplay their hesitations and U-turns. There was a significant risk that the interview would be perceived as a selection interview, as I would be conducting it with my own students or with others who could have been and were undoubtedly aware of my position. For these reasons I decided to work with Camille Marthon, an interviewer who was closer to the applicants in terms of age and status, making it easier for the interviewees to discuss the rationales behind the trajectories they followed or considered. Camille was roughly the same age as the interviewees and was herself weighing career options after having completed a master's in social science research, where she wrote a dissertation on international youth mobility and its uses in subsequent trajectories. Where interviews conducted by myself might have been experienced as interrogations, the greater social proximity between interviewer and interviewee was conducive to bringing out the maieutic dimension in the interview setting; the interview can, in such cases, encourage reflection on oneself and one's own condition and projections into the future. These 'double socioanalys[e]s' (Bourdieu 1999: 611) are sufficiently framed by the interview template to be fully exploitable while allowing for freer expression than in a more formal interview setting or in the impersonal, terse form of a questionnaire response. On some occasions, we also used a few interviews made in similar conditions by students in the *Sciences sociales du politique* master's programme at the IEP of Strasbourg, within the framework of a workshop on field investigation conducted by Sébastien Michon.

## Notes

1 'Windows dresser, advertising designer', 'interior designer', 'textile designer', 'professional worker in visual and applied arts'.
2 Data provided by the statistical department of the educational authorities for the region of Strasbourg (*rectorat de l'académie de Strasbourg, 2008*)

# Bibliography

Abbing, H. (2002), *Why are Artists Poor: The Exceptional Economy of the Arts*, Amsterdam: Amsterdam University Press.

Abbott, A. (1988), *The System of Professions*, Chicago: University of Chicago Press.

Abraham, Y-M. (2007), 'Du souci scolaire au sérieux managérial, ou comment devenir un "HEC"', *Revue française de sociologie*, 1(48), pp. 37–66.

Agrikoliansky, E. *et al.* (2005), *Radiographie du mouvement altermondialiste*, Paris: La Dispute.

Allen, K., Quinn, J., Hollingworth, S. and Rose, A. (2013), 'Becoming Employable Students and "Ideal" Creative Workers: Exclusion and Inequality in Higher Education Work Placements', *British Journal of Sociology of Education*, 34(3), pp. 431–52.

Arnaud, L. and Guionnet, C. (eds) (2005), *Les frontières du politique. Enquêtes sur les processus de politisation et dépolitisation*, Rennes: Presses universitaires de Rennes, pp. 11–25.

Ashton, D. and Noonan, C. (eds) (2013), *Cultural Work and Higher Education*, Basingstoke: Palgrave Macmillan.

Balasinski, J. and Mathieu, L. (eds) (2006), *Art et contestation*, Rennes: Presses universitaires de Rennes.

Baudelot, C. and Gollac, M. (2003), *Travailler pour être heureux? Le bonheur et le travail en France*, Paris: Fayard.

Baudelot, C. and Establet, R. (1992), *Allez les filles!*, Paris: Points Seuil.

Beaud, S. (2003), *80 % au bac... et après? Les enfants de la démocratisation scolaire*, Paris: La Découverte.

Becker, H. (1982), *Art Worlds*, Berkeley and Los Angeles: University of California Press.

Beckman, G.D. (ed.) (2010), *Disciplining the Arts: Teaching Entrepreneurship in Context*, Lanham: Rowman and Littlefield.

Bennett, T., Savage, M., Silva, E., Warde, A., Gayo-Cal, M., Wright, D. (2009), *Culture, Class, Distinction*, Abington: Routledge.

Bense Ferreira Alves, C. and Leblanc, F. (2013), 'Les rétributions: un incessant travail d'articulation', *Sociétés contemporaines*, 91, pp. 5–15.

Bodin, R. (2009), 'Les signes de l'élection. Repérer et vérifier la conformation des dispositions professionnelles des élèves éducateurs spécialisés', *Actes de la recherche en sciences sociales*, 178, pp. 80–7.

Boltanski, L. (1987), *The Making of a Class: Cadres in French Society*, Cambridge: Cambridge University Press.

Boltanski, L., Darré, Y. and Schiltz, M-A. (1984), 'La dénonciation', *Actes de la recherche en sciences sociales*, 51, pp. 3–40.

Boltanski, L. and Chiapello, E. (2005), *The New Spirit of Capitalism*, New York: Verso.
Bouquillion, P. (ed.) (2012), *Creative Economy, Creative industries. Des notions à traduire*, Paris: Presses Universitaires de Vincennes.
Bourdieu, P. (1978), 'Classement, déclassement, reclassement', *Actes de la recherche en sciences sociales*, 24, pp. 2–22.
Bourdieu, P. (1979), 'Les trois états du capital culturel', *Actes de la recherche en sciences sociales*, 30, pp. 3–6.
Bourdieu, P. (1984), *Distinction: A Social Critique of the Judgment of Taste*, Cambridge: Harvard University Press.
Bourdieu, P. (1987a) 'The Biographical Illusion', *Working Papers and Proceedings of the Centre for Psychosocial Studies*, ed. R.J. Parmentier and G. Urban, pp. 1–7.
Bourdieu, P. (1987b), 'The Invention of the Artist's Life', *Everyday Life*, 73, pp. 7–103.
Bourdieu, P. (1990), *Homo Academicus*, Palo Alto: Stanford University Press.
Bourdieu, P. (1991), 'Le champ littéraire', *Actes de la recherche en sciences sociales*, 89, pp. 3–46.
Bourdieu, P. (1996a), *The Rules of Art: Genesis and Structure of the Literary Field*, Palo Alto, Stanford University Press.
Bourdieu, P. (1996b), 'La double vérité du travail', *Actes de la recherche en sciences sociales*, 114, pp. 89–90.
Bourdieu, P. (1999), 'Understanding', *in The Weight of the World: Social Suffering in Contemporary Society*, Cambridge: Polity Press, pp. 607–26.
Bourdieu, P. (2000), *Pascalian Meditations*, Palo Alto: Stanford University Press.
Bourdieu, P. (2001), *Masculine Domination*, Cambridge: Polity.
Bourdieu, P. (2014), 'The Future of Class and the Causality of the Probable', in A. Christoforou and M. Lainé (eds), *Re-Thinking Economics: Exploring the Work of Pierre Bourdieu*, London: Routledge.
Bourdieu, P. and Darbel, A. (1991), *The Love of Art: European Art Museums and Their Public*, Stanford: Stanford University Press.
Bourdieu, P. and Passeron, J-C. (1979), *The Inheritors: French Students and their Relations to Culture*, Chicago: University of Chicago Press.
Bryson, B. (1996), 'Anything but heavy metal: symbolic exclusion and musical dislikes', *American Sociological Review*, 61(5), pp. 884–99.
Bureau, M-C., Perrenoud, M. and Shapiro, R. (eds), 2009, *L'artiste pluriel. Démultiplier l'activité pour vivre de son art*, Villeneuve-d'Ascq: Presses universitaires du Septentrion.
Buscatto, M. (2003), 'Chanteuse de jazz n'est point métier d'homme. L'accord imparfait entre voix et instrument en France', *Revue française de sociologie*, 44(1), pp. 35–62.
Cacouault-Bitaud, M. (2007), *Professeurs... mais femmes. Carrières et vies privées des enseignantes du secondaire au XXe siècle*, Paris: La Découverte.
Cacouault-Bitaud, M. and Ravet, H. (eds) (2008), 'Les femmes, les arts et la culture', special issue, *Travail, genre et sociétés*, 1(19).
Casey, B. *et al.* (1995), 'Employment in the Cultural Sector', *Cultural Trends*, 7(25), pp. 87–97.
Chamboredon, J-C. (1991), 'Classes scolaires, classes d'âge, classes sociales. Les fonctions de scansion temporelle du système de formation', *Enquête*, 6 [http://enquete.revues.org/document144.html].
Chiapello, E. (1998), *Artistes versus managers*, Paris: Métailié.
Chapoulie, J-M. (1987), *Les professeurs de l'enseignement secondaire: un métier de classe moyenne*, Paris: Éditions de la Maison des sciences de l'homme.

Charle, C. (1992), 'Le temps des hommes doubles', *Revue d'histoire moderne et contemporaine*, 39–1, janvier-mars, pp. 73–86.

Charle, C. (2008), 'Les directeurs de théâtre, entre spéculation et vocation', *in Théâtre en capitales. Naissance de la société du spectacle à Paris, Berlin, Londres et Vienne*, Paris: Albin Michel, pp. 54–101.

Charles, F. and Cibois, P. (2010), 'L'évolution de l'origine sociale des enseignants du primaire sur la longue durée: retour sur une question controversée', *Sociétés contemporaines*, 77, pp. 31–55.

Chaumier, S. (2006), 'Les formations aux métiers de la culture: de la génération spontanée au désir de régulation', *U-culture(s)*, 1, pp. 56–61.

Chauvel, L. (1998), *Le destin des générations. Structure sociale et cohortes en France au XXᵉ siècle*, Paris: PUF.

Chenu, A. (2002), 'Une institution sans intention. La sociologie en France depuis l'après-guerre', *Actes de la recherche en sciences sociales*, 141–2, pp. 46–61.

Cléron, E. and Patureau, F. (2009), 'L'emploi dans le secteur culturel', *Culture chiffres*, 1.

Coll. (1992), *Formation et emploi culturel, les formations de 3e cycle d'administrateurs culturels en question*, Grenoble: ministère de la Culture, Université Grenoble II, Observatoire des politiques culturelles.

Collins, R. (1988), 'Women and men in the class structure', *Journal of Family Issues*, 9(1), pp. 27–50.

Collovald, A. (2001), 'De la défense des "pauvres nécessiteux" à l'humanitaire expert. Reconversion et métamorphoses d'une cause politique', *Politix*, 14(56), pp. 135–61.

Conlin, P. (2014), 'The cultural intermediary in plutocratic times', *European Journal of Cultural Studies*, pp. 1–18 (online).

Convert, B. (2003), 'Des hiérarchies maintenues. Espace des disciplines, morphologie de l'offre scolaire et choix d'orientation en France, 1987–2001', *Actes de la recherche en sciences sociales*, 149, pp. 61–73.

Convert, B. (2006), *Les impasses de la démocratisation scolaire. Sur une prétendue crise des vocations scientifiques*, Paris: Raisons d'agir.

Convert, B. (2010), 'Espace de l'enseignement supérieur et stratégies étudiantes', *Actes de la recherche en sciences sociales*, 183, pp. 14–31.

Coulangeon, P. (2003), 'Quel est le rôle de l'école dans la démocratisation de l'accès aux équipements culturels ?', *in Le(s) public(s) de la culture*, Paris: Presses de Sciences Po, pp. 245–62.

Coulangeon, P. (2004), *Les musiciens interprètes en France. Portrait d'une profession*, Paris: Documentation française.

Coulangeon, P. (2013), 'Changing Policies, Challenging Theories and Persisting Inequalities: Social Disparities in Cultural Participation in France from 1981 to 2008', *Poetics* 41(2), pp. 177–209.

CURAPP (1998), *La politique ailleurs*, Paris: PUF.

Darbus, F. and Hély, M. (2010), 'Travailler dans l'économie sociale et solidaire: aspirations, représentations et dispositions. Une étude auprès des adhérents de l'association Ressources solidaires', *Revue internationale de l'économie sociale*, 317, pp. 68–86.

Dauvin, P. and Siméant, J. (2002), *Le travail humanitaire. Les acteurs des ONG, du siège au terrain*, Paris: Presses de Sciences Po.

De Saint Martin, M. (1996), 'Les reconversions culturelles: l'exemple de la noblesse', *Hermès*, 20, pp. 183–90.

Demazière, D. and Gadéa, C. (eds) (2009), *Sociologie des groupes professionnels. Acquis récents et nouveaux défis*, Paris: La Découverte.

Desrosières, A. (1992), 'Séries longues et conventions d'équivalence', *Genèses*, 9, pp. 92–7.

DeVereaux, C. (ed.) (2009), 'Arts and Cultural Management: The State of the Field', *Journal of Arts Management, Law and Society*, 38(4).

DeVereaux, C. (ed.) (2011), *Cultural Management and Its Boundaries, Past, Present, and Future*, Helsinki, HUMAK University Press.

DeVereaux, C. and Vartiainen, P. (eds) (2009), *The Science and Art of Cultural Management*, Helsinki, HUMAK University Press.

DiMaggio, P. (1987), *Managers of the arts: the careers and opinions of administrators of US resident theatres, art museums, orchestras and community arts agencies*, Washington: Seven Locks Press.

Donnat, O. (2004), 'La féminisation des pratiques culturelles', *in* Thierry Blöss, (ed.), *La dialectique des rapports hommes-femmes*, Paris: PUF, pp. 423–31.

Donnat, O. (2009), *Les Pratiques culturelles des Français à l'ère numérique, enquête 2008*, Paris: ministère de la Culture et de la communication, La Découverte.

Dorn, C.M. (1992), 'Arts administration: a field of dreams?' *Journal of Arts Management, Law, and Society*, 22(3), pp. 241–51.

Draelants, H. and Darchy-Koechlinn, B. (2011), 'Flaunting one's academic pedigree? Self-presentation of students from elite French schools', *British Journal of Sociology of Education*, 3(1), pp. 17–34.

Dressayre, P. (2002), 'Le métier de directeur des affaires culturelles de ville', *L'observatoire*, 23, pp. 23–7.

Dubois, V. (2006), 'Du militantisme à la gestion culturelle', *in* Christophe Gaubert, Marie-Hélène Lechien and Sylvie Tissot (eds), *Reconversions militantes*, Limoges: Presses universitaires de Limoges, pp. 139–62.

Dubois, V. (2012a), *La politique culturelle. Genèse d'une catégorie d'intervention publique*, Paris: Belin.

Dubois, V. (2012b), 'Cultural Democratisation in the Struggle between Public Intellectuals and the State. The Debate on the 'Theatre of the People' in France (1895–1905)', *International Journal of Cultural Policy*, vol. 18(5), pp. 593–606.

Dubois, V., Méon, J-M. and Pierru, E. (2013), *The Sociology of Wind Bands: Amateur Music Between Cultural Domination and Autonomy*, Aldershot: Ashgate.

Dubois, V. (2014), 'What has become of the "new petite bourgeoisie"? The case of cultural managers in France', *in* Coulangeon, Ph. and Duval, J. (eds), *The Routledge Companion to Bourdieu's 'Distinction'*, Milton Park-New York, Routledge, pp. 78–93.

Duval, J. (2015), 'Evolutions of tastes in films and changes in field theory', in Ph. Coulangeon, J. Duval, (eds), *The Routledge Companion to Bourdieu's Distinction*, Milton Park-New York, Routledge, pp. 94–108.

ENCATC (2003), Training in cultural policy and management. International directory of training centres. Europe, Russian federation, Caucasus, Central Asia, Paris: UNESCO.

Evrard, Y. (1990), 'La formation des managers culturels', *Mediaspouvoirs*, 17, pp. 137–47.

Evrard, Y., and Colbert, F. (2000), 'Arts Management: A New Discipline Entering the Millennium?', *International Journal of Arts Management*, 2(2), pp. 4–13.

Farges, G. (2011), 'Le statut social des enseignants français au prisme du renouvellement générationnel', *Revue européenne des sciences sociales*, 49(1), pp. 157–78.

Fassin, D. (2000), 'La supplique. Stratégies rhétoriques et constructions identitaires dans les demandes d'aide d'urgence', *Annales. Histoire, Sciences Sociales*, 55(5), pp. 955–81.

Feist, A. (2000), *Cultural employment in Europe*, Cultural policies research and development unit, Policy note n. 8, Strasbourg: Council of Europe.

Ferrand, M. (2004), *Féminin, masculin*, Paris: La Découverte.

Ferrand, M., Imbert, F. and Marry, C. (1999), *L'excellence scolaire: une affaire de famille. Le cas des normaliennes et normaliens scientifiques*, Paris: l'Harmattan.

Freidson, E. (1986), 'Les professions artistiques comme défi à l'analyse sociologique', *Revue française de sociologie*, 27(3), pp. 431–43.

Fridman, V. and Ollivier, M. (2004), 'Ouverture ostentatoire à la diversité et cosmopolitisme: vers une nouvelle configuration discursive?', *Sociologie et sociétés*, 36(1), pp. 105–26.

Garnham, N. (2005), 'From Cultural to Creative Industries: An Analysis of the Implications of the "Creative Industries" Approach to Arts and Media Policy Making in the United Kingdom', *International Journal of Cultural Policy*, 11(1), pp. 15–29.

Geay, B. (2002), *Profession: instituteur*, Paris: Seuil.

Georgakakis, D. (1995), 'Comment enseigner ce qui ne s'apprend pas. Rationalisations de la "communication de masse" et pratiques pédagogiques en école privée', *Politix*, 29, pp. 158–85.

Girard, C., Moutarde, P. and Pébrier, S. (2006), *Étude sur la formation à la direction des établissements culturels du spectacle vivant*, Paris: ministère de la Culture.

Girard, D. (2012), 'Sur le tard, sur le tas… et ailleurs', *in* Isabelle Mathieu et Claude Patriat, (eds), *L'université et les formations aux métiers de la culture. La diagonale du flou*, Dijon: Éditions universitaires de Dijon, pp. 31–40.

Glevarec, H. (2005), 'La fin du modèle classique de la légitimité culturelle. Hétérogénéisation des ordres de légitimité et régime contemporain de justice culturelle. L'exemple du champ musical', *in* É. Maigret, É. Mac (eds), *Penser les médiacultures. Nouvelles pratiques et nouvelles approches de la représentation du monde*, Paris: Armand Colin/Ina, pp. 69–102.

Goetschel, P. and Yon, J-C. (eds) (2008), *Les directeurs de théâtre, XIXe-XXe siècles, histoire d'une profession*, Paris: Publications de la Sorbonne.

Gouyon, M. (2010), 'Une typologie de l'emploi salarié dans le secteur culturel en 2007', *Culture chiffres*, 3.

Gouyon, M. and Patureau, F. (2012), 'Le salariat dans le secteur culturel en 2009: flexibilité et pluriactivité', *Culture chiffres*, 2.

Gouyon, M. and Patureau, F. (2014) 'Vingt ans d'évolution de l'emploi dans les professions culturelles (1991–2011)', *Culture chiffres*, 6.

Gripsrud, J., Hovden, J.F. and Moe, H. (2011), 'Changing Relations: Class, Education and Cultural Capital', *Poetics*, 39(6), pp. 507–29.

Halbwachs, M. (1972), 'Matière et société', *in Classes sociales et morphologie*, Paris: Minuit, pp. 58–94.

Hatzfeld, H. (2005), *Faire de la politique autrement. Les expériences inachevées des années 1970*, Rennes: ADELS – Presses universitaires de Rennes.

Herron, D. G. *et al.* (1998), 'The Effect of Gender on the Career Advancement of Arts Managers', *Journal of Arts Management, Law and Society*, 28(1), pp. 27–40.

Hesmondhalgh, D. and Baker, S. (2010). *Creative Labour: Media Work in Three Cultural Industries*, Abingdon, New York: Routledge.

Hinves, J. (2012), 'Becoming a Cultural Entrepreneur: Creative Industries, Culture-led Regeneration and Identity', *in* Jonathan Paquette (ed.), *Cultural Policy, Work and Identity: The Creation, Renewal and Negotiation of Professional Subjectivities*, Farnham: Ashgate, pp. 161–79.

Hutchens, J. and Zoe, V. (1985), 'Curricular considerations in arts administration: a comparison of views from the field', *Journal of Arts Management and Law*, 15(2), pp. 7–28.

Hua, Z. (2007), 'Presentation of self in application letters', *in* Zhua Hua, Paul Seedhouse, Li Wei, Vivian Cook, (eds), *Language learning and teaching as social inter-action*, Basingstoke: Palgrave, pp. 126–47.

IBF (2013), *The Attractiveness of the Teaching Profession in Europe*, Luxembourg: Publications Office of the European Union.

Jamet, D. (1991), *Les formations à l'administration et à la gestion dans le domaine culturel en France*, ministère de la Culture, département des études et de la prospective, Paris.

Jeanpierre, L. and Roueff, O. (eds.) (2014), *La culture et ses intermédiaires dans les arts, le numérique et les industries créatives*, Paris: Editions des archives contemporaines.

Jeffri, J. (1983), 'Training arts managers: views from the field', *Journal of Arts Management and Law*, 13(2), pp. 5–28.

Jouvenet, M. (2003), *Figures actuelles du musicien. Sociologie des cultures musicales et professionnelles du rap et des musiques électroniques*, thèse de sociologie, Paris: EHESS.

Kirchberg, V. and Zembylas, T. (2010), 'Arts management: a sociological inquiry', *Journal of Arts Management, Law and Society*, 40(1), pp. 1–5.

Kris, E. and Kurz, O. (1981), *Legend, Myth and Magic in the Image of the Artist – A Historical Experiment*, New Haven: Yale University Press.

Kuesters, I. (2010), 'Arts Managers as Liaisons Between Finance and Art: a Qualitative Study Inspired by the Theory of Functional Differentiation', *Journal of Arts Management, Law and Society*, 2010, 40(1), pp. 43–57.

Lafarge, G. (2008), 'Les conditions sociales de l'insertion professionnelle. Destins croisés de deux populations étudiantes d'IUT', *Actes de la recherche en sciences sociales*, 175, pp. 40–53.

Lafarge, G. and Marchetti, D. (2011), 'Les portes fermées du journalisme. L'espace social des étudiants des formations "reconnues"', *Actes de la recherche en sciences sociales*, 189, pp. 72–100.

Lahire, B. (2004), *La culture des individus*, Paris: La Découverte.

Lahire, B. (2006), *La condition littéraire*, Paris: La Découverte.

Lahire, B. (2008), 'De la réflexivité dans la vie quotidienne: journal personnel, autobiographie et autres écritures de soi', *Sociologie et sociétés*, 40(2), pp. 165–79.

Lamont, M. (1992), *Money, Morals and Manners. The Culture of the French and the American Upper-Middle Class*, Chicago: University of Chicago Press.

Le Roux, B. and Rouanet, H., (2004), *Geometric Data Analyisis: From Correspondance Analysis to Structured Data Analysis*, Dordrecht: Kluwer.

Lecoutre, M. (1995), 'Le cheminement d'insertion professionnelle des étudiants sortis de cinq formations de 3ème cycle à l'administration et à la gestion du secteur culturel', Centre d'études et de recherche du groupe ESC (Clermont-Ferrand).

Lecoutre, M. (2006), 'Le capital social dans les transitions écoles entreprises', *in* Antoine Bevort, Michel Lallement, (eds), *Le capital social. Performance, équité et réciprocité*, Paris: La Découverte.

Le Gall, B. and Soulié, C. (2009), 'Administrative reform and the new conflict of the faculties at French universities', *Laboratorium*, 1, pp. 83–97.

Lemêtre, C. (2009), *Entre démocratisations scolaire et culturelle: sociologie du baccalauréat théâtre (1989–2009)*, thèse de sociologie, Université de Nantes.

Lizé, W., Naudier, D. and Roueff, O. (2011), *Intermédiaires du travail artistique. À la frontière de l'art et du commerce*, Paris, Documentation française.

Lizé, W., Naudier, D. and Sofio, S. (eds.) (2014), *Les stratèges de la notoriété. Intermédiaires et consécration dans les univers artistiques*, Paris: Editions des archives contemporaines.

Lozach, U. (2012), *Ne pas choisir, ne pas déchoir. La professionnalisation inaccomplie des étudiants de Sciences Po*, mémoire de master Sciences sociales du politique, Strasbourg.

Luck, S. (2010), 'Activist distinction in the 21st century: The new petite bourgeoisie's commitment in radical-left movements', paper presented at the workshop *La distinction, 30 ans après*, Paris, 4–6 November.

Mangset, P. (1995), 'Risks and Benefits of Decentralisation: The Development of Local Cultural Administration in Norway', *European Journal of Cultural Policy* 2(1), pp. 67–86.

Marchetti, D. (2012), *Une sociologie relationnelle de la production des biens culturels de grande diffusion. L'exemple de l'information journalistique*, mémoire d'habilitation à diriger les recherches, Université de Strasbourg.

Marry, C. (2000), 'Filles et garçons à l'école', *in* Agnès Van Zanten (ed.), *L'école: l'état des savoirs*, Paris: La Découverte, 2000, pp. 283–92.

Martin, C. (2008), 'Les formations à l'administration et à la gestion de la culture: bilan et perspectives', *Culture études*, Paris: ministère de la Culture.

Marx, K. (1993), *Grundrisse: Foundations of the Critique of Political Economy*, London: Penguin Books (first published in German in 1939).

Mathieu, I. (2011), *L'action culturelle et ses métiers*, Paris: PUF.

Mathieu, I. (2012), 'La culture sur le métier', *in* Isabelle Mathieu et Claude Patriat (eds), *L'université et les formations aux métiers de la culture*, pp. 121–40.

Mathieu, I. and Patriat, C. (eds) (2012), *L'université et les formations aux métiers de la culture. La diagonale du flou*, Dijon: Éditions universitaires de Dijon.

Matz, K. (2012), 'La culture au service du développement économique ou la neutralisation politique', *in* Vincent Dubois *et al.*, *Le politique, l'artiste et le gestionnaire. (Re)configurations locales et (dé)politisation de la culture*, Bellecombe-en-Bauges: Éditions du Croquant, pp. 153–69.

Mauger, G. (1994), 'Gauchisme, contre-culture et néo-libéralisme. Pour une histoire de la génération de mai 68', *in* CURAPP, *L'identité politique*, Paris: PUF, pp. 208–12.

Mauger, G. (ed.) (2006a), *L'accès à la vie d'artiste. Sélection et consécration artistiques*, Bellecombe-en-Bauges: Éditions du Croquant.

Mauger, G. (ed.) (2006b), *Droits d'entrée. Modalités et conditions d'accès dans les univers artistiques*, Paris: Éditions de la Maison des sciences de l'homme.

Menger, P.-M. (1998), *La profession de comédien. Formations, activités et carrières dans la démultiplication de soi*, Paris: La Documentation Française.

Menger, P.-M. (1994), 'Être artiste par intermittence: la flexibilité du travail et le risque professionnel dans les arts du spectacle', *Travail et emploi*, 60, pp. 4–22.

Menger, P.-M. (2003), *Portrait de l'artiste en travailleur*, Paris: Seuil/La république des idées.

Menger, P.-M. (2005a), *Les intermittents du spectacle. Sociologie d'une exception*, Paris: Éditions de l'EHESS.

Menger, P.-M. (2005b), 'Les professions culturelles: un système incomplet de relations sociales', *in* Guy Saez (ed.), *Institutions et vie culturelles*, Paris: La Documentation française.

Menger, P-M. (2014), *The Economics of Creativity. Art and Achievement under Uncertainty*, Cambridge: Harvard University Press.

Michon, S. (2008), 'Les effets des contextes d'études sur la politisation', *Revue française de pédagogie*, 163, pp. 63–75.

Michon, S. (2009), 'La construction de connaissances et de compétences spécifiques à une carrière dans l'action publique européenne: formation et insertion professionnelle des étudiants d'un master', [halshs.archives-ouvertes.fr/halshs-00361592].

Michon, S. (2012), 'Faire carrière dans les métiers de l'Europe politique: dispositions, savoirs spécifiques et types de carrière. Enquête auprès d'élèves et d'anciens élèves de masters "Politiques européennes"', *Politique européenne*, 38, pp. 185–93.

Millet, M. and Moreau, M. (2011), *La société des diplômes*, Paris: La Dispute.

MKW *et al.* (2001), *Exploitation and development of the job potential in the cultural sector in the age of digitalisation*, Brussels: European Commission DG Employment and Social Affairs.

Montoya, N. (2008), 'Médiation et médiateurs culturels: quelques problèmes de définition dans la construction d'une activité professionnelle', *Lien social et Politiques*, 60, pp. 25–35.

Moulin, R. and Passeron, J-C. (1985), *Les Artistes: essai de morphologie sociale*, Paris: La documentation française.

Moulinier, P. (1983), *La formation des administrateurs culturels*, Développement culturel, dossier documentaire 28–29, Paris, UNESCO.

Muel-Dreyfus, F. (1983), *Le métier d'éducateur*, Paris: Minuit.

Naudier, D. (2000), *La cause littéraire des femmes. Modes d'accès et modalités de consécration des femmes dans le champ littéraire (1970–98)*, thèse de doctorat de sociologie, Paris: EHESS.

Nauze-Fichet, E. and Tomasini, M. (2005), 'Parcours des jeunes à la sortie du système éducatif et déclassement salarial', *Économie et statistique*, 388–9, pp. 57–83.

Neilson, B. and Coté, M. (2014), 'Are We All Cultural Workers Now?', *Journal of Cultural Economy*, 7(1), pp. 2–11.

Neveu, E. (1994), *Une société de communication?*, Paris: Montchrestien.

Neveu, E. (2000), 'Le genre du journalisme. Des ambivalences de la féminisation d'une profession', *Politix*, 13(51), pp. 179–212.

Nixon, S. and du Gay, P. (2002), 'Who Needs Cultural Intermediaries?', *Cultural Studies*, 16(4), pp. 495–500.

Noël, S. (2010), *L'édition indépendante « critique » en France au tournant du XXIème siècle. Une identité instable dans le champ éditorial*, thèse de doctorat en sociologie, Paris: EHESS.

Noël, S. (2012a), *L'édition indépendante critique: engagements politiques et intellectuels*, Villeurbanne: Presses de l'ENSSIB.

Noël, S. (2012b), 'Maintenir l'économie à distance dans l'univers des biens symboliques: le cas de l'édition indépendante « critique »', *Revue française de socio-économie*, 2(10), pp. 73–92.

O'Brien, J. and Feist, A. (1995), *Employment in the arts and cultural industries: an analysis of the 1991 census*, London: Arts Council of England.

Octobre, S. (1999), 'Profession, segments professionnels et identité. L'évolution des conservateurs de musées', *Revue française de sociologie*, 40–2, pp. 357–83.

Orange, S. (2010), 'Le choix du BTS. Entre construction et encadrement des aspirations des bacheliers d'origine populaire', *Actes de la recherche en sciences sociales*, 183, p. 32–47.

Passeron, J-C. (1965), 'Changement et permanence dans le monde intellectuel. De l'après-guerre à la croissance continue', Colloque d'Arras, 12–13 juin.

Passeron, J-C. (1982), 'L'inflation des diplômes. Remarques sur l'usage de quelques concepts analogiques en sociologie', *Revue française de sociologie*, 23(4), pp. 551–84.

Passeron, J-C. (2013), *Sociological Reasoning: A Non-Popperian Space of Argumentation*, Oxford: The Bardwell Press.

Pavis, F. (2010), 'Une discipline "utile" dans l'enseignement supérieur: promotion et appropriations de la gestion (1965–75)', *Mouvement social*, 4(233), pp. 127–42.

Pène, S. (1997), 'Lettre administrative et espace social', *in* Daniel Fabre (ed.), *Par écrit: ethnologie des écritures quotidiennes*, Paris: Éditions MSH, pp. 201–17.

Périer, P. (2004), 'Une crise des vocations? Accès au métier et socialisation professionnelle des enseignants du secondaire', *Revue française de pédagogie*, 147, pp. 79–90.

Perrot, M. (1987), 'Qu'est-ce qu'un métier de femme?', *Le mouvement social*, 140, pp. 3–8.

Peterson, R.A. (1986), 'The role of formal accountability in the shift from impresario to arts administrator', *in* Raymonde Moulin (ed.) *Sociologie de l'art*, Paris: La documentation française, pp. 111–34.

Peterson, R.A. (1987), 'From impresario to arts administrator: formal accountability in nonprofit cultural organizations', *in* Paul DiMaggio (ed.), *Nonprofit enterprise in the arts. Studies in mission and constraint*, New York-Oxford: Oxford University Press, pp. 161–83.

Peugny, C. (2009), *Le déclassement*, Paris: Grasset.

Peyrin, A. (2008), 'Démocratiser les musées: une profession intellectuelle au féminin', *Travail, genre et sociétés*, 1(19), pp. 65–85.

Peyrin, A. (2010), *Être médiateur au musée. Sociologie d'un métier en trompe-l'œil*, Paris: La documentation française.

Pinto, L. (1991), 'Déconstruire Beaubourg. Art, politique et architecture', *Genèses*, 6, pp. 98–124.

Pinto, V. (2014) *À l'école du salariat. Les étudiants et leurs "petits boulots"*, Paris: PUF.

Poliak, C. (2002), 'Manières profanes de "parler de soi"', *Genèses*, 47, pp. 4–20.

Pollard E. (2013), 'Making Your Way: Empirical Evidence from a Survey of 3,500 Graduates', *in* Daniel Ashton and Caitriona Noonan (eds), *Cultural Work and Higher Education*, Basingstoke: Palgrave Macmillan, pp. 45–67.

Pudal, B. (2003), 'La vocation communiste et ses récits', *in* Jacques Lagroye (ed.), *La politisation*, Paris: Belin.

Quemin, A. (2009), 'Femmes et artistes. La difficile voie du succès dans le secteur de l'art contemporain', juin 2009, http://elles.centrepompidou.fr/blog/?p=167

Rambach, A. and Rambach, M. (2001), *Les intellos précaires*, Paris: Hachette.

Rannou, J. and Roharik, I. (2006), *Les danseurs, un métier d'engagement*, Paris: La Documentation française.

Ravet, H. (2006), 'L'accès des femmes aux professions artistiques. Un double droit d'entrée dans le champ musical', *in* Gérard Mauger (dir.), *L'accès à la vie d'artiste. Sélection et consécration artistiques*, Bellecombe-en-Bauges: Éditions du Croquant.

Reay, D., David, M.E. and Ball, S.J. (2005), *Degrees of Choice: Class, Race, Gender and Higher Education*, Stoke-on-Trent: Trentham Books.

Redaelli, E. (2012), 'American Cultural Policy and the Rise of Arts Management Programs: The Creation of a New Professional Identity', *in* Jonathan Paquette (ed.), *Cultural Policy, Work and Identity: The Creation, Renewal and Negotiation of Professional Subjectivities*, Farnham: Ashgate, pp. 145–59.

Rémond, E. (1999), 'Pourquoi veulent-ils devenir journalistes?', *Communication et langages*, 119, pp. 4–23.

Retière, J-M. (2001), 'En retard pour l'aide d'urgence... Analyse de courriers de demandeurs (FUS 1998)', *Revue française des affaires sociales*, 1, pp. 167–83.

Reynaud, B. (1999), 'L'emprise des groupes. Sur l'édition française au début des années 1980', *Actes de la recherche en sciences sociales*, 130, pp. 3–10.

Rolfe, H. (1995), 'A Learning Culture? Trends in Vocational Education and Training in the Cultural Sector', *Cultural Trends*, 7(27), pp. 27–42.

Roueff, O. (2001), 'Bohème militante, radicalité musicale: un "air de famille". La sensibilité des musiques improvisées au militantisme radical', *Sociétés et représentations*, 1(11), pp. 407–32.

Roussel, V. (ed.) (2010), *Les artistes et la politique*, Saint-Denis: Presses universitaires de Vincennes.

Rozier, S. (2001), *L'entreprise-providence. Mécénat des entreprises et transformations de l'action publique dans la France des années 1960–2000*, thèse de science politique, Paris: Université Paris 1.

Sapiro, G. (ed.) (2007a), 'Vocations artistiques', *Actes de la recherche en sciences sociales*, 168.

Sapiro, G. (2007b), 'La vocation artistique entre don et don de soi', *Actes de la recherche en sciences sociales*, 168, pp. 4–11.

Savage, M. *et al.* (1992), *Property, Bureaucracy, and Culture: Middle-Class Formation in Contemporary Britain*, London; New York: Routledge.

Savage, M. *et al.* (2013), 'A new model of social class? Findings from the BBC's Great British Class survey experiment', *Sociology*, 47(2), pp. 219–50.

SECEB documents (2006), *The Bologna Process and Cultural Education*, Brussels: ENCATC.

Seibel, B. (1988), *Au nom du livre. Analyse sociale d'une profession: les bibliothécaires*, Paris: La Documentation Française.

Serre, D. (2012), 'Le capital culturel dans tous ses états', *Actes de la recherche en sciences sociales*, 191–2, pp. 4–13.

Sikes, M. (2000), 'Higher education training in arts administration: a millennial and metaphoric reappraisal', *Journal of Arts Management, Law, and Society*, 30(2), pp. 91–101.

Simonet, M. (2010), *Le travail bénévole. Engagement citoyen ou travail gratuit?*, Paris: La Dispute.

Sinigaglia, J. (2014a), 'The Intermittent Workers' Movement: Between a Demobilizing Precarity and Mobilizing Precarious Workers', *Sociétés contemporaines* (online).

Sinigaglia, J. (2014b), 'Happiness as a Reward for Artistic Work: A Social Norm, from Injunction to Incorporation', *Sociétés contemporaines* (online).

Smith Maguire, J. (2014), 'Bourdieu on Cultural Intermediaries', *in* Smith Maguire, J. and Matthews, J. (eds), *The Cultural Intermediaries Reader*, London: Sage, pp. 15–24.

Smith Maguire, J., and Matthews, J. (2012), 'Are We All Cultural Intermediaries Now? An Introduction to Cultural Intermediaries in Context', *European Journal of Cultural Studies* 15(5), pp. 551–62.

Smith Maguire, J. and Matthews, J. (eds) (2014), *The Cultural Intermediaries Reader*, London: SAGE.

Solaroli, M. (2014), 'Vecchi e nuovi intermediari culturali', *Studi Culturali*, 11(3), pp. 371–6.

Sorignet, P.-E. (2010), *Danser. Enquête sur les coulisses d'une vocation*, Paris: La Découverte.

Soulié, C. (2008), 'Montée de l'esprit gestionnaire et actualisation du conflit des facultés en France', *in* Franz Schultheis *et al.* (ed.). *Le cauchemar de Humboldt. Les réformes de l'enseignement supérieur européen*, Paris: Raisons d'agir, pp. 89–104.

Sternal, M. (2007), 'Cultural Policy and Cultural Management Related Training: Challenges for Higher Education in Europe', *The Journal of Arts Management, Law, and Society*, 37(1), pp. 65–78.

Suaud, C. (1978), *La vocation*, Paris: Minuit.

Suteu, C. (2006), *Another brick in the wall. A critical review of cultural management education in Europe*, Amsterdam: Boekmanstudies.

Tchouikina, S. (2010), 'The crisis in Russian cultural management: Western influences and the formation of new professional identities in the 1990s–2000s', *Journal of arts management, law and society*, 40(1), pp. 76–91.

Urfalino, P. (1993), 'La philosophie de l'État esthétique', *Politix*, 24, 1993, pp. 20–35.

Varela, X. (2013), 'Core Consensus, Strategic Variations: Mapping Arts Management Graduate Education in the United States', *Journal of Arts Management, Law, and Society*, 43(2), pp. 74–87.

Verger, A. (1982), 'L'artiste saisi par l'école. Classements scolaires et "vocation" artistique', *Actes de la recherche en sciences sociales*, 42, pp. 19–32.

Wagner, A-C. (2007), 'La place du voyage dans la formation des élites', *Actes de la recherche en sciences sociales*, 170, pp. 58–65.

Weber, M. (1992), *Essais sur la théorie de la science*, Paris: Plon (Agora).

Zadora, E. (2008), 'Les établissements d'enseignement supérieur artistique et culturel. Effectifs et diplômes. Année scolaire 2006–7', *Culture chiffres*, 1.

# Index

Abbing, H. 6, 109
Abbott, A. 22, 29
Abraham, Y-M. 113
Agrikoliansky, E. 115
Allen, K. 112
Arnaud, L. 115
Arts, artists: artistic training 48–9, 76, 79; artistic activities 78–80, 127; artistic vocation 6, 53, 65, 76–80, 90; artists' lifestyle (bohemia): 33, 110, 113, 119
Arts/cultural management (as an academic discipline) xvi, 4–5, 6, 10–1, 15–6, 23, 25–34, 38, 56, 78–80, 111
Ashton, D. 13, 36 n31
Association of Arts Administration Educators 16, 26, 54 n2
Austria 29
Avant-garde 103

Balasinski, J. 114
Ball, S.J. 31
Baltic countries 29
Baudelot, C. 2, 11 n3, 41, 66, 107
Beaud, S. 53
Becker, H. 2
Beckman, G.D. 113
Bennett, T. xiv, xix
Bense Ferreira Alves, C. 107
Bodin, R. 67
Boltanski, L. xix, 3, 64, 106, 107, 111
Bouquillion, P. 111
Bourdieu, P. xiv–xvi, xviii, 1, 2, 7, 9, 11 n4, 15, 22, 23, 24, 29, 40, 41, 45, 67, 75, 81, 88, 94, 106, 107, 111, 113–14, 116, 119, 120, 129
Bryson, B. 104
Bulgaria 29
Bureau, M-C. 20
Buscatto, M. 54 n13

Cacouault-Bitaud, M. 41, 54 n13
Capital: cultural xv, xvii, xix, 8, 22, 23, 38, 45, 48–9, 53, 65, 88, 98, 102, 106; educational xviii, 7–9, 10, 15, 22–3, 25, 32–3, 38, 40, 44–8, 50, 52–3, 56, 61, 75, 79, 81–3, 86, 87–9, 104, 106, 120; literary 87–9; social 9, 10, 22, 49, 59, 81, 83, 86, 96 n34, 120; symbolic 41, 83, 89
Casey, B. 34 n1
Chamboredon, JC. 82–3
Chapoulie, J-M. 75
Charle, C. 35 n12
Charles, F. 87
Chaumier, S. 27
Chauvel, L. 9, 32, 85
Chenu, A. 47
Chiapello, E. xix, 3, 106, 107, 111
Cibois, P. 87
Cinema 30, 49, 100–1, 103, 104, 113, 116, 127
Civil service, civil servants xvi, 17, 21, 22, 23, 27, 36 n26, 42, 94 n1, 123
Cléron, E. 96 n32
Colbert, F. 4
Collins, R. 41
Collovald, A. 115
Conlin, P. xviii
Convert, B. 6, 25, 40, 55 n21
Coulangeon, P. xvi, 45, 48, 78, 105
Council of Europe 26, 118 n15
Creative economy xvi, xix, 3, 13, 111
Critique (see New spirit of capitalism; Economy; Politics)
Croatia 29
Cultural democratization 24, 70, 84–5, 116
Cultural employment xvi, 12–5, 21–2, 36 n39, 128; development of xvi, 12–9;

employment conditions in the cultural
field 7–8, 14, 19–21, 33, 55 n20, 94 n7
Cultural genres (see also tastes) 98, 100–6,
117 n, 127
Cultural heritage 20, 23, 28, 39, 54 n3, 96
n32, 98–100, 102, 127
Cultural intermediaries xiv, xvii–xviii, 2, 3,
9, 15, 24, 35 n12, 81, 97
Cultural policy xvi, 13, 16, 18, 26, 72, 105,
123
Cultural practices xvi, 40, 45, 48–9, 50–1,
53, 55 n19, 64, 83, 87, 92–3, 97–100,
125, 127
Cultural tastes (see also genres) xvi, xix, 6,
48, 64, 67, 87, 97–101, 103–5, 106, 117
n1, 127
CURAPP 115

Darbel, A. 40
Darbus, F. 121
Darchy-Koechlinn, B. 65
Darré, Y. 64
Dauvin, P. 7, 116, 121
David, M.E. 31
De Saint Martin, M. 85
Demazière, D. 3, 22
Desrosières, A. 13
DeVereaux, C. 4
DiMaggio, P. 3, 16, 21, 26, 39
Direct observation 6, 129
Disinterestedness (see Money)
Donnat, O. 40, 49, 55 n19
Dorn, C.M. 26
Downgrading (downclassing): social xv, 9,
87; educational xv, 9, 63, 83; strategies
against 9–10, 25, 62, 83, 87–9, 119
Draelants, H. 65
Dressayre, P. 39
du Gay, P. xvii, xviii
Dubois, V. xviii, 13, 16, 18, 21, 27, 72, 74,
105, 106, 116, 117 n6
Duval, J. 101

Eclectism (omnivorousness) 70, 97, 101,
104–5, 117
Economics (academic discipline) xv, 28,
37 n48, 37 n49, 47, 51, 52, 84, 91–3, 98,
112–13
Economy, and culture xvi, 17–8, 110, 119;
attitudes toward 105, 111–14 (see also
New spirit of capitalism)
Establet, R. 41
European comparisons 12–3, 18, 19–21,
29, 31, 74, 109, 111

European Network of Cultural
Administration Training Centres
(ENCATC) 26, 27, 36 n37
European Union 14, 26
Evrard, Y. 4, 36

Family backgrounds 48, 53–4, 57, 120,
126; relatives in the cultural field 48,
85–7
Farges, G. 74
Fassin, D. 64
Feist, A. 34 n1
Feminization 38–40
Ferrand, M. 54
Freidson, E. 6
Fridman, V. 105

Gadéa, C. 3, 22
Garnham, N. 111
Gayo-Cal, M. xiv, xix
Geay, B. 87
Gender 1, 5, 7, 8, 10, 38–42, 48, 50, 61,
65, 78, 109, 126
Generation 8–10, 22, 32–3, 39, 46, 80,
85–7, 115–16, 128
Georgakakis, D. 27
Germany 29
Girard, C. 27
Girard, D. 27
Glevarec, H. 105
Goetschel, P. 35 n12
Gollac, M. 2, 11 n3, 66, 107
Gouyon, M. 19, 20, 34 n3, 36 n28
Greece 29
Gripsrud, J. 117 n1
Guionnet, C. 115

Halbwachs, M. 34 n2, 44
Hatzfeld, H. 115
Health (occupations in the health sector)
43–4, 45
Hély, M. 121
Herron, D. G. 3
Higher classes (backgrounds) 9, 38, 42–5,
52, 54, 55 n18, 87, 89, 90, 105, 107,
114, 122
Higher education xv, 25, 40, 45–7, 53,
69–70, 83, 113–14, 126; transformations
in the HE system 8, 12, 25–6, 28, 31–4,
36 n31, 36 n32, 45–7
Hinves, J. 18
Hollingworth, S. 112
Hovden, J.F. 117 n1
Hua, Z. 64

Humanitarian aid 94 n1, 116
Humanities (academic discipline) xv, 7, 8, 25, 28, 30, 36 n32, 37 n45, 39, 47, 51, 74, 88, 94 n1, 95 n15, 114
Hutchens, J. 4

Imbert, F. 54 n14
Indetermination (social infinitude, dream of social flight) xix, 9, 21–4, 68–9, 81–5, 119
International Association of Arts and Cultural Management (AIMAC) 4
Internships 22, 50, 56, 58, 76, 78–80, 83, 86, 126
Interviews 6, 11, 61–3, 125, 129–30
Italy 29

Jamet, D. 36 n38, 37 n45
Jeanpierre, L. xiv, 3
Jeffri, J. 4
Journalism 7, 14, 18, 23, 34 n6, 35 n14, 38, 42, 46–7, 54 n4, 55 n16, 55 n24, 57, 67, 81, 85, 89, 94 n1, 95 n24, 110, 119, 128
Jouvenet, M. 80

Kirchberg, V. 4
Kris, E. 65
Kuesters, I. 3
Kurz, O. 65

Labour market xvi, xix, 12–3, 29, 64, 106, 116, 119
Lafarge, G. 7, 42, 54 n5, 55 n24, 120
Lahire, B. 54 n13, 64, 128
Lamont, M. xvi, xix
Law (academic discipline) 28, 29, 37 n49, 39, 47, 51, 58, 61, 79, 93, 94 n1, 124
Le Gall, B. 114
Le Roux, B. 5
Leblanc, F. 107
Lecoutre, M. 34, 95 n28, 96 n34
Legitimate culture (cultural legitimism, highbrow culture) xvi, 83, 87, 97–106, 127
Lemêtre, C. 40, 78
Libraries xvi, 23; librarians 2, 14, 22, 40–1, 44, 95 n23, 128
Lizé, W. xiv, 3, 24
Local authorities 4, 16–7, 18, 23, 30, 35 n10, 36 n26, 70–1
Lower classes (backgrounds) 53, 57, 61, 82–3, 91–4, 98, 110

Lozach, U. 62, 89, 96 n37
Luck, S. 115

Mainstream culture 31, 99, 103
Management (academic discipline) xvi, xix, 3, 18–9, 27–9, 30, 36 n34, 41, 47, 51, 78–9, 89–90, 94 n1, 98, 111–14, 125
Mangset, P. 11 n5, 18
Marchetti, D. 7, 42, 54 n5, 55 n24, 110
Marry, C. 40, 42, 54 n14
Martin, C. 5, 9, 27, 28, 34, 37 n43, 37 n48
Marx, K. 2, 31, 76
Mathieu, I. 24, 27, 28, 37 n45, 48, 55 n20, 94 n7
Mathieu, L. 114
Matthews, J. xiv, xvii, xviii, 3
Matz, K. 112
Mauger, G. 6, 22, 56, 78, 79, 80, 118 n20
MCA (Multiple Correspondence Analysis) 5, 50, 55 n27, 59, 97
Media (see Journalism)
Menger, P-M. xvi, 6, 14, 19, 20, 21, 35 n20, 35 n23, 79, 107, 109
Méon, J-M. 106
Methodology 4–6, 50, 59, 98, 124–30
Michon, S. 114, 121, 130
Middle classes xiv–xv, xix, 3, 8–9, 10, 81, 82–3, 110, 122; lower xviii, 8–9, 53, 81, 82–3, 87–8, 95 n23, 95 n27; upper xiv, 9, 10, 15, 80, 81, 82, 87–9, 90, 97,106
Middlebrow culture 103–4, 117 n3
Millet, M. 22
Ministry of Culture 6, 13, 17, 18, 27, 30, 34 n7, 38, 124, 128
Moe, H. 117 n1
Money attitudes toward xv, 109–10; non-monetary rewards xvii, 2, 6–7, 9–10, 11 n3, 89, 106–8, 119–20
Montoya, N. 24
Moreau, M. 22
Motivation letters (see also narratives of vocation) 12, 63–7, 129
Moulin, R. 13
Moulinier, P. 26
Moutarde, P. 27
Muel-Dreyfus, F. 24, 78
Museums (curators) 2, 14, 30, 100, 128

Naudier, D. 3, 24, 54 n13
Nauze-Fichet, E. 9
Netherlands (The) 29
Neveu, E. 27, 34 n6, 54 n4
New petite bourgeoisie xviii, 81, 87–8, 115

New spirit of capitalism xix, 106, 111–14
Nixon, S. xvii, xviii
Noël, S. 66, 112
Noonan, C. 13, 36 n31
Norway (see also Scandinavian countries)
    11 n5, 18, 117 n1

O'Brien, J. 34 n1
Octobre, S. 35 n12, 45, 95 n29
Ollivier, M. 105
Omnivorousness (see Eclectism)
Orange, S. 95 n27

Passeron, J-C. xv, xvii, 13, 34 n5, 45, 106,
    120
Patriat, C. 27
Patureau, F. 19, 34 n3, 96 n32
Pavis, F. 36 n34
Pébrier, S. 27
Pène, S. 64
Performing arts xvi, 3, 11 n3, 17–9, 19–21,
    30, 33, 34 n5, 35 n21, 36 n28, 37 n51,
    39, 47, 51, 54 n3, 54 n10, 67–8, 79, 81,
    85, 87, 95 n24, 100, 118 n21, 128
Périer, P. 74
Perrenoud, M. 20
Perrot, M. 39
Peterson, R.A. 15
Peugny, C. 9, 83
Peyrin, A. 3, 24, 41
Pierru, E. 106
Pinto, L. 72
Pinto, V. 58
Poland 29
Poliak, C. 64
Political science (academic discipline) 37
    n49, 39, 51, 61
Politics (political attitudes) 105, 112,
    114–17, 118 n21, 126
Pollard E. 35 n24, 109,117 n9
Prestige (see Symbolic capital)
Professionalization (of cultural managers)
    xvi, 6–7, 16–7, 21–2, 26–7, 120
Publishing sector 3, 18–9, 29–30, 32, 39,
    68, 96 n32, 112, 124, 128
Pudal, B. 63

Quemin, A. 54 n13
Questionnaire 5, 32, 42, 50, 55 n16, 57,
    61–5, 67, 94 n4, 98, 104, 124–30
Quinn, J. 112

Rambach, A. 110
Rambach, M. 110

Rannou, J. 20
Ravet, H. 54 n13
Reay, D. 31
Redaelli, E. 16, 26
Relationship to the object of study 123–4
Rémond, E. 64
Reproduction: professional 8, 81, 85–7;
    crisis of 9, 120, 122; social xiv, xv–xvi,
    4, 122
Retière, J-M. 64
Reynaud, B. 112
Roharik, I. 20
Rolfe, H. 31, 34 n1
Romania 29
Rose, A. 112
Rouanet, H. 5
Roueff, O. xiv, 3, 24, 94 n8, 118 n21, 122 n1
Roussel, V. 114
Rozier, S. 112
Russia 103

Sapiro, G. 6, 78
Savage, M. xiv, xix
Scandinavian countries (see also Norway)
    11 n5, 18, 29, 117 n1
Schiltz, M.-A. 64
Seibel, B. 41, 85, 95 n23
Self-assertion 41, 89–94
Self-fulfillment xix, 1, 6, 10, 24, 64, 78,
    81, 107–9, 113–14, 121
Serre, D. 22
Shapiro, R. 20
Sikes, M. 26
Silva, E. xiv, xix
Siméant, J. 7, 116, 121
Simonet, M. 120
Sinigaglia, J. 107, 117 n12, 118 n21
Smith Maguire, J. xiv, xvii, xviii, 3
Social sciences (academic discipline) xv,
    25, 28, 37 n45, 47
Sofio, S. 3
Solaroli, M. xiv, 3
Sorignet, P.-E. 41, 75, 78, 90
Soulié, C. 25, 114
Spain 29
Sponsorship (private funding) 6, 16
Sternal, M. 26, 29
Suaud, C. 2, 54
Suteu, C. 29
Switzerland 29

Tchouikina, S. 3
Teaching occupations 2, 7–8, 10, 23, 25,
    40, 41, 44, 58, 67, 73–5, 87–9

Television 49, 83, 96 n32, 98–100, 127
Tomasini, M. 9
Traditional occupations 73–80, 121
Training programmes in cultural
    management 4–5, 25–34, 56, 100;
    development of xvi, xviii, 8–9, 15–7,
    25–8, 118; structure of supply of 26–30,
    38–9, 40; effects of 22, 25, 31–4, 120

UK xvi, xix, 13, 20, 31, 34 n1, 35 n24,
    109, 117 n9
UNESCO 26
Upward social mobility 8–9, 81–5, 88, 119
Urfalino, P. 74
USA xvi, 2, 16, 26

Varela, X. 26, 28
Vartiainen, P. 4
Verger, A. 78

Visual arts 17, 20, 22, 47, 48, 54 n3, 54
    n13, 58, 79, 84, 87, 99, 127
Vocation: concept of xiv, xvii, xix, 1–2,
    6–8, 11 n1, 15, 25, 38, 53, 58, 67, 75–
    80, 83, 90, 121–2; narratives of 63–7,
    75–80, 129

Wagner, A-C. 62
Warde, A. xiv, xix
Weber, M. 2, 107
Welfare (occupations in) (see also Health)
    42–4, 121
Wright, D. xiv, xix

Yon, J-C. 35 n12

Zadora, E. 54 n3
Zembylas, T. 4
Zoe, V. 4

For Product Safety Concerns and Information please contact our EU
representative GPSR@taylorandfrancis.com
Taylor & Francis Verlag GmbH, Kaufingerstraße 24, 80331 München, Germany

www.ingramcontent.com/pod-product-compliance
Ingram Content Group UK Ltd.
Pitfield, Milton Keynes, MK11 3LW, UK
UKHW020948180425
457613UK00019B/577